INTRODUCTION TO HUMAN SERVICES
AND SOCIAL CHANGE

INTRODUCTION TO HUMAN SERVICES AND SOCIAL CHANGE

History, Practice, and Policy

LORI M. GARDINIER, EMILY A. MANN,
MATTHEW R. LEE, AND LYDIA P. OGDEN

OXFORD
UNIVERSITY PRESS

OXFORD
UNIVERSITY PRESS

Oxford University Press is a department of the University of Oxford.
It furthers the University's objective of excellence in research, scholarship,
and education by publishing worldwide. Oxford is a registered trade mark
of Oxford University Press in the UK and in certain other countries.

Published in the United States of America by Oxford University Press
198 Madison Avenue, New York, NY 10016, United States of America.

For titles covered by Section 112 of the US Higher Education Opportunity
Act, please visit www.oup.com/us/he for the latest information about
pricing and alternate formats.

Library of Congress Cataloging-in-Publication Data

Names: Gardinier, Lori, author.
Title: Introduction to human services and social change : history,
    practice, and policy / Lori M. Gardinier, Emily A. Mann, Matthew R. Lee,
    and Lydia P. Ogden.
Description: New York, NY : Oxford University Press, [2023] | Includes
    bibliographical references and index. | Summary: "Introduction to Human
    Services and Social Change: History, Practice, and Policy is a core,
    introductory text that provides a foundation for future human service
    professionals interested in the intersection of theory, research, and
    practice. Providing an exciting blend of theory and research, the text
    uses frameworks derived from contemporary learning science to provide
    students with thought-provoking opportunities to apply concepts to
    service learning, case studies, and historical and contemporary
    events"—Provided by publisher.
Identifiers: LCCN 2023011452 (print) | LCCN 2023011453 (ebook) | ISBN
    9780197524411 (paperback) | ISBN 9780197524435 (epub) | ISBN
    9780197524428 (ebook)
Subjects: LCSH: Human services. | Social service. | Social change.
Classification: LCC HV40 .G3658 2023 (print) | LCC HV40 (ebook) | DDC
    361.3/2—dc23/eng/20230601
LC record available at https://lccn.loc.gov/2023011452
LC ebook record available at https://lccn.loc.gov/2023011453

Printed by Marquis, Canada

To Our Students

BRIEF CONTENTS

CONTENTS

PREFACE

Throughout history, humans have created informal and formal networks of mutual and communal support for others. As societies developed, organized responses expanded to include government initiatives and those of civil society, defined as a community of citizens linked by common interests and collective activity. In the United States, we often define these actions as human services. According to the National Organization of Human Services (n.d.), human services practitioners are "uniquely approaching the objective of meeting human needs through an interdisciplinary knowledge base, focusing on prevention as well as remediation of problems, and maintaining a commitment to improving the overall quality of life of service populations."

Human service work is social change work. Social change work acknowledges inequities and problems in the world and seeks to address them. One major component of social change work is addressing one of the most persistent correlates of negative outcomes: poverty. The wealth and resources in the United States surpass those of most countries throughout the world, yet many individuals, families, and communities lack access to nutrient-rich food, safe and affordable housing, a living wage, mental health services, quality education, or medical care. Human services professionals are at the forefront of preventing and responding to these issues, both in the US and abroad. Although addressing poverty and economic inequality is a foundation of social change work, human services professionals also address diverse issues associated with promoting social and racial justice. This textbook examines the ways human services professionals address the impact of historic and contemporary issues that impact individuals, families, and communities.

In this text, you will notice that many terms, such as human services, social services, charity, nonprofits, and social welfare, are used. Broadly speaking, these terms are referencing organizations or agencies that strive to support people or change social conditions.

Some people identify as a human services practitioner, especially those who work in direct service of individuals and families. Others working in this space may not identify with that label. You may hear people say that they work in the *nonprofit sector* or as a *community organizer*. The textbook uses language to reflect context or situational members of the field. However, what we are trying to describe are different organized efforts to address social change work.

The social change sector is critical to individual and societal well-being. The sector encompasses small local programs and also includes large national policies. The federal government in the US spends more than $1 trillion on social programs such as food assistance programs, public housing, and Medicare (Lecy & Thornton, 2016). Under this umbrella of social programs are a complex range of services, including foster care, anti-poverty programs, and public health care programs for low-income individuals. In the US, nonprofit social services constitute more than 1.56 million organizations and 5.4 percent of the country's gross domestic product (McKeever, 2018. There is a long and complex history of the development of social change systems. This book considers some of the major influences of the sector and highlights some of the pathways and barriers to effective social change work.

THE HUMAN SERVICES PRACTITIONER

This book will introduce you to the ways that individuals can support and advance social change work. This book intentionally emphasizes techniques and strategies that have shown impacts, while concurrently elevating emerging ways of thinking about social change. We provide frameworks for understanding social problems and highlight the complexity of working within the human service sector.

Engaging in social change work requires constant self-reflection on what we believe and value, how we interact with others, and how to work toward leaving this world better than we found it. Work in human service and social change fields requires an interdisciplinary understanding of systems, human development, social interactions, systems of oppression, and the levers of power. We need to look critically at history and at current approaches to ensure that individuals and systems intending to do "good" are not perpetuating harm and power differentials. Movements such as Black Lives Matter have held up a mirror to our individual actions and institutions and offered opportunities to consider the ways that racial profiling and differential use of force impact Black, Indigenous, and people of color (BIPOC) communities.

Self-reflection is important within our profession. Like many professions in our society, human services organizations and professionals have inflicted harm on individuals and communities. It is not enough to intend to "do good"; as a field, we must be self-critical and advocate for anti-oppressive policies and organizations that reduce the need for human services.

Human services practitioners have always occupied an interesting space of responding to the world as it is, trying to make life better within the existing systems, and fighting for new ways to change. To do this, we must engage in a constant process of critique of both ourselves and the field. Perhaps when you read about some of the historical programs and practices discussed in this book, you will be critical for their approach. In 100 years, how do you imagine people will view our current way of practicing? What do you think they will not understand about the reasons for our systems and programs? What can we do to be working toward systems and practices that promote quality of life for all members of our society?

ORGANIZATION OF THE BOOK

This book comprises 12 chapters. Some courses will structure their content to align with their chronological flow, and others will not. Each chapter stands on its own; however, ideas transfer between chapters. Each chapter provides assessment questions and reflection questions to both make sure you understand the ideas and promote deeper thought about the ideas raised. In addition, the chapters provide questions about service-learning. We recognize that many classes will not contain a service-learning component; however, we hope you will use these questions to consider any previous or anticipated volunteer or field experiences. We believe this will help you ground the ideas from the reading into your past, current, or future field experiences and deepen your learning.

In Chapter 1, we define the scope of practice of a human services professional in direct practice, programs, and policy. Specifically, we examine how human services professionals play a role in preventing and addressing social problems. This prevention orientation shapes our understanding of the innovative ways in which human services practitioners help individuals, families, and communities adapt to adversity, reduce risk factors, and increase protective factors. Chapter 2 explores the early history of people and organizations dedicated to human services, highlighting seminal program models, global dynamics, power dynamics, and how certain historical debates persist today. Using a historical lens, we hope to illuminate the conditions that influence the field. In Chapter 3, we explore the theoretical frameworks that have been used to understand and respond to social problems. These frames serve to situate the different interventions that human services professionals and organizations use to address societal challenges. Chapter 4 provides the essential features of direct practice human services work. You will gain an understanding of how these relationships differ from other relationships and how the direct services process takes place. You will learn about key aspects of direct practice and client advocacy and become familiar with the tasks and responsibilities of practitioners who work as case managers. In Chapter 5, we continue our examination of direct services by providing an overview of the complex interaction of skills, knowledge, and attitudes that inform ethical human service counseling. After considering techniques of direct practice, we examine specific ethical considerations for this work in Chapter 6, where we explore how our own personal experiences, beliefs, and biases impact ethical practice. This chapter is intentionally placed in the middle of the book because the ideas, theories, and examples straddle both direct practice and systems change work. Chapter 7 explores theories and practices for understanding cultural diversity and identity. We examine different types of identities and discuss contemporary approaches to effective communication in a multicultural society. In Chapter 8, we discuss organizational interventions such as government agencies and private for-profit and nonprofit organizations, along with informal organizations such as mutual aid networks. Chapter 9 examines community development and organizing as tools for social change work. Activism and community organizing are methods used to empower individuals and groups to create lasting change for larger groups and communities. Black Lives Matter, Stop Asian Hate, #MeToo, and Occupy Wall Street are some examples of social change movements. These movements use "people power" to reimagine historical trends and change systems. Chapter 10 examines the role of social policy. Policies are rules, a plan, or method of action that governments and organizations create and implement to guide their operations. In human services, policy influences how we practice and what resources are available to individuals, families, and communities. Human services professionals need to understand social policy from both a historical perspective and the current role social policy plays in contemporary life. In this chapter, we discuss a range of social policies and explore how these policies directly and indirectly impact the health and welfare of children, families, and communities. This chapter, along with Chapter 9, highlights the multiple ways social change work can happen: through grassroots movements and political actions.

One of the unique features of this book is found in Chapter 11 with the addition of our attention to globalization as it relates to human services. Globalization describes the interdependence and interconnectedness of international systems, which include economies, governments, businesses, and media. Human services organizations and the people they serve are affected by global forces, including the economy and politics of their home nation. Last, Chapter 12 considers the role of stress and burnout and how human services professionals can address the challenges of working in a field associated with trauma. Having this understanding is critical to the practitioner's well-being and to their understanding of the clients and community that they serve.

This text provides an overview of key issues in the field of human services and the diverse roles human service practitioners take to engage in social change work. However, this text cannot provide access and depth to all topics that are important in our field. We acknowledge this is only one of many sources necessary to understand the complexity of the human service field. We acknowledge that many important topics are not addressed. We hope your education and practice in the field of human service will be supported by themes and terms from this text, but that you also spend your time learning and experiencing material that may have been missed or underrepresented in this textbook.

REFERENCES

Lecy, J., & Thornton, J. (2016). What big data can tell us about government awards to the nonprofit sector: Using the FAADS. *Nonprofit and Voluntary Sector Quarterly, 45*(5), 1052–1069.

National Organization of Human Services. (n.d.). *About human services.* https://www
.nationalhumanservices.org

ACKNOWLEDGMENTS

This book was truly a collaborative process between the authors, students, and Oxford University Press. Our editors and the staff at Oxford University Press have been critical supporters, including Grace Howard, Alyssa Quinones, Alyssa Palazzo, Sherith Pankratz, and Emma Stens. We especially thank Tonya Martin for her incredible editing work.

This book is the product of shared knowledge, dialogue, and experience within the Human Services Program at Northeastern University. We acknowledge Rebecca Riccio as a co-author of Chapter 8, and the overall perspective that she brings to our work. Thank you to Alexa Arena and Denise Horn for providing content expertise. We acknowledge the countless students who have trusted us with their learning, and the alumni who are working in social change space. Several students played a direct role in supporting the development of this book, including Charlotte Grossman, Jasmine Gutierrez, Claire Molinich, and Monica Vega.

Lori Gardinier acknowledges her husband, Jared Ingersoll, for being a constant source of support; I'm deeply grateful for the depth of thought that you bring into our lives. Thank you to my children Arden Ingersoll and Larkin Gardinier for inspiring me through your individual pursuits. Thank you to my friends who supported this and so many projects. I acknowledge my first social work professor, Dr. Eddie Davis, for asking me the right questions at the right time and for seeing potential in me. Dr. Davis, and many of my professors at SUNY College at Buffalo, modeled student–professor relationships that informed my teaching philosophy. I am grateful to be part of a supportive and innovative academic community at Northeastern University. I am eternally grateful to my co-authors and contributors Emily Mann, Matt Lee, Lydia Ogden, and Rebecca Riccio. Also, thank you to Margot Abels, Natalia Stone, and Lisa Worsh for your commitment to making the Human Services Program an impactful, supportive, and student-centered community. Thank you to the thousands of students who keep me motivated to learn and evolve as an educator and human.

Emily Mann acknowledges the love and support of her family, Eli, Ruthie, and Ron Sandler. Thank you to my parents Barbara Mann and Lenny Mann; my stepparents Fern Mann and Peter Josyph; and my parents-in-law, Karen Sandler, Howard Sandler, and Caryl Sandler. Within this extended family are many role models for academic curiosity, persistence, patience, advocacy, and action. To my students and colleagues in the Human Services Program at Northeastern University, thank you for your pride and passion for the field. Thank you Lori Gardinier, Matt Lee, Lydia Ogden, Rebecca Riccio, Margot Abels, Natalia Stone, and all my students who think, write, and debate many of the topics in this book. I also thank my teachers, mentors, and advisors, specifically Kathleen McCartney and Arthur Reynolds. I would not be here without their support and encouragement.

Matt Lee acknowledges, in no particular order, Cori Ng, Steve Altamuro, Mikaela Altamuro, Doreen Lee-Bierce, Josh Hong, Tara O'Rourke, Ochion Jewell, Tracee Ng, Robyn Ng, Andowah Newton, Chaz Olajide, Isabel Gutiérrez-Bergman, Roland Lange, Hunter Swanson, and Emily Kohl for keeping him motivated during the Zoom era of writing this work, and prioritizing family, community, and health. Your encouragement was a sign of true friendship and support. Thank you of course to the wonderful co-authors of this book. This was a team effort, and endless gratitude goes to Lori for having the vision to bring us together. Many thanks as well to the amazing students at Northeastern University, whose candor, ambition, and dedication to social change really inspired some of the creative and needed sections of the textbook that address the kinds of intersectional issues you all care about so much.

Lydia Ogden is grateful to the Human Services Department at Northeastern University, especially her co-authors on this book: Dr. Lori Gardner, Dr. Emily Mann, and Dr. Mathew Lee. They provided the opportunity to work on this project, and their support, encouragement, and diligence made her participation in writing this book possible. I also extend gratitude to the many students who, over the years, shared their experiences in fieldwork placements and internships in a way that has helped focus the content of this book. I also thank the Simmons University School of Social Work for providing time to work on scholarship such as this. Finally, I thank my family—Thad, Miles, Nate, Anja, Lenny, and, of course, Mom and Dad—for their support of this project among many others.

Oxford University Press facilitated many rounds of review from educators across the country. We acknowledge their thoughtful feedback and suggestions. These reviewers include Susan Holbrook (Southwestern Illinois College), Carmen Monico (Elon University), Barbara Carl (The Pennsylvania State University), Lisa Dunkley (East Tennessee State University), Taryl Holbrook (Florida State College at Jacksonville), Najmah Thomas (University of South Carolina Beaufort), Tami Foy (California State University, Fullerton), Jacquelyn Baker-Sennett (Western Washington University), Kristie Haga (Wytheville Community College), Christine Wilkey (Saint Mary-of-the-Woods College), Deidra Rogers (East Tennessee State University), Jennifer Arny (Central Ohio Technical College), Hillary Ellerman (Auburn University), Constance Walsh (Fullerton College), Mark Kilwein (Clarion University of Pennsylvania), Linda Long (College of DuPage), Tami Long (University of Alabama), Ed Bonilla (Middlesex Community College), Jyotsna Kalavar (Georgia Gwinnett College), Marc McCann (The Pennsylvania State University), Amy Warmingham (University of Mount Olive), Abigail Akande (The Pennsylvania State University–Abington College), Claire Critchlow (Metropolitan State University of Denver), Mirelle Cohen (Olympic College), Jayne Barnes (Nashua Community College), Asmita Saha (Auburn University), Kara Finch (Stanly Community College), Cathleen Ferrick (York County Community College), Rebecca Hubble (New River Community College), Susan McIntyre (Hillsborough Community College), Rana Gautam (University of North Georgia), Judith Castonguay (Community College of Vermont), Shanna Davis (Eastern Washington University), Jennifer Ung Loh (SOAS University of London), Pamela Schmidt (Bunker Hill Community College), and our anonymous reviewers.

ABOUT THE AUTHORS

Lori M. Gardinier is the Director of the Human Services Program at Northeastern University and a Senior Research Associate at the Dukakis Center for Urban and Regional Policy. As a social worker, she has practiced in anti-poverty/social justice organization and as a counselor in agencies addressing intimate partner violence. In her role at Northeastern, she is a leader in experiential education practice in both local and global settings. She has developed partnerships with many of Boston's nonprofit organizations through her own practice and her continued implementation of service-learning partnerships. She has also established experiential education programs with nonprofits in Benin, Costa Rica, India, Japan, Mexico, the United Kingdom, and Zambia. Her research and nonprofit evaluation work span social movement studies, sexual violence, youth development, harm reduction, nonprofit networks, and best practice in experiential education.

Emily A. Mann is a Teaching Professor in the Human Services Program and a Senior Research Associate at the Dukakis Center for Urban and Regional Policy at Northeastern University. She is a founding member of the Northeastern University Public Evaluation Lab (NU-PEL), which is a hub for community-based evaluation. Her teaching focuses on child and adolescent development, social research methods, social policy, and prevention science. Her current research examines educational and clinical interventions and includes several community-based program evaluations.

Matthew R. Lee is a Teaching Professor in the Human Services Program at Northeastern University. He has taught courses in counseling theory and practice, cross-cultural psychology, and ethnic identity and conflict. His research examines campus climate and advocacy for diversity and inclusion, and Asian American mental health and experiences of microaggressions as they relate to phenotype.

Lydia P. Ogden is an Associate Professor at Simmons University School of Social Work. She has taught widely across human services and social work curricula, including courses on counseling, mental health assessment and diagnosis, substance use, working with those living with serious mental illnesses, and research methods. Her scholarship and teaching are informed by her direct social work practice experience with persons living with mental health challenges. Her current research focuses on using the science of well-being to improve the lives of people living with serious mental illness, as well as those who serve them via direct practice.

CHAPTER 1

Human Services Practice

Learning Objectives

After completing this chapter, you will be able to:
1.1. Define *human services*.
1.2. Name and describe the three major domains of human services work and provide examples of jobs within each domain.
1.3. Explain the nature of prevention science and describe the principles of effective prevention programs.
1.4. Describe the harm reduction approach to human services.
1.5. Explain how restorative justice differs from traditional criminal justice solutions.

In this chapter, we define the scope of practice of a human services professional and focus on the role of human services in direct practice, programs, and policy. We explore how human services professionals play a role in preventing and addressing social problems. This prevention, intervention, and treatment orientation shapes our understanding of the innovative ways in which human services practitioners help individuals, families, and communities adapt to adversity, reduce risk factors, and increase protective factors.

1.1 WHAT IS HUMAN SERVICES?

The field of **human services** encompasses a wide range of occupations centered on the goals of helping people meet basic human needs and solving social problems. The term **social problem** refers to any condition or behavior that has negative consequences for large numbers of people, such as poverty, crime, hunger, homelessness, joblessness, and racism. The National Organization for Human Services describes the field of human services as "approaching the objective of meeting human needs through an interdisciplinary knowledge base, focusing on prevention as well as remediation of problems, and maintaining a commitment to improving the overall quality of life of service populations" (Stinchcomb, 2021).

Human services *direct practice* focuses on the individual, couple, family, or group level. It may also involve addressing systems in proximity to the individual, such as a peer group or school system. Human services professionals working in this capacity may be case managers, counselors, social workers, or advocates.

Human services *programs* are organizations and networks that work with individuals or groups to provide goods and services, or work toward the broad goals of the human services profession. Programs may include educational interventions, such as after-school programs, or provide basic resources, such as a food pantry.

A *policy* is a set of ideas, a plan, or course of action officially established by a group such as an organization, business, or governmental body. Human service policies (U.S. Department of Health and Human Services, n.d.) are enacted or implemented at the local, state, or federal level and reflect legislative initiatives. Human service policies reflect social welfare objectives such as the protection of vulnerable populations in promoting education, public health, safe and stable housing, job training and employment, and child welfare. Human service policy can also reflect nongovernmental initiatives, for example, policies related to human resources in the workplace such as organizational policy on maternity and family leave.

Interconnectivity

The domains of practice, program, and policy do not operate in isolation; they are interconnected (Figure 1.1). People performing a direct service function are often doing so within programs. Policies can influence the resources that clients have access to and funding that programs receive. Furthermore, programs and direct service providers attempt to influence policy in several ways. Programs may participate in coalitions and networks that participate in direct and indirect lobbying activities seeking to reform policy. Second, programs can function as incubators for best practices that are then applied by local, state, and federal governments. When proven to be effective, those ideas can be brought to scale and replicated through larger government programing. Often, some of the most impactful programs are those that are implemented in partnerships with nonprofit organizations, government, and private business. This approach is referred to as a multisectoral solution. We provide examples of these models in Chapter 3.

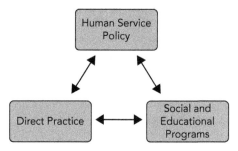

FIGURE 1.1   The Interconnectivity of Three Domains

Intersectionality

The study and practice of human services considers human behavior within the social and political environment, and the complex interplay between these forces. Examining practices, programs, and policies offers an intersectional exploration of the field. *Intersectionality* is defined as the interconnectivity among multiple social identities and inequalities, such as gender, race/ethnicity, social class, age, disability, LGBTQ+ identity, immigration status, religious or cultural identity, and more (Crenshaw, 1989; Murphy-Erby et al., 2010, p. 679). Intersectionality considers the contributions of complex factors within and between individuals, families, communities, and the broader social and economic system, by especially considering how people experience the impact of different types of oppression or privilege.

Intersectionality highlights the complexity, nuance, and uniqueness of human experiences. For example, sexism does not affect all women in the same way. Black trans women experience different social barriers compared to immigrant women of West Indian descent. Although sexism may seem like a common risk for all women, the experience of sexism may impact women differently based on their social location. The term **social location** refers to the unique way that factors such as race, class, gender, age, language, immigration status, ability, religion, sexual orientation, and geography shape a person's experience. The lens of intersectionality improves how we understand the different types of work human services professionals practice.

1.2 TYPES OF HUMAN SERVICES WORK

Who Are Human Services Professionals? What Do Human Services Professionals Do?

Human services professionals work in nonprofit organizations, private companies, and within governmental agencies to support individual, family, and community well-being. Throughout different sectors, human services professionals consider individual, family, and community needs, and address these needs through the implementation of practices, programs, and policies. Human services professionals work in a wide range of fields, such as health care, education, and social work.

Human services professionals work in three different types or domains of practice (Figure 1.2): micro (direct practice), meso (programs and other initiatives), and macro (policy). They work to prevent, intervene, and treat social problems that may negatively impact the health and well-being of individuals, families, and communities. In addition, human services practitioners also work to enhance access and opportunities to maximize wellness. Subsequent chapters delve into the nuances, skills, and knowledge associated with many of the various practice modalities introduced in this chapter.

Human service work is performed in multiple settings across the life course. **Life course theory** (LCT) considers individual development over time, from birth to death and highlights how human development is impacted by the time and place of development, developmental pathways or trajectories, interdependency, human agency or decision-making, diversity, and the balance of individual and developmental risk and protective factors (Elder, 1998; Hutchison, 2011). LCT considers the context of human

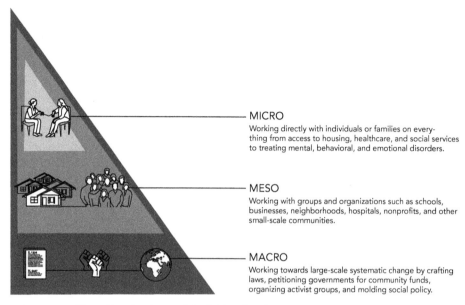

FIGURE 1.2   Three Practice Areas of Social Work: Micro, Meso, Macro

development and explores how specific experiences and social changes interact with growing and changing human beings.

Generalist Knowledge and Skills

Training of emerging human services professionals at the undergraduate level includes both theoretical content and skill development. Meaningful engagement in the field requires both an understanding of *why* social problems emerge and *how* to engage in planned change efforts. Generalist practice knowledge and skills are those that can adapt and support many different populations in a variety of settings. The values, knowledge, and skills of generalist practice are transferable within and between practice communities. Generalist practices can include direct practice and human services work in programs and policy. Below, we discuss these three areas of practice and define them as micro, meso, and macro practice. These domains align with areas of practice in social work but can be applied to human services practice and social change efforts more broadly. We further discuss the relevance of micro, meso, and macro practice in Chapter 3.

Micro Practice

Micro practice refers to providing services directly to individuals, families, and groups. We discuss this in detail in Chapters 4 and 5. It is the most common form of human services work. This type of practice may include case work, counseling, and direct personal or health care. Direct service work can be done within all sectors (public, private, and governmental) and can be found within mental health and health care systems, educational systems, and criminal justice systems. *Case management* is a direct practice tool that aims to coordinate client care. A case manager performs a range of activities, including planning or coordinating an array of health and social service programs to meet a particular client's needs.

Pine Street Inn in Boston, Massachusetts, is the largest homeless services provider in New England (Pine Street Inn, 2020). At the Pine Street Inn, human services professionals work with individuals who lack access to permanent housing. Pine Street Inn refers to people who use their services as "guests." Other similar organizations might use labels such as "resident" or "client." Word choices can be important ways to signal the values and philosophy of an organization and the relationships they hope to have with people who are using their services. In a direct service staff position, a human services professional might support their guest in the process of identifying longer term housing opportunities. They could work with the guest to explain the process for accessing public housing or assist with completing an application. If a guest is seeking training or employment assistance or help with recovery from a substance use disorder, this is also something that a human services professional might support. Job titles associated with micro-level practice include case manager, school social worker, hospital social worker, and crisis intervention counselor.

Meso Practice

Although direct practice may be the most familiar form of human/social service delivery, it is not the only mechanism of practice. Broader practice within groups, nonprofit organizations, institutions, and communities is defined as **meso practice**. Meso practice can include program planning and management, community organizing, community and economic development, and advocacy and activism (Jacobson, 2001). Pine Street Inn is a nonprofit organization working in a meso capacity and providing direct services. Pine Street Inn provides a range of services that include housing, emergency services, and workforce development for nearly 2,000 unhoused people each day. Another type of meso practice is community organizing. Community organizing is generally understood to be coordinated collective efforts on the part of a group to advocate for change (Box 1.1). Examples include organizing better public transportation, improvements to schools, or community safety. We discuss community organizing at length in Chapter 9. Job titles within meso-level practice include youth program coordinator, shelter director, or community organizer.

Macro Practice

Macro practice involves working to create large-scale systemic change. The term **social policy** refers to governmental policies designed to improve human welfare, such as measures related to health, education, housing, and criminal justice. The goal of social policy

---

BOX 1.1   United Way

United Way can trace some of its roots to the development and collaboration of the Charity Organization Society movement (discussed in Chapter 2) of the 19th century. As social service organizations began to systematically consider the economic and social predictors of poverty, small independent charities soon realized the complexity of their mission and considered the benefits of collaboration. Collaboration and cooperation within and between agencies streamlined the ways in which social services were requested and delivered to those in need. The first United Way began in 1918 in Chicago, Illinois "to encourage and stimulate collective community planning, and the development of better standards of community organization for social work" (Hansan, 2013, p. 1). Approximately four decades later, United Way had expanded to a national model, with more than 30,000 partner agencies, including local, state, national, and federal agencies. Today, the United Way has a broad mission to "mobilize the caring power of communities around the world to advance the common good" by focusing its work in three main areas: health, education, and financial stability (United Way, 2020).

is to foster personal, familial, and community well-being. Human services professionals can work to foster social policy that directly or indirectly improves outcomes for children, families, and communities and strives toward a more equitable society. Schoon and Bynner (2003) described implications for the development of social policy that are summarized here:

- Implement policy that addresses prevention rather than crisis intervention. Social policy should aim to prevent social problems by providing access to programs and practices. Early identification and intervention programs can prevent the occurrence of the problem, delay the onset of the problem, and reduce the magnitude and severity of the problem (Durlak, 1995).
- Implement asset-based policy that identifies and bolsters personal, family, and community strengths. Often, we identify problems and seek to solve them, rather than considering assets within the community that can be expanded.
- Implement policy that examines the predictors and processes associated with positive development. It is necessary to understand the precursors of positive adaptation and maladaptation and implement practices and programs that can address these factors. For example, if policy is seeking to address school failure and drop out, the root causes must be considered. Early educational interventions and developmentally appropriate school-based remediations may be a part of the predictive model of school failure. Other factors also need to be addressed, such as the role of race/ethnicity, family socioeconomic status, gender, disability status, student social–emotional functioning, and the broader community context.
- Implement policy that considers the interconnections between people and their communities. Policymakers should engage with key stakeholders in the community in developing solutions to social problems.
- Implement developmental policy that addresses the ongoing assets and risks within individuals, families, and communities over their lifetime. Interventions that are specific to one place and time may not effectively impact developmental outcomes. For example, although it is important to consider the role of early interventions, such as high-quality preschool, these programs may not address subsequent family or community risk that occurs after the cessation of the intervention (Lowenstein, 2011). Developmental policies include interventions throughout the life course.

Human services professionals have a unique and in-depth understanding of the ways that social policies positively and negatively impact individuals and communities. With this perspective, they can work directly and indirectly to influence social policy. Direct actions may include lobbying and advocacy. Indirect actions may include the educational development or social or emotional support of individuals and groups as they prepare to self-advocate (Banks, 1999). Human services professionals may work on a macro level with a nonprofit organization whose primary aim is to change policy, such as the National Alliance to End Homelessness. Although the work that organizations such as Pine Street Inn engage in is critical, are there also solutions at the macro level that could reduce the need for such services? Macro-level human services professionals work in organizations that provide a voice for policies that would better address issues of homelessness, such as advocating for the creation of affordable housing or expansion of subsidized housing.

Human services professionals may also participate in professional organizations that develop policy and advocacy priorities. For example, the National Association of Social Workers (NASW) has identified issues such as child welfare and student loan forgiveness as legislative priorities. Professional organizations such as NASW support research and legislative priorities about policy issues and create strategies for advocacy (NASW, n.d.). Job titles associated with macro-level practice include policy director, legislative aide, and coordinator of advocacy for behavioral health.

1.3 WHAT IS PREVENTION SCIENCE?

Human services professionals work in both proactive and reactive ways within micro, meso, and macro practice. Proactive approaches seek to support positive human growth and development and prevent or limit negative outcomes. Reactive approaches address existing social problems and implement treatments. Some human services practice can be considered both proactive (to prevent or limit negative outcomes) and reactive (working to address existing social problems and reduce further harm).

The National Prevention Science Coalition defines **prevention science** as "evidence-based strategies that reduce risk factors and enhance protective factors to improve the health and wellbeing of individuals, families, and communities" (National Science Coalition, 2019). Prevention science seeks to avoid negative health and social outcomes and strengthen conditions that allow people and communities to thrive. Prevention science developed within the field of health sciences, but it has been broadly applied to fields of medicine, psychology, social work, and education. A prevention perspective can be applied in many ways to help address the onset, duration, and severity of social problems (Coie et al., 1993).

Preventive interventions are introduced before the onset of a problem. *Universal preventive interventions* are targeted to all or most individuals in a population. *Selective interventions* target individuals at risk of a problem. *Indicated interventions* target individuals most at risk of a problem and are often associated with treatment programs (Gordon, 1983).

Universal prevention can be applied in many fields, from universal access to free public education to large-scale prevention efforts that use mass media campaigns to address public health concerns, such as the benefits of hand-washing to prevent the spread of a virus. These universal approaches seek to reduce risks associated with the onset or severity of a social problem.

Applying Prevention Science

The Substance Abuse and Mental Health Services Administration (SAMHSA, 2020) has estimated that approximately 140 million Americans use alcohol and 11.5 percent are heavy drinkers. This report concluded that 14.5 million people live with an alcohol use disorder (SAMHSA, 2020). The National Institute on Drug Abuse (2020a) estimated the costs of substance use disorder as $740 billion annually, which reflects costs associated with health care, the criminal justice system, and lost employment and work productivity. Focusing on prevention of substance use disorders is critical given its social and economic impacts.

Universal prevention programs have been initiated in school and community settings targeting individual youth and their families to address challenges with substance use. Programs that seek to prevent substance use and abuse among children and adolescents focus on reducing risk factors associated with the onset of substance use disorder and promoting protective attributes that reduce risk. Applying holistic and developmentally relevant strategies and programs that are "evidence based," meaning that they have been shown to have an impact, is important when providing prevention programing.

Principles of Effective Prevention Programs

The National Institute on Drug Abuse (NIDA) has outlined 11 prevention principles to consider when developing and implementing effective substance use disorder prevention programs (Table 1.1). Many of these principles apply to the development of other types of prevention programs, such as high school completion and violence prevention.

Treatment Responses

Prevention and intervention practices and programs may not always eliminate or reduce the problem of substance use disorder. The National Institute on Drug Abuse (2020b) recognizes that a range of care that includes individualized treatment programs can be crucial to successfully address issues of substance use disorder. It identifies both medical and mental health services as beneficial for someone living with substance use disorder. Treatment modalities may include behavioral counseling or medication. Outpatient treatment approaches may also be utilized, where people reside outside of a facility but participate in robust therapeutic treatment. Other individuals may pursue treatment in

TABLE 1.1   NIDA's 11 Principles of Effective Prevention Programs

Principle No.	Description
1	Prevention programs should enhance protective factors and reverse or reduce risk factors.
2	Prevention programs should address all forms of drug abuse.
3	Prevention programs should address risk and protective factors within the broader community.
4	Prevention programs should address specific risks, such as age, gender, and ethnicity.
5	Family-based prevention programs should enhance family functioning and include parenting skills and training in drug education.
6	Prevention programs can start as early as preschool to address early predictors of substance abuse, such as aggressive behavior, poor social skills, and academic difficulty.
7	Prevention programs can be implemented in elementary school to enhance academic and social functioning.
8	Prevention programs for middle and high school students should continue to foster school connections to support student study habits; communication; positive peer relationships; self-efficacy; and drug resistance skills, attitudes, and beliefs.
9	Prevention programs can be targeted to general populations, rather than targeted groups. These interventions reduce labeling and promote school and community shared values.
10	Combined family-school programs and partnerships can be more effective than single programs.
11	Broader school, community, and media programs and campaigns are most effective when they share consistent messages and information.

Source: Robertson et al. (2003).

a residential rehabilitation facility, where they may participate in therapeutic groups, individual counseling, and family therapy and, in some instances, they may receive medication. Provision of wraparound services, meaning comprehensive and holistic, is critical to success. These might include access to employment, training, or educational support. Individuals may also need housing or legal services.

Among the best known resources for individuals living with substance use disorder are mutual support group models such as Alcoholics Anonymous (AA) and Narcotics Anonymous (NA). These self-help and support group programs are based on 12-step models grounded in a set of principles designed to foster group process and uplift members of the group. Support groups are led by their own members, and although AA is the best known, other examples include Sex and Love Addicts Anonymous, Overeaters Anonymous, and Gamblers Anonymous. The use of self-help groups such as AA and NA has been very effective for many people.

1.4 HARM REDUCTION

Historically, people have viewed sobriety or abstinence as the goal of treatment; however, a **harm reduction** model provides an alternative perspective. According to Foy (2017), **harm reduction** is any activity or policy that aims to reduce the potential harm of a particular activity. For example, people struggling with substance use may seek a sobriety approach in which they fully abstain from drugs and alcohol. For others, this approach might not be aligned with their needs or current situation. Harm reduction suggests that abstinence approaches are not the only way to have a positive impact on individuals and communities (Leslie et al., 2008). Harm reduction models provide a different way of thinking about issues that recognizes how social and economic factors contribute to individual behavior while promoting policy and programmatic that reduce immediate- and long-term risks.

Harm Reduction International (2020) asserts these principles:

- Keep people alive and encourage positive change in their lives.
- Reduce the harms of drug laws and policy.
- Offer alternatives to approaches that seek to prevent or end drug use.

Examples of activities using a harm reduction approach include the following:

- Needle and syringe exchange programs
- Opioid substitution therapies such as methadone and buprenorphine
- Supervised injection sites
- Overdose prevention interventions such as naloxone

Shifting from an abstinence-only approach to a harm reduction model has been critical to the fight against the opioid crisis (Wallace et al., 2018). Like harm reduction, decriminalization also prioritizes health and safety. The Portugal model, for example, shifted its focus away from incarcerating drug users to providing improved treatment and other services designed to reduce harm. The decriminalization of drugs in Portugal has resulted in fewer drug-related deaths, incarcerations, and HIV diagnosis (Transform Drug Policy Foundation, 2021).

1.5 RETHINKING RESPONSES

Once a social problem manifests, we need to consider what systems and institutions are best equipped to respond and how we can reduce the risk of future harm. As discussed previously, human services intersect with many systems. The interconnections between human services and the criminal justice system are considerable. In the case of crime, how can our systems better respond to the needs of victims and offenders? **Restorative justice** is an approach emphasizing accountability, making amends, and, when desired, facilitated meetings between victims, offenders, and other persons. Criminologist and pioneer of social justice Howard Zehr (2015) has asserted that the three core pillars of restorative justice ask:

- Harms and needs: Who was harmed? What was the harm? How can it be repaired?
- Obligations: Who is responsible and accountable and how can they repair the harm?
- Engagement: Victims and offenders have active roles in the justice process.

Restorative justice models seek to use a community versus criminal justice approach to reduce some of the negative outcomes associated with traditional forms of punishment, such as incarceration. These approaches include activities such as facilitated dialogue, during which restitution agreements and plans are created. Often, contracts are created in which offenders are mandated to apologize and do community service to compensate for a victim's loss. Human services professionals may interact with the restorative justice model when supporting clients who are involved in the criminal justice system. These approaches can respond to our social problems while reducing risks for future harm. Restorative justice models are being explored as a approach for resolving conflict in school settings. Some college campuses are exploring the use of restorative justice approaches in cases of sexual assault. Viewing restorative justice through a prevention science lens, this approach can reduce the risks associated with holding a criminal record, including being unhoused or unemployed.

SPOTLIGHT ON SERVICE-LEARNING

Reflecting on a human services profession you have encountered, is it performing micro, meso, or macro practice? Consider a human services organization you have served with. How many of its services and programs focus on prevention?

SUMMARY

- The field of human services is defined as a range of occupations centered on the goals of helping people meet basic human needs and solving social problems. Human services professionals work to meet human needs through an interdisciplinary knowledge base focused on prevention, intervention, and treatment of social problems. Human services are services that work to enhance the quality of life of individuals, families, and communities.
- The three types of human services work are micro, meso, and macro practice.
- Micro practice refers to providing services at the micro level, via one-on-one practice. Direct practice that involves interactions with individuals, families, and

groups is the most common form of human services work. This type of practice may include case work, counseling, and direct personal or health care.

- Meso practice includes practice within families, groups, nonprofit organizations, institutions, and communities. Meso practice can include program planning and management, community organizing, community and economic development, and advocacy and activism. This type of practice may include program coordination, directing and managing social service organization, or community organizing.
- Macro practice involves working to create large-scale systemic change. Developing and implementing social policy is one way to engage in macro practice. Direct actions may include lobbying and advocacy. Macro practitioners can work to create, implement, and advocate for community needs at the federal, state, or local level.
- Prevention science is an evidence-based approach that considers micro, meso, and macro risk and protective factors. Specifically, prevention science practices work to reduce risk and enhance protective factors through prevention, intervention, and treatment programs. There is a strong focus on trying to prevent or minimize the impacts of social problems before they manifest.
- Harm reduction is any activity or policy that aims to reduce the potential harm of a particular activity. Harm reduction suggests that abstinence approaches are not the only way to have a positive impact on individuals and communities. The goal of harm reduction approaches is to reduce the negative impacts of an issue without an exclusive focus on elimination or abstinence.

REVIEW QUESTIONS

Assessment Questions

1. What is the difference between micro, meso, and macro practice? What are examples of each?
2. Why is prevention science needed in the field of human services and how is it implemented?
3. How does the prevention science model help us think about addressing social problems such as substance use disorder? How can prevention, intervention, and treatment models be applied to this issue?
4. What are the characteristics of a harm reduction approach?

Reflection Questions

1. Why are interconnectivity and intersectionality such important ideas in the field of human services? How can we ensure that these ideas are always considered when considering new solutions to social problems?
2. Think of an issue such as housing or juvenile crime. How might a human services professional support a client using direct practice, program, or policy approaches?
3. What is an issue that is traditionally addressed by reactive approaches that could be addressed by the principles of prevention science, and how would that be executed?
4. What are other examples of when a harm reduction approach might be beneficial? Consider both the benefits and drawbacks of this type of approach.

REFERENCES

Banks, S. (1999). The social professions and social policy: Proactive or reactive? *European Journal of Social Work, 2*(3), 327–339.

Coie, J. D., Watt, N. F., West, S. G., Hawkins, J. D., Asarnow, J. R., Markman, H. J., Ramey, S. L., Shure, M. B., & Long, B. (1993). The science of prevention: A conceptual framework and some directions for a national research program. *American Psychologist, 48*(10), 1013–1022.

Crenshaw, K. W. (1989). Demarginalizing the intersection of race and sex: A Black feminist critique of antidiscrimination doctrine, feminist theory, and antiracist politics. *University of Chicago Legal Forum, 14*, 538–554.

Durlak, J. A. (1995). *School-based prevention programs for children and adolescents.* SAGE.

Elder, G. H., Jr. (1998). The life course as developmental theory. *Child Development, 69*(1), 1–12.

Foy, S. (2017). *Solution focused harm reduction: Working effectively with people who misuse substances.* Springer.

Gordon, R. S., Jr. (1983). An operational classification of disease prevention. *Public Health Reports, 98*(2), 107–109.

Hansan, J. E. (2013). *United Way of America.* Retrieved March 5, 2020, from https://socialwelfare.library.vcu.edu/eras/civil-war-reconstruction/united-way-of-america

Harm Reduction International. (2020). *What is harm reduction?* https://www.hri.global/what-is-harm-reduction

Hutchison, E. D. (2011). Life course theory. In R. J. R. Levesque (Ed.), *Encyclopedia of adolescence.* Springer.

Jacobson, W. B. (2001). Beyond therapy: Bringing social work back to human services reform. *Social Work, 46*(1), 51–61.

Leslie, K. M., Canadian Paediatric Society, & Adolescent Health Committee. (2008). Harm reduction: An approach to reducing risky health behaviours in adolescents. *Paediatrics & Child Health, 13*(1), 53–56.

Lowenstein, A. E. (2011). Early care and education as educational panacea: What do we really know about its effectiveness? *Educational Policy, 25*(1), 92–114.

Murphy-Erby, Y., Christy-McMullin, K., Stauss, K., & Schriver, J. (2010). Multi-systems life course: A new practice perspective and its application in advanced practice with racial and ethnic populations. *Journal of Human Behavior in the Social Environment, 20*(5), 672–687.

National Institute of Mental Health. https://www.nimh.nih.gov/about/advisory-boards-and-groups/namhc/reports/priorities-for-prevention-research-at-nimh

National Association of Social Workers. (n.d.). *Advocacy.* Retrieved March 16, 2021, from https://www.socialworkers.org/Advocacy

National Institute on Drug Abuse. (2020a). *Trends & statistics.* Retrieved June 8, 2020, from https://www.drugabuse.gov/related-topics/trends-statistics#supplemental-references-for-economic-costs

National Institute on Drug Abuse. (2020b, July 24). *Treatment.* https://www.drugabuse.gov/publications/drugfacts/treatment-approaches-drug-addiction

National Science Coalition. (2019). What is Prevention Science? https://www.npscoalition.org/prevention-science

Pine Street Inn. (2020). *Pine Street Inn home.* https://www.pinestreetinn.org

Robertson, E. B., David, S. L., & Rao, S. A. (2003). *Preventing drug use among children and adolescents: A research-based guide for parents, educators, and community leaders.* Diane Publishing. https://d14rmgtrwzf5a.cloudfront.net/sites/default/files/preventingdruguse_2_1.pdf

Schoon, I., & Bynner, J. (2003). Risk and resilience in the life course: Implications for interventions and social policies. *Journal of Youth Studies, 6*(1), 21–31.

Stinchcomb, J. (2021). *What is human services.* National Organization for Human Services. https://www.Nationalhumanservices.Org/What-Is-Human-Services.

Substance Abuse and Mental Health Services Administration. (2020). *Key substance use and mental health indicators in the United States: Results from the 2019 National Survey on Drug Use and Health* (HHS Publication No. PEP20-07-01-001, NSDUH Series H-55). Center for Behavioral Health Statistics and

Quality, Substance Abuse and Mental Health Services Administration. https://www.samhsa.gov/data

Transform Drug Policy Foundation. (2021, May 13). *Drug decriminalisation in Portugal: Setting the record straight.* https://transformdrugs.org/blog/drug-decriminalisation-in-portugal-setting-the-record-straight

United Way. (2020). *Our mission.* Retrieved June 9, 2020, from https://www.unitedway.org/our-impact/mission

U.S. Department of Health and Human Services. (n.d.). *Office of Human Services Policy.* Office of the Assistant Secretary for Planning and Evaluation. Retrieved March 16, 2021, from https://aspe.hhs.gov/office-human-services-policy

Wallace, B., Barber, K., & Pauly, B. B. (2018). Sheltering risks: Implementation of harm reduction in homeless shelters during an overdose emergency. *International Journal of Drug Policy, 53,* 83–89.

Zehr, H. (2015). *The little book of restorative justice: Revised and updated.* Simon & Schuster.

CHAPTER 2

Early History of the Human Services Field

Learning Objectives

After completing this chapter, you will be able to:

2.1. Describe the nature and purpose of early social services and nonprofit organizations.

2.2. Describe how poverty was viewed in the colonial United States.

2.3. Explain how colonial-era institutions categorized "worthy" and "unworthy" poor.

2.4. Describe the development of the nonprofit sector in the United Kingdom.

2.5. Define *scientific charity* and *social Darwinism* and explain how these concepts shaped social programs.

2.6. Describe the settlement house movement and its influence on assistance for the poor.

2.7. List late-19th- and early 20th-century social programs that were established to protect children from abuse and neglect.

2.8. Describe the growth and funding for social programs in the 1900s.

The configuration and scope of support for those in need have long been debated. Is it the job of the government (the state) to support people in need? Or is it best left to religious institutions or the family? Maybe institutions outside of government are best suited to provide assistance? It can be argued that our government serves the masses, and civil society should support those with needs that remain unmet. Perhaps the government should address some needs but not others. Whatever the configuration, there are benefits and limitations to social support from the government, business, and civil society sectors. When debating "Whose role is it anyway?" we are also asking questions about power. Who has power and why? How do power imbalances perpetuate inequality? Who has the resources and ability to respond to social inequality? What does the presence or absence of power afford a person or a community? What historical conditions have compounded or disrupted power dynamics? In this chapter, we explore the early history of people and organizations dedicated to social service, highlighting seminal program models, global dynamics, power dynamic, and how certain core historical debates persist today.

2.1 EARLY SOCIAL SERVICES AND NONPROFIT ORGANIZATIONS

United States models were heavily influenced by those in Europe, specifically England. During European feudalism, between the 9th and 15th centuries, the roles of individuals in society and systems of support were clearly codified. Roles and social and economic status were delineated. Christian monasteries, where basic food and shelter were provided, represented one of the only supplemental supports for those in need during this time (Box 2.1; Dyer, 2012). Monasteries served this role in England until their dissolution by King Henry VIII in the 1530s (Higginbotham, 2011). As feudalism was declining, and cities and towns were developing, new approaches to address social and economic challenges emerged. In addition, between 1348 and 1349, one-third to one-half of the British population perished as a result of the bubonic plague pandemic known as the Black Death, which decimated its labor force and inspired surviving workers the opportunity to command a higher wage. As a result of this shortage, the Ordinance of Labourers was passed in 1349, establishing a set of rules governing labor and wages (Quigley, 2015. The ordinance was designed to ensure that "able-bodied" individuals were contributing to Britain's economy. It also sought to control wages among laborers, who found themselves with greater negotiating power during the labor shortage. Many historians mark this ordinance as the start of what would become known as the British Poor Laws, a set of policies designed to regulate and respond to poverty.

The British Poor Laws evolved over a 500-year period. These laws had several aims, including controlling the labor force and determining who would receive and administer poor relief and under what circumstances; and to assert control of behaviors deemed undesirable, such as street begging. Local parishes were charged with implementing a "poor rate" which taxed parish households; those funds, in turn, supported relief efforts. In some instances, "able-bodied" people who refused to work could be imprisoned. In 1601, Queen Elizabeth refined the Poor Laws, making "relieving want" an obligation of the state (Trattner, 2007). The Elizabethan Poor Laws also made parents legally obligated to support their children and grandchildren, and adult children were legally obligated to provide for parents and grandparents (Trattner, 2007).

BOX 2.1 Religion and Responding to Need

Among all major religions, leaders use historical texts to call for charity and support of those in most need. Within the Qur'an, there is a focus on the need for justice and cooperation among the children of Allah. The role of tithing within Judaism and Christianity reflects this call to charity as well. Dāna is the practice of cultivating generosity in Hinduism and Buddhism. Although there have been many interpretations and critiques of these practices, faith communities have played an important and sometimes complex role in responding to human needs.

2.2 POVERTY IN THE 13 COLONIES

The best way of doing good to the poor, is not making them easier in poverty, but leading
or driving them out of it.

—Benjamin Franklin (1766/1987, pp. 587–588)

Early settlers in colonial states replicated many of the European approaches. Generally
residing in homogeneous communities, colonists could typically depend on neighborly
support (Trattner, 2007). Quigley (1996) explains that the colonial laws emphasized
localized responsibility for the poor. Furthermore, he explains that the colonial Poor
Laws only obligated towns to care for their own poor and that poverty-stricken strangers
were not welcome in communities. Quigley states, "People who were poor but new to the
area were forcefully instructed to return to where they came from and subject to jail if
they disobeyed their order of banishment" (p. 64).

The early colonies were deeply rooted in Calvinistic beliefs, or what is often
referred to as the Protestant work ethic. John Calvin, a 16th-century French theologian
(Figure 2.1), believed that selected individuals were predestined for heaven, meaning
that a person's eternal fate was predetermined. It was not possible to know for certain
who the chosen ones were, but one indicator was "earthly success."

Calvinistic values favored work, thrift, and economic independence. Kahl (2005)
explains:

The most certain mark of election [for heaven] was proving one's faith in a worldly activity, and success in a worldly occupation and wealth became an absolute sign that one was
saved by God from the start, while poverty became the certain sign of damnation! The
Calvinist creation of the Protestant work ethos and the strict and systematic

FIGURE 2.1 John Calvin (1509–1564)

requirements about what constitutes a life that increases the glory of God (e.g., personal responsibility, individualism, discipline, and asceticism) made poverty appear to be the punishment for laziness and sinful behavior. Good works were a necessary but not a sufficient sign of being chosen. (p. 107)

2.3 INSTITUTIONAL RESPONSES

During the colonial era, the previously discussed values were deeply embedded in dominant institutions, laws, perspectives, and responses to the poor. The British distinctions between the "worthy" and "unworthy" poor carried over to the 13 colonies that would eventually become the United States. The "worthy poor" in historical language included widows, orphans, or those with a visible physical disability. The politicians and the public in both the US and the UK became weary of outdoor relief models (Trattner, 2007). During the eighteenth and nineteenth centuries governments in both Britain and the U.S. would favor institutional models such as workhouses or poorhouses, an approach that was consistent with Calvinistic values (Trattner, 2007). Workhouses were housing institutions set up by the state for those unable to support themselves. They were a response to poverty that provided relief where the poor lived and worked (Figure 2.2). In 1834, the English Poor Laws were amended to expand the workhouse model. Although this approach had been applied previously, the Poor Laws now codified their usage. Family members in workhouses were separated from each other, and for elders, the workhouse was often their residence until they died.

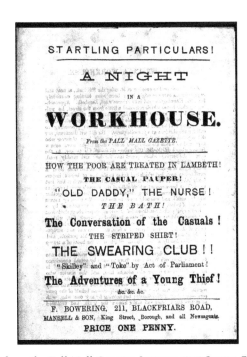

FIGURE 2.2 Excerpt from the Pall Mall Gazette, January 1866 *Source*: Colin Waters/Alamy Stock Photo

Although built with both cost and morals in mind, workhouses soon became places of stigma (Higginbotham, 2011). Charles Dickens was a political journalist covering parliament during the inception of these workhouse policies. Dickens was so disturbed by the workhouse approach that it is said to have inspired him to write *Oliver Twist* (1838). This novel contains one of the most well-known depictions of the workhouse program, narrating the harsh conditions experienced by both adults and children.

Mental Health Needs

The previous approaches aimed to address economic and social struggle. Concurrently, the imperative to create responses to mental health care was also growing. Historically, individuals living with mental health challenges were poorly understood and poorly cared for. Care options were limited to family support, the prison system, or other relief programs. Society's understanding of mental health has evolved over centuries. Researchers and mental health providers today benefit from centuries of knowledge about the human brain and how emotions are processed, as well as the influence of the social environment and human relationships. Although contemporary systems of care remain inadequate, advances in psychopharmacology and talk therapy have accelerated in the past 70 years.

Bethlem Hospital was founded in London, UK in the 13th century for individuals affected by mental distress and with no place else to go. It became known as a hospital for individuals who had "gone mad." Bethlem became known as "bedlam," and given the hospital's reputation and notoriety for abuse, the word *bedlam* became synonymous with chaos and "madness." Impoverished people who were deemed not psychologically well enough for workhouses were often called "Tom o'Bedlams" and were sent to places such as Bethlem Hospital. As a result, these hospitals removed people from society deemed to be a public nuisance. Recognizing that they were not suitable for prison or the workhouses, this was perceived to be a humane option (Jay, 2016). Many of these earliest psychiatric hospitals, however, were opulent on the outside and inhospitable on the inside, housing residents in deplorable conditions in which they were often chained and subjected to physical abuse.

In the late 1700s, reformers such as William Tuke advocated for a different approach to mental health that focused on treatment and recovery. Tuke's "moral treatment" approach centered on the belief that people could become well and should be treated with dignity and respect. This new model of care fueled the first hospital of its kind called The Retreat in York, England, focusing on a therapeutic approach that centered individual rights and wellness at the core of treatment, and did not use chains to restrict residents. The Retreat is still in operation today. The growth of these facilities throughout the United Kingdom and Europe would become part what is now called the asylum movement. The word asylum was originally defined as a "place of refuge"; however, the word connotes a very different meaning now (Box 2.2). The Museum of the Mind on the outskirts of London provides exhibits on the historical and contemporary issues related to mental health and is also adjacent to the modern-day Bethlem hospital.

In the early years of the United States, there were few facilities designed for the express purpose of caring for individuals in need of mental health services. In the 1800s, Dorothea Dix, a nurse, educator, and activist who had her own challenges with

BOX 2.2   Language

Language has a unique ability to reflect the values and beliefs in a society. Historically, people experiencing psychological distress were referred to as "lunatics." This word choice reflected the historical perceptions that symptoms had a lunar (moon) relationship. "Insane" was another word that was commonly used, meaning mad, or without sound mind or reason. Although insane is a word that we currently use, it is generally limited to legal language or in casual settings, not within the human services or medical fields. As the text in this chapter suggests, the original meaning of the word asylum did not carry with it the same connotation as today. Currently, we use a broader umbrella to consider mental health to include how we feel, think, act, make decisions, and relate to others in our lives. Many people will label mental illness as neurodivergence or the status of having a diagnosis such as bipolar disorder or schizophrenia. However, these labels do not fully reflect people's experiences or identity, because mental health and illness can exist on a continuum and not always in a discrete category or diagnosis. There are many ways to be healthy or well, and people often experience challenges (e.g., mental, social, occupational) along a continuum. Furthermore, the presence, absence, or severity of mental health challenges vary at different points in people's lives. Thus, the language and terms that we currently use for mental illness may become antiquated in response to changing cultural forces and our evolving understanding of the human experience.

depression, toured The Retreat and was inspired by the work of Tuke and others. She was so motivated to have an impact on these issues, upon returning home to the United States, she began working in a women's prison in Cambridge, Massachusetts. Appalled with the conditions there, she advocated for better mental health care and was instrumental in the creation of state mental health facilities. Her efforts resulted in the creation of the state hospital model that was used throughout the US. These facilities were designed in the spirit of The Retreat model—a place of refuge. Facilities were thoughtfully designed with the intent to promote wellness. Many had large windows to promote natural light, and were often situated on beautiful grounds providing recreation in addition to other forms of therapeutic opportunities (Box 2.3). It is important to also recognize that these models of mental health services were less available for some people in society. For example, many in the African American community have historically utilized the church as a primary support for well-being (Dempsey et al., 2016) rather than retreat facilities. Differences in utilizations can stem from discrimination or familial or cultural norms around support.

The promise of the state hospital system was never fully realized. State funds were reduced, resulting in poor management. There was a lack of viable and effective treatments. In the absence of contemporary treatments, these were also places where inhumane experimental treatments were performed, such as insulin shock therapy, electroconvulsive therapies (ECTs), and prefrontal lobotomies. Although ECTs and some psychosurgeries are performed today, these procedures are performed discriminately, judiciously, with consent, and with anesthesia.

By the 1950s, more pharmacological treatments became available for mental illness, and in the 1960s, federal policies shifted funding into community-based treatment approaches in the United States. This confluence of factors resulted in the closure of many of these state hospitals, or what is often referred to as deinstitutionalization. Contemporary researchers suggest that deinstitutionalization is a misnomer because many people in need of intensive mental health care ended up in other institutional settings such as

BOX 2.3	Buffalo State Asylum for the Insane

The state hospital in Buffalo, New York, serves as an example of the enlightened asylum model (Figure 2.3). Opened in 1880, this state-of-the-art facility sat on more than 200 acres of land. Landscape designer Frederick Law Olmsted, famous for designing Central Park in New York City, created a park-like environment that was intended to promote wellness. The hospital was in operation until the 1970s, and it is registered on the National Register of Historic Places.

FIGURE 2.3   Hotel Henry, formerly the Buffalo Asylum for the Insane, in Buffalo, NY
Source: © Christopher Payne /Esto for the image.

the prison system. The term trans-institutionalization may better describe the experiences of people shifting from state hospitals to other institutions. Although advances have been made to mental health care, many people in need of services find themselves in the prison system or other institutions that are ill-equipped to appropriately provide care.

2.4 THE DEVELOPMENT OF THE NONPROFIT SECTOR: LONDON'S EAST END

Social problems received increased attention in economically segregated London. In the 1800s, there was a period of growth and expansion of charitable organizations (Ball & Sunderland, 2001). As Charles Dickens described in *A Tale of Two Cities* (1859), the West End was home to people of affluence and influence, whereas the East End housed laborers, immigrants, and those with limited economic resources. The East End's location near the docks made it a hub for global commerce and also a center of "unsavory" activities, such as alcohol consumption and sex work (Booth, 2014).

The East End attracted two types of "outsiders." The first group included well-intentioned charity workers, students, and philanthropists seeking to understand and respond to poverty. Many of the most enduring and influential charities have their roots here, including the Salvation Army, the Jewish Board of Guardians (now Jewish Care), and Toynbee Hall (discussed later). The second group consisted of poverty tourists who

BOX 2.4	Poverty Tourism in India

The practice of "slumming" exists today and provokes significant moral concerns. Companies have established "slum" tours throughout the world, including India. Tours of Indian poverty advertise themselves as "reality tours" offering "authentic" experiences of India. They often claim to focus on debunking popular negative depictions of Indian poverty, such as those portrayed in the award-winning film, *Slumdog Millionaire* (Meschkank, 2011). Whereas proponents stress that poverty tours can promote education and charity, critics condemn these tours as voyeuristic and exploitative.

One of the largest issues surrounding poverty tourism is that residents have no opportunity to consent or object. Even when tour agencies claim to provide a mutually beneficial experience, they are doing so without access to a resident's perspective. In reality, these views fail to account for the wide range of potential negative impacts on residents, including violation of privacy, degradation, disrespect, misrepresentation, and perpetuation of social relegation (Whyte et al., 2011).

engaged in "slumming"—visiting the East End to observe its residents as a form of entertainment (Koven, 2006). "Slum journalists" and "slum novelists" wrote accounts of East End social goings-on for entertainment purposes (Box 2.4).

To many, the East End represented what William Booth, founder of the Salvation Army (Figure 2.4), described as "Darkest England" in his book *In Darkest England, and the Way Out*, published in 1890. The book's title was based on British explorer Henry Morton Stanley's *Through the Dark Continent* and *Darkest Africa*. The phrase "Darkest Africa" was meant to depict, to a mostly middle and upper-class white Christian readership, a place of "savages," the "uncivilized," and the "godless" in need of saving (Booth,

FIGURE 2.4   William Booth (1829–1912)

2014). Similarly, many believed that the East End was a place of savages and people in need of "saving."

Racism and classism were prevalent in the early history of the European and US conceptualization of socially and economically disadvantaged people and communities. Booth, a former Methodist minister, established the Salvation Army in 1865 to provide service through mission work to people who were unwelcome at traditional churches. Tice (1992) explains, "the *Salvationist's* **duty** was to inject a Christian ethic into industrial society and to intervene when the state neglected the poor" (p. 64). The Salvation Army expanded to the United States and ultimately to 131 countries, and it is one of the most widely known organizations of its kind (Salvation Army International Trust, 2019). Their approach would soon be at odds with the emerging thinking about how poverty relief should emphasize "worthiness."

2.5 SCIENTIFIC CHARITY AND SOCIAL DARWINISM

Charles Darwin was a 19th-century English naturalist who revolutionized modern Western society with development of the theory of evolution by natural selection. Darwin's 1859 book *On the Origin of Species* book summarized his observation of finches during a five week visit to the Galapagos Archipelago in Ecuador, South America. It was during this voyage that Darwin first began to infer the evolution of species based on their environment and the practices of adaptation to one's environment over generations (Sulloway, 1982).

A growing group of social reformers started to reject previous models of what they saw as "indiscriminate relief" or charity regardless of social and economic behavior. Committed to what they saw as a better way to respond to poverty, a new approach emerged under the auspices of "scientific charity," sometimes referred to as "scientific philanthropy." Scientific charity was grounded in theories of social Darwinism. This expansive and influential approach would again find itself in conflict with emerging norms. Profound questions arose from Darwin's research and its ability to help understand social order. Eddy (2010) explains,

> Darwinism raised many moral issues in the human social context of the late nineteenth century. Did the natural world provide a basis or model for moral action for human beings? Would the authority of science come to replace the authority of theology? What could be said about human nature from a Darwinist perspective and did that mesh with the theological anthropology of the day? Were human beings more fundamentally committed to communion or to combat with each other? Was the natural moral law one of competition or of cooperation? (p. 22)

Herbert Spencer, an English philosopher who coined the term "survival of the fittest," believed that government and charitable intervention to poverty weakened society. Martin (2012) explains: "Although Spencer's theory of social superiority was developed in advance of Darwin's theory, his followers relied upon Darwin's theory of natural selection for scientific validity of social Darwinism" (p. 25). The core principle of this approach was that charity should work along with and not against natural selection (Gettleman, 1963). Keeping with their goals of what they saw as better coordinated, more targeted interventions to people deemed worthy, they believed scientific charity would be the best way to eliminate poverty. A stark contrast with the Salvation Army, Tice (1992) explains, "For Salvationists, the dichotomy of worthiness and un-worthiness that characterized the work of scientific charity was irrelevant since the redemptive powers of God undercut such distinctions" (p. 64).

The most well-known proponent of the scientific charity approach was the Charitable Organization Society (COS). COS emerged from several charitable organizations working in London around 1869 (see Humphreys, 2001; Kendall, 2000). The core ideas were to distinguish the poor into worthy and unworthy poor, organize a system of giving, and implement what would become early casework. Proponents of this approach believed that poverty solutions could be systematized. Ziliak (2004) explains that in order to understand poverty,

> you had to get up close to it. To understand poor people you had to "befriend" them individually, studying each "case." And to improve poor people—as the COS desired to do—you had of course to construct an ideal of them. (p. 434)

COS interventions designated people as worthy or unworthy based on case evaluations. Humphreys (2001) explains:

> The veracity and background of each impoverished applicant would first be methodically investigated. Individuals judged to be deserving of, and likely to benefit from, assistance would be directed to the most appropriate charitable agency to develop their rehabilitation into society. (p. 1)

In the United States, COS began as a protest against the unsatisfactory operation of private and public charity efforts during the Long Depression of 1873–1878 (Bremner, 1956). The U.S. COS movement was primarily led by Josephine Shaw Lowell (Figure 2.5),

FIGURE 2.5   Josephine Lowell (1843–1905)

a member of Boston's elite upper class who became a formidable social reformer and philanthropist. She became the first female commissioner of the New York State Board of Charities and a founder of the New York City COS. Lowell, and colleagues sought to "teach the rich how to give and the poor how to live" (Waugh, 2001, p. 218). Lowell believed that charity and public assistance should be granted "only when starvation is imminent." The COS movement believed that charity should not make life too comfortable for low-income people; they believed, perhaps based on a Calvinist "work ethic," that "excessive" charity would weaken society.

Mary Richmond (Figure 2.6), a leader in the COS movement, sought to professionalize social work with the publication of her book *Social Diagnosis* (1917) and her work with the Red Cross Home Service (Franklin, 1986). Richmond's commitment to the establishment of a casework approach created the foundation for much of contemporary practice. Her philosophy de-emphasized social reform and aspired to establish social work as a technical profession. Franklin (1986) explains,

> Her book not only facilitated an easier transition to the helping processes as a technical service analogous to that of a doctor or lawyer, but, more importantly, it defined social diagnosis as the attempt to make as exact a definition as possible in relation to the other human beings upon whom he (the person) in any way depends or who depends upon him, and in relation to the social institutions in his community. (p. 517)

There were ultimately 52 COS locations in the US, where the COS model was influential in philanthropy and nonprofit operations. The COS of Denver, Colorado, established in 1877, eventually developed into United Way (Hansan, 2013). In 1898, the First Summer School in Philanthropic Work was established in New York by COS as the first school of social work. In 1904, the expanded program was renamed the New York

FIGURE 2.6 Mary Ellen Richmond (1861–1928) *Source*: History and Art Collection/Alamy Stock Photo

School of Philanthropy. By 1940, the school became officially associated with Columbia University as the Columbia University School of Social Work and extended its program to include graduate degrees (Columbia School of Social Work, n.d.).

The critical role that COS played in formalizing social work practice and the non-profit sector is undeniable. However, COS's emphasis on individual behavior and limited attention to social environment and structural forces created tensions with other leaders and organizations that emerged during the late 19th and early 20th centuries.

2.6 SETTLEMENT HOUSE MOVEMENT

> There can hardly be anything more opposed to conventional charity than the social settlement. . . . The settlements are not charitable institutions. They are, on the contrary, illustrations of social equality and democracy.
>
> —Francis Greenwood Peabody (1898, p. 329)

During the late 1880s, the settlement house movement took root in London's East End. In 1884, Samuel and Henrietta Barnett, social activists and philanthropists, founded Toynbee Hall, which was established with the purpose of providing an opportunity for Oxford and Cambridge University students to live and work with the poor. Toynbee Hall originated the global concept of the **settlement house** as a way to provide social services for poor workers while creating a community of learning and fellowship.

The early settlement house movement included some who subscribed to the ideas of scientific charity. However, its founders quickly adopted a philosophy of "practical socialism," promoting national health care, family leave, and a robust social welfare state. Settlements quickly spread throughout the United Kingdom and the world.

Hull House

Many U.S. thought leaders visited Toynbee Hall and were inspired by its approach. After spending three months at Toynbee Hall, social activist Stanton Coit established the first settlement house in New York City in 1886. Social reformer and activist Jane Addams visited Toynbee Hall in 1888 and, with her collaborator Ellen Gates Starr, founded the most well-known settlement, Chicago's Hull House, in 1889 (Figure 2.7).

Many leaders at Hull House were among a first generation of female college graduates (Box 2.5). Although they were educated, meaningful leadership and employment opportunities were limited for women. This generation of female graduates felt a sense of obligation to do something useful with their education, and they set in motion some of the most important social reforms and activities, such as kindergarten, citizenship classes, penny banks, and the creation of community playgrounds. The settlement house movement also led to subsequent social welfare and juvenile justice policy (Reinders, 1982).

African American and Black Communities

The settlement house movement has been criticized for ignoring African American communities and focusing primarily on immigrant communities from Western Europe (Lasch-Quinn, 1993). Although many settlement houses were concentrated in major

FIGURE 2.7   Postcard depicting Hull House in Chicago

| BOX 2.5 | Jane Addams |

After Hull House made Jane Addams famous, in 1909 she became the first female president of the National Conference of Social Work (Figure 2.8). In 1911, she was named the first head of the National Federation of Settlements. Addams also served as the first vice president of the National American Woman Suffrage Association. By the start of World War I, Addams turned her philanthropy toward the creation of a political movement pushing for pacifism and peace. In 1914, Addams, along with other social work professionals, created the American Union Against Militarism. She was investigated by the U.S. Federal Bureau of Investigation in the 1920s, and Herbert Hoover described her as "the most dangerous woman in America." Addams' foundational work in promoting international peace, particularly through a feminist lens, won her the Nobel Peace Prize in 1931 (Alonso, 1995).

FIGURE 2.8   Jane Addams (1860–1935)
Source: Prismatic Pictures/Bridgeman Images

northern cities, several were established in the South, including the Locust Street Social Settlement House in Hampton, Virginia, the first settlement house for African Americans. Locust Street was founded by Janie Porter Barrett (Figure 2.9), whose mother was formerly enslaved. Barrett was a leader in education and child welfare in Virginia over many decades. Barrett's approach to social reform included interracial cooperation and relied on relationships with members and leaders of White women's organizations (including Jane Addams') to support her agenda. Through this networking, Barrett was able to establish a rehabilitation center for at-risk African American girls, known as the Virginia Industrial School for Colored Girls. By 1920, the Virginia State Legislature began providing funds to establish educational institutions for White youth, modeled after the work of Barrett's institution (Social Welfare History Project, 2017).

The Robert Shaw Settlement House was incorporated in 1908 in Boston. Many leaders from the local African American community were involved in this settlement that provided cultural activities, youth clubs, vocational training, and programs serving the elderly. Robert Shaw Settlement House was named for the colonel who led one of the first African American regiments in the Civil War. He was also the brother of Josephine Shaw Lowell, leader of COS.

The settlement house movement's relationship with racial justice was complex. Although it is fair to critique how and who was served by these organizations, one must also recognize the incremental contributions that were made toward racial justice.

Photo by Foster, Richmond, Va.
MRS. JANIE PORTER BARRETT

FIGURE 2.9 Janie Porter Barrett (1865–1948)

Leaders from the settlement house movement served as founders and advocates for the National Association for the Advancement of Colored People (NAACP), and many recognized the impact of racism and segregation on African Americans and used research and legislative efforts to fight discrimination and prejudice (Moore, 1994).

International Settlements

The settlement house movement expanded far beyond the United Kingdom and the United States. In Japan, organizations were established by college students from Tokyo Imperial University in the spirit of the movement (Perkins, 2019). In the early 1900s, Japanese college students were very active in earthquake disaster response and sought to continue their efforts into anti-poverty programs. Many Christian missionaries also sought to replicate the settlement house approach in Japan (Ogawa, 2004). Also in the early 1900s, Russian philanthropists established a settlement house in Moscow to improve community conditions and provide early childhood education ("The First Social Settlement in Russia," 1912). The settlement house model could also be found in Canada, Hungary, and beyond (Berry, 2020).

2.7 CHILDREN AND YOUTH

Much like London during the 1800s, the conditions in some U.S. urban centers were crowded and often unsanitary. Several depressions strained cities, workers, and families. This reality included large numbers of unhoused youth, particularly in New York City. Some were orphans; others had been pushed out of a family residence due to crowding. Some still had attachments to family but were engaged in criminal activity. The rising number of youths living in these conditions became a growing societal concern (Rivlin & Manzo, 1988). Orphanages were the predominant model of care for unhoused children during this time. Other children lived and worked as apprentices in various trades. All of these responses were ad hoc, insufficient, and fraught with challenges.

Orphan Trains

Very few government interventions or laws existed to protect children in the 19th and early 20th centuries. Robust child labor laws, foster care, or government-run child welfare programs did not exist. Charles Brace, founder of the Child Aid Society, devised a program that became known as the orphan trains. Under this approach, children who were unhoused or came from families that were unable to care for them traveled by train from New York City to the Midwest and to Canada and were adopted by families (Figure 2.10). Some children were adopted by people who wanted to expand their families, and others were adopted to provide labor on family farms and for small businesses. Approximately 150,000 children were part of the orphan train program. In some instances, children were "auctioned" off at train platforms. Those who were auctioned would wear their best clothing and sometimes display their talents in hopes that someone would take them. Some were lucky enough to be placed with loving families. Many others were treated as nothing more than an inexpensive form of labor (Cook, 1995). While some children were eventually reunited with their families later in life, others remained in their new communities.

FIGURE 2.10   Children riding an orphan train *Source*: National Orphan Train Complex

Child Migration Scheme

Some practices in England significantly influenced U.S. models for organized responses to poverty. However, the U.S. orphan train model provided the basis for a UK program known as the Child Migration Scheme. In response to a growing population and inspired by the orphan train model, between the 1920s and the 1970s, more than 130,000 British children were relocated to former colonies. Global economic ambitions and racial motives influenced this program. The children came from vulnerable backgrounds. Some were orphans, and others were led to believe that they were. Children who were part of this program traveled by boat to Canada, Australia, New Zealand, and Rhodesia (now Zimbabwe). Both physical and psychological abuse were widely reported, and the UK and Australian governments have since apologized for their actions.

Native American Children and Reeducation

European activities and relationships with Indigenous communities throughout the United States were morally, economically, and politically problematic. Given the atrocities perpetrated against Native Americans, it is unsurprising that relationships were strained with people of European descent. Adams (1995) explains that in the late 1800s, philanthropists believed that one of the "solutions" to the "Indian problem" was education. Policymakers and philanthropists believed that education would be the key to promoting assimilation. The prevailing belief from assimilationists was that Native American youth should adopt Christian values and a more individualistic mindset. These institutions deemphasized values that were integral within Native American communities, such as focusing on collective and community good. To meet these goals, "Indian boarding schools" were created. The schools did not allow children to practice their customs or use their language. This model was used for approximately 100 years, starting around the 1870s. There were more than 400 federally funded schools during this time that were "reeducating" Native American youth (Pember, 2019). Parents were often coerced into sending their children to these schools, and contact with family was discouraged. Many children experienced psychological, physical, and/or sexual abuse. The U.S. Department of the Interior reported in 2022 that more than 500 child deaths were determined to originate from 19 federal Indian boarding schools (Newland, 2022).

Protection from Abuse and Neglect

In the absence of child welfare laws, there was little law enforcement could do in instances of neglect or abuse. A seminal case is that of Mary Ellen Wilson in 1874. At age 18 months, she was surrendered to the New York City's Department of Charities by her mother. A man named Thomas Wilson asserted that he was her "illegitimate" father, and he and his wife adopted her. Wilson died soon after, and his wife remarried. Abused, neglected, and forced into servitude, Mary Ellen was a prisoner unable to leave their New York City apartment. Although neighbors never saw her, they could hear the abuse, and reports were made to the authorities at the Department of Public Charities and Correction. Mary Ellen's situation came to the attention of mission worker Etta Angell Wheeler, who was able to see the child briefly. Jalongo (2006) explains,

> Mary Ellen's appearance was shocking. Severe bruises were visible on her arms and legs. She was nine but was barely the size of a typical 5-year-old. Although it was winter and the apartment was cold, the frail child was clothed in only summer dress and wore no socks or shoes. She stood on a wooden box to reach the sink and wash dishes and did not utter a word; a heavy, braided leather whip was on the table. As terrible as Mary Ellen's physical condition was, it was the look of sheer misery on the unloved child's face that made Etta Wheeler determined to become her advocate. She first contacted the police department, but they could do nothing unless someone had actually witnessed the assault. She tried to work through Children's Charities and they could provide food and clothing but did not have the power to remove a child from a guardian's custody. (p. 2)

Etta Wheeler approached Henry Bergh for help. Bergh was an animal rights advocate and founder of the American Society for the Prevention of Cruelty to Animals. Together they pursued legal action for her removal and were successful. More cases came to Bergh's attention, and along with politician Elbridge Gerry and respected philanthropist John D. Wright, he established the New York Society for Prevention of Cruelty to Children, widely recognized as the first child welfare organization in the United States (The New York Society for the Prevention of Cruelty to Children, 2017).

Foster Care

Organized child-saving activities in the United States in the 1800s and early 1900s primarily focused on the needs of newly arrived White children; African American children were not the focus (Peebles-Wilkins, 1995). Concerned about the lack of foster homes for

African American children, Fredericka Douglass Sprague Perry, the granddaughter of famous abolitionist Frederick Douglass, worked with other advocates to establish the Colored Big Sister Home for Girls in Kansas City, Missouri. According to Peebles-Wilkins, "The Colored Big Sisters Home existed as a state-contracted private institution through the 1940s" (p. 143). By the 1950s, the number of children in institutions began to substantially decrease. This was due to the start of family placement and a foster care system that today supports a population of more than 500,000 US children (Sabini, 2017).

2.8 GROWTH AND FUNDING FOR SOCIAL PROGRAMS

The period from the late 1800s to post-World War II was economically dynamic and characterized by limited social reforms. Government interventions were not keeping pace with social needs and the changing structures of society. With urbanization, family sizes were contracting, and community cohesion and social integration became more important. Robert Putnam's book, *Bowling Alone* (2000), explains the role wealthy industrialists played in establishing some of the most important institutions of our society through philanthropy. In addition to supporting charitable organizations, philanthropists supported the creation of hospitals, universities, museums, and other community organizations. Their wealth and the extent of their philanthropic investment ensured that some of their names are still familiar to us today, such as Andrew Carnegie and John D. Rockefeller. Bill and Melinda Gates and Warren Buffet are likely to be familiar names to future generations. Although these individuals had significance in shaping the story, it remains a complex tale.

Thomas Perkins was a wealthy and influential Boston merchant who made many important investments in the city. He helped fund the Perkins School for the Blind, a vanguard in education for people with vision and hearing impairments. He also supported Massachusetts General Hospital, a global leader in health care and research. He helped fund libraries, museums, and many social causes. However, much of his family wealth was amassed in the trading of enslaved people, animal fur, and engaging in the opioid trade.

Concurrent to industrialist philanthropic investment, the working and middle classes were also establishing important organizations, such as workers unions, volunteer fire departments, and community organizations. The middle class was also able to engage in charitable giving due to revisions in the early 20th-century tax law. Some of the changes encouraged philanthropic giving to charities by people of modest means, increasing and diversifying the voices investing in charitable causes.

The early 20th century was a time of rapid social reform fueled by many of the nonprofit and civil society organizations described previously. Not surprisingly, charitable giving declined during the Great Depression (1929–1939). However, this period was the impetus for the first large-scale federal investment in social reform. The New Deal was a program instituted by President Franklin D. Roosevelt in 1933 to provide economic relief and create jobs. It included reforms in industry, finance, agriculture, labor, housing, and many of the social policies that are discussed later in this book.

This would be the first of many US government investments in social welfare. As the economic and political landscape evolved over the next several decades, so did the nonprofit and human services field. Increased government funding and corporate giving, coupled with major and small-scale donors, fostered the growth of one of the largest sectors in U.S. society. Currently, 80 percent of private charitable giving comes from individuals, including gifts from bequests (wills and trusts). Corporations also play a role in funding nonprofits and human services. Ethical questions about the structure of philanthropy are still an issue today. Although wealth has benefited nonprofit institutions and social causes, questions arise about the concentration of power predominantly in the hands of wealthy White men (Callahan, 2017).

By the 1970s, government funding for the sector surpassed private donations. Many private nonprofit organizations depend heavily on government funding to provide services. It could be argued that these organizations are "quasi-governmental" because of the influence that the government has on their practices and funding. Another term used to describe this relationship is the "shadow state," meaning that the entanglements between government and private nonprofits essentially render the organizations indistinguishable from government.

Human services is rooted in a complex history that is influenced by evolving philosophies, funding, and perspectives about how best to respond to social and economic conditions and promote well-being. Continuing to analyze how intersecting institutions, power, and resources impact individuals and communities will help in the design of ethical programs, services, and structural changes in the future.

SPOTLIGHT ON SERVICE-LEARNING

Students who are concurrently engaging a human services organization for this class or in extracurricular clubs may reflect on how history influences their work. Consider the content from this chapter as it relates to a current or past experience with a human services organization.

1. How have social issues and responses to those issues changed in the US over the past 200 years?
2. Are you currently working or volunteering with a human services program? If so, what can you learn about the history of the organization? Has its focus or approach changed over the years?
3. What role does private philanthropy play in supporting your organization? Take a look at your organization's most recent annual report. What can you learn about its sources of funding?

SUMMARY

- Human services organizations were created as a form of support for those in need and improve our collective well-being. Some organizations may be funded by the government, whereas others are private nonprofits, which are mission-driven organizations established for purposes other than generating profit.
- Much of US social policy and practice was influenced by early European opinions and policies. Many British beliefs, such as the distinction between "worthy" and "unworthy" poor and the negative attitudes to those who were not working, were carried over to the United States. These beliefs were apparent in the colonial version of Britain's Poor Laws, which criminalized unemployment and begging.

- The 13 colonies were deeply rooted in Calvinistic beliefs, which valued work, thrift, and economic independence. Many believed an individual's fate was pre-determined, with poverty as a sign of damnation. Poverty was seen as a punishment for laziness and sinful behavior and thus looked down upon. Anyone who was seen to be in a situation due to their own bad decisions or laziness was considered to be "unworthy poor," whereas widows and orphans were considered to be "worthy poor."

- Institutional care for individuals living with mental health challenges have often been insufficient and inhumane. Often, the conditions were deplorable, with people chained and subjected to physical abuse. In the 1700s, the approach shifted based on the belief that people could become well and should be treated with respect. Thus, The Retreat model was designed as a place of refuge, carefully designed to promote wellness. In the 20th century, as more pharmacological treatments became available and funding shifted, there was a move to deinstitutionalize.

- Many social services organizations have their roots in London's East End, where laborers, immigrants, and those with limited economic resources were housed. Organizations such as the Salvation Army, the Jewish Board of Guardians (now Jewish Care), and Toynbee Hall all started there.

- Social Darwinism was a theory that humans follow the same process of natural selection that plants and animals follow. Scientific charity was grounded in this theory, with the premise that charity should work along with and not against natural selection. This entailed more targeted interventions to those deemed worthy, with the goal of eliminating poverty.

- The settlement house movement began with the establishment of settlement houses as a way to provide social services for poor workers while creating a community of learning and fellowship. The houses first began with the purpose of providing an opportunity for university students to live and work with the poor.

- After the case of Mary Ellen's abuse, Etta Wheeler and Henry Bergh sought legal action that eventually led to the creation of the New York Society for Prevention of Cruelty to Children as one of the first child welfare organizations. Prior to this, children were provided with minimal protection with regard to abuse and neglect.

- Social programs are funded partially by wealthy philanthropist individuals as well as smaller charitable giving donations by average citizens. There are also contributions from government funding and corporate giving.

REVIEW QUESTIONS

Assessment Questions

1. What is marked as the beginning of the Poor Laws? How did they change over time?
2. What is scientific charity? How did the Charitable Organization Society apply this approach?
3. What are settlement houses? What were the core philosophies?
4. How did the United States and United Kingdom handle children experiencing poverty?

Reflection Questions

1. How has the response to mental health problems in history shaped modern-day society's view and response?
2. What were some of the strengths and limitations of the settlement house movement?
3. Consider some of the historical beliefs mentioned in this chapter, such as "worthy" or "unworthy" poor. Are any elements present in today's society? If so, what beliefs and how are they represented?
4. What flaws might there be in the way social programs are funded in the United States? What changes could be made to improve the system?

REFERENCES

Adams, D. W. (1995). *Education for extinction: American Indians and the boarding school experience, 1875–1928.* University Press of Kansas.

Alonso, H. H. (1995). Nobel Peace Laureates, Jane Addams and Emily Greene Balch: Two women of the Women's International League for Peace and Freedom. *Journal of Women's History, 7*(2), 6–26.

Ball, M., & Sunderland, D. T. (2001). *An economic history of London 1800–1914* (Vol. 22). Routledge.

Berry, M. E. (2020). *Settlement Movement 1886–1986: One hundred years on urban frontiers.* Social Welfare History Project. https://socialwelfare.library.vcu.edu/settlement-houses/settlement-movement-1886-1986

Booth, W. (2014). *In darkest England and the way out.* Cambridge University Press.

Bremner, R. (1956). Scientific philanthropy, 1873–93. *Social Service Review, 30*(1), 168.

Callahan, D. (2017). *The givers: Wealth, power, and philanthropy in a new gilded age.* Vintage.

Columbia School of Social Work. (n.d.). *Historical timeline.* https://socialwork.columbia.edu/about/historical-timeline

Cook, J. F. (1995). A history of placing-out: The orphan trains. *Child Welfare, 74*(1), 181–197.

Dempsey, K., Butler, S. K., & Gaither, L. (2016). Black churches and mental health professionals: Can this collaboration work? *Journal of Black Studies, 47*(1), 73–87.

Dyer, C. (2012). Poverty and its relief in late medieval England. *Past & Present, 216*(1), 41–78.

Eddy, B. (2010). Struggle or mutual aid: Jane Addams, Petr Kropotkin, and the progressive encounter with social Darwinism. *The Pluralist, 5*(1), 21–43.

Franklin, B. (1987). *On the price of corn and the management of the poor.* Library of America. (Original work published 1766)

Franklin, D. (1986). Mary Richmond and Jane Addams: From moral certainty to rational inquiry in social work practice. *Social Service Review, 60*(4), 504–525.

Gettleman, M. (1963). Charity and social classes in the United States, 1874–1900, I. *American Journal of Economics and Sociology, 22*(2), 313–329.

Hansan, J. E. (2013). *United Way of America.* Retrieved May 7, 2020, from https://socialwelfare.library.vcu.edu/eras/civil-war-reconstruction/united-way-of-america

Higginbotham, P. (2011). *Life in a Victorian workhouse: From 1834 to 1930.* Pitkin.

Humphreys, R. (2001). Beginnings of the London Charity Organization Society. In *Poor relief and charity 1869–1945* (pp. 1–22). Palgrave Macmillan.

Jalongo, M. (2006). The story of Mary Ellen Wilson: Tracing the origins of child protection in America." *Early Childhood Education Journal, 34*(1), 1–4.

Jay, M. (2016). *This way madness lies: The asylum and beyond.* Thames & Hudso.

Kahl, S. (2005). The religious roots of modern poverty policy: Catholic, Lutheran, and reformed Protestant traditions compared. *Archives Européennes De Sociologie, 46*(1), 91–126.

Kendall, K. A. (2000). World-wide beginnings of social work education. *Indian Journal of Social Work, 61*(2), 141–156.

Koven, S. (2006). *Slumming: Sexual and social politics in Victorian London.* Princeton University Press.

Lasch-Quinn, E. (1993). The mainstream settlement movement and blacks. *Black Neighbors: Race and the Limits of Reform in the American Settlement House Movement, 1890-1945*, 29–46.

Martin, M. (2012). Philosophical and religious influences on social welfare policy in the United States: The ongoing effect of Reformed theology and social Darwinism on attitudes toward the poor and social welfare policy and practice. *Journal of Social Work, 12*(1), 51–64.

Meschkank, J. (2011). Investigations into slum tourism in Mumbai: Poverty tourism and the tensions between different constructions of reality. *GeoJournal, 76*(1), 47–62.

Moore, L. S. (1994). Social workers and the development of the NAACP. *Journal of Sociology & Social Welfare, 21*, 125.

Newland, B. (2022). *Federal Indian boarding school initiative investigative report*. U.S. Department of the Interior.

Ogawa, M. (2004). "Hull-House" in Downtown Tokyo: The transplantation of a settlement house from the United States into Japan and the North American Missionary Women, 1919–1945. *Journal of World History, 15*(3), 359–387.

Peabody, F. G. (1898). Social settlements. In National Conference of Charities and Corrections (Ed.), *Proceedings of National Conference of Charities and Corrections, at the annual session held in Toronto: Issue 24* (pp. 329–332). Press of Geo H. Ellis.

Peebles-Wilkins, W. (1995). Janie Porter Barrett and the Virginia Industrial School for Colored Girls: Community response to the needs of African American children. *Child Welfare, 74*(1), 143.

Pember, M. (2019, March 8). Death by civilization: Thousands of Native American children were forced to attend boarding schools created to strip them of their culture. My mother was one of them. *The Atlantic.*

Perkins, C. (2019, July). From the ashes of the Great Kantō Earthquake: the Tokyo imperial university settlement. In *Japan Forum* (Vol. 31, No. 3, pp. 408–433). Routledge.

Quigley, W. P. (1996). Five Hundred Years of English Poor Laws,1349-1834: Regulating the Working and Nonworking Poor, pages 5–11.

Quigley, W. P. (1996). Work or starve: Regulation of the poor in colonial America. *University of San Francisco Law Review, 31*(1), 35–83.

Reinders, R. C. (1982). Toynbee Hall and the American settlement movement. *Social Service Review, 56*(1), 39–54.

Rivlin, L., & Manzo, L. (1988). Homeless children in New York City: A view from the 19th century. *Children's Environments Quarterly, 5*(1), 26–33.

Sabini, C. (2017). *Foster care: A history*. The NALS Docket. https://www.nals.org/blogpost/1359892/290477/Foster-Care-A-History

Salvation Army International Trust (2019). Annual Report 2019-2020 by Salvation Army IHQ

Social Welfare History Project. (2017). Janie Porter Barrett (1865–1948): Founder of the Locust Street Social Settlement (1890) and the Virginia Industrial School for Colored Girls (1915). http://socialwelfare.library.vcu.edu/settlement-houses/barrett-janie-porter-1865-1948-african-american-social-welfare-activist

Sulloway, F. J. (1982). Darwin and his finches: The evolution of a legend. *Journal of the History of Biology, 15*(1), 1–53.

The first social settlement in Russia. (1912, August 3). *Outlook (1893–1924), 101*, 752.

The New York Society for the Prevention of Cruelty to Children. (2017). *History*. https://nyspcc.org/about-the-new-york-society-for-the-prevention-of-cruelty-to-children/history

Tice, K. (1992). The battle for benevolence: Scientific disciplinary control vs. "indiscriminate relief": Lexington Associated Charities and the Salvation Army, 1900–1918. *Journal of Sociology and Social Welfare, 19*(2), 59–77.

Trattner, W. I. (2007). *From poor law to welfare state: A history of social welfare in America*. Simon & Schuster.

Waugh, J. (2001). "Give this man work!" Josephine Shaw Lowell, the Charity Organization Society of the City of New York, and the Depression of 1893. *Social Science History, 25*(2), 217–246.

Whyte, K. P., Selinger, E., & Outterson, K. (2011). Poverty tourism and the problem of consent. *Journal of Global Ethics, 7*(3), 337–348.

Ziliak, S. (2004). Self-reliance before the welfare state: Evidence from the charity organization movement in the United States. *Journal of Economic History, 64*(2), 433–461.

CHAPTER 3

Understanding and Responding to Social Problems

Learning Objectives

After completing this chapter, you will be able to:

3.1. Describe characteristics of "wicked problems."

3.2. Describe some common attitudes about social problems.

3.3. Name and explain various models used to address social problems.

3.4. Define *evidence-based practice* and explain how these methods are used in the human services profession.

3.5. Describe the benefits of multisectoral collaboration in responding to social problems.

Recall from Chapter 1 that social problems are conditions or behaviors that result in negative consequences for large numbers of people. Social problems such as poverty, homelessness, and unemployment are complex because they arise due to multiple, interdependent factors. Responses to social problems must address the complex nature of the individual and structural factors that impact the magnitude, significance, and prevalence of the problems. In this chapter, we explore the theoretical frameworks that have been used to understand and respond to social problems.

3.1 WICKED PROBLEMS

Rittel and Webber (1973) coined the term "wicked problems," asserting that social problems differ from scientific problems in that they are not fully solvable. Wicked problems vary due to diverse causes and situations. No single formula can be applied in attempting to resolve wicked problems. Wicked problems also do not present clear criteria for when a solution has been reached. They are often symptoms of larger problems with conditions that frequently change.

Poverty is a wicked problem that leads to other social problems, such as lack of access to health care and quality education. Poverty is experienced differently in different regions of the world and is affected by micro, meso, and macro forces. Although wicked problems are complex and seemingly intractable, human services professionals apply practices, programs, and policies to address negative impacts on individuals, families, and communities. In the case of poverty, coordinated and multisectoral responses are required.

Although the mission and specific objectives of human services organizations vary, their efforts to respond to existing social problems and prevent future problems are a shared goal. To accomplish this goal, we need to understand how and why complex social problems develop and how we can most effectively minimize harm, promote safety and success, and create lasting, positive change in our communities.

3.2 ATTITUDES ABOUT SOCIAL PROBLEMS

Society perceives certain groups or populations as being worthy of investing resources, and others as less worthy. Chapter 2 demonstrated how these distinctions between worthy and unworthy were ingrained in policies and civil society solutions. Groups such as children and elders, or individuals with a visible disability, often receive more societal support than those who are post-incarcerated, undocumented, or have invisible disabilities. Individuals who are perceived to be responsible for their challenges, such as those with a history of substance use or criminal behavior, often receive less support from both civil society and government organizations. Perceptions about "personal responsibility" can influence attitudes about government and nonprofit responses. This differentiation is apparent in current social welfare policies, nonprofit organizational responses, and attitudes toward those who are not able to fully participate in society.

Perceptions of Substance Use Disorder

Historically, drug or alcohol use disorders have been perceived as a personal choice or moral failing (Barry et al., 2014). Medical, social, and legal responses have reflected this bias. Traditional substance use prevention focused on personal choice, and the consequences to substance use were often punitive. As research on substance use became more sophisticated, a new definition emerged in policy and practice. Substance use disorders (SUDs) are referred to as the use of drugs and alcohol that impacts daily life, and they are associated with many physical and mental health challenges. This reframing has slowly begun to impact how society views SUDs and has changed the design of social responses. Rather than consider SUDs as solely an individual problem, with the response being individual treatment, a broader approach considers factors outside the individual experience, including family, education, traumatic events, and employment. In cases such as opioid use disorder, factors including access to prescription pain relievers and medical pain management are entering into an expanded model of both prevention and treatment.

Beliefs About Individuals and Communities

Most people have compassion for individuals living with cancer. However, this empathy can be variable when someone is perceived to be responsible for their plight. For example, a person who has lung cancer and was a long-term smoker may be perceived with less empathy than a person with a family history of breast cancer. Why is this? Social psychologists Lerner and Miller (1978) referred to this phenomenon as **just world belief**, the notion that you get what you deserve, and you deserve what you get. This belief can be empowering when life successes are frequent. However, we know that life is more random than we would like, and working hard does not always result in success or victory. The idea that we can control what happens to us is very reassuring, but it is often not the case. The just world belief can promote an **empathy gap** and influence how we respond to certain individuals. An empathy gap is a form of bias that prevents us from being able to understand the perspectives and experiences of others. The just world belief can predict some rather socially negative beliefs and attitudes, given people may not be able to empathize with others experiencing more harmful social problems; such attitudes include brutality, oppression, and different forms of discrimination (Sidanius & Pratto, 1999).

A complex mix of information, experiences, and institutions influences what we believe about the world and other people. We may not always understand where our beliefs come from or how bias may shape our worldview and perceptions of others. Our subjective experiences and beliefs are often so powerful that it can be difficult to perceive people, events, or social phenomena objectively. Psychologists describe these mental shortcuts as **schemas**.

Although these frameworks can be useful as we try to interpret the world around us, they can prevent human services professionals from seeing individuals and communities objectively. Our subjective experiences and mindsets can make us suspicious of information that is inconsistent with our understanding of the world. **Confirmation bias** is when we select information that is consistent with our existing beliefs and reject information that is inconsistent. This bias is increasingly being discussed regarding social media. The self-selecting of information and relationships that affirm what we believe to be true about the world is sometimes referred to as an **echo chamber** because we may surround ourselves with influences and people who reflect to us what we already believe.

Attribution Theory

Confirmation bias and stereotypes can make it difficult to objectively determine the cause of a social issue and/or to view a social problem and individuals objectively. How we understand social problems often drives how we respond to them. Understanding the *why* behind a problem is referred to as **attribution theory**. In other words, what frames or forces are we using to explain and understand the causes of behavior or events? Many people from Western cultures often overemphasize individual personality traits, moods, or emotional states when explaining a complex behavior, such as suggesting people make poor choices and that is the cause of poverty. This type of attribution is called a **dispositional attribution** (Heine, 2020), and it contrasts with explanations that emphasize environmental, structural, and policy-based reasoning, such as when we characterize poverty as being caused by poor access to safe and clean living environments, and policies that do not provide adequate funding and care to underresourced communities. This second type of attribution is called a **situational attribution** (Heine, 2020). Both types of attributions matter in understanding the multiple causes of complex problems, so it is most comprehensive to understand both the individual factors and the cultural or structural factors that contribute to social problems in order to develop appropriate solutions.

3.3 MODELS FOR ADDRESSING SOCIAL PROBLEMS

Various theoretical frameworks have been used to guide human services practice. Models are used to visualize and frame social issues and can provide a specific orientation or call to action to solve social problems. Different models for addressing social problems may focus on unique causes and correlates of the problem. For example, one model may focus on the role of the individual, whereas another model may focus on the role of the community, society, or government. To frame our understanding of poverty, for example, do we first examine individual actions and choices, or social and institutional forces such as a lack of access to education, employment, or health care? How do both individual and social factors impact the experience of poverty?

Medical Model

Sometimes human services professionals need to react to a social problem quickly and efficiently. A complex framework may not be best suited to tackle the specific needs of individuals, families, or communities in crisis. A **medical model** is based on assessment, diagnosis, and treatment of a problem, and it generally assesses a condition due to its biological, genetic, or physical causes. For example, in the case of a child who has fallen on the playground and is taken to the emergency room, best practice calls for a swift evaluation of the cause of the injury to address the child's pain, identify an accurate diagnosis, and implement a clear treatment plan.

Medical models are most common in settings in which timely treatment is essential to meet immediate needs. For example, if a client with a history of a SUD relapses, the client may be assessed, determined to be in need of additional treatment, and recommended to participate in inpatient substance abuse treatment. If an individual is experiencing a major episode of depression, a medical professional might recommend an antidepressant or other pharmaceutical intervention and, in some cases, hospitalization. In other cases, the focus must be expanded to consider the health, wellness, and safety of the broader community. A social model is an alternative perspective that considers the role of the individual and the broader environment.

Ecological Model

An ecological model (Bronfenbrenner, 1977) differs from a medical model. An **ecological model** offers a holistic perspective on both human development and the broader context that shapes development (Figure 3.1). A contextual ecological model begins to answer some of the broader questions about the individual and the situation. It considers both the individual and the structural causes of a problem, and it explores how individual and structural factors interact or impact each other. This approach identifies the importance of the interactions between a growing and developing individual and the personal, family, school, and community environment. In the example above, the client who enters an inpatient substance use disorder treatment center may also benefit from an ecological assessment. Are there factors related to the client's personal or family relationships, housing, work environment, or community that are associated with the relapse? If so, in addition to treatment, the client may benefit from ecological interventions to address factors that are correlated with a SUD. For example, an ecological approach may examine the safety of the client's housing, the stress associated with their work, or family

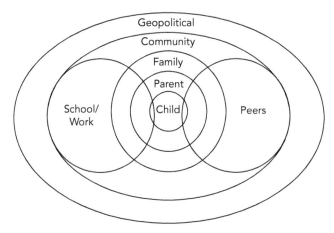

FIGURE 3.1 The ecological model is based on the interaction of individual and structural factors. *Source*: Used with permission of Blackwell Publishing, from *Child Development*, A. Sameroff, *81*, 1, 2010; permission conveyed through Copyright Clearance Center, Inc.

factors such as the spouse's support. Notice that this type of analysis can help advance a strengths perspective (see Chapter 4) that empowers a client by considering of some of their personal and relational strengths.

Human services professionals work within and across sectors to address the root causes of social problems. In Chapter 1, the terms micro, meso, and macro were used to describe types of social services practice: *micro* refers to direct practice, *meso* to programs and other initiatives, and *macro* to policy. These terms (plus one more) are also used to describe the various systems or environmental elements that influence human development and experience:

- Micro-level systems are close to the individual's experience and include temperament, ability, or perceived capacity.
- Meso-level systems are further removed and may include relationships with family and peers.
- Exo-level systems include the environments in which daily activities occur, such as school, neighborhood, workplace, and the immediate community.
- Macro-level systems include the social and political environment and cultural norms and may have more of an indirect impact on daily life and family functioning.

Within each of the ecological spheres, the experiences of individuals differ. Human development is a unique experience, based on our individual characteristics and how these characteristics or traits interact with the closer and more distant environments.

Certain factors are protective of a person's development and support positive outcomes. Other factors and experiences may be negative and promote disease or dysfunction. Risk factors are those that may impede development and contribute to negative outcomes. Protective and risk factors are ecological, from within the child/individual, family, school, community, and political sphere (Bogenschneider, 1996; Fraser, 1997). Risk factors associated with interpersonal violence are shown in Figure 3.2.

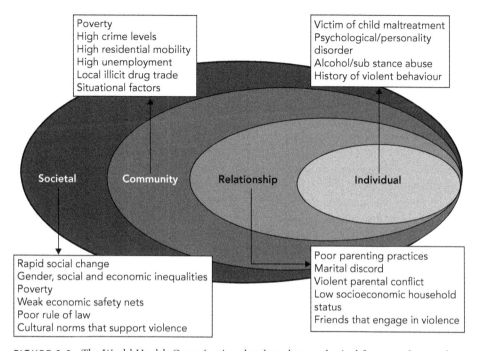

Poverty
High crime levels
High residential mobility
High unemployment
Local illicit drug trade
Situational factors

Victim of child maltreatment
Psychological/personality
disorder
Alcohol/sub stance abuse
History of violent behaviour

Societal   Community   Relationship   Individual

Rapid social change
Gender, social and economic inequalities
Poverty
Weak economic safety nets
Poor rule of law
Cultural norms that support violence

Poor parenting practices
Marital discord
Violent parental conflict
Low socioeconomic household
status
Friends that engage in violence

FIGURE 3.2   The World Health Organization developed an ecological framework to understand the complex predictors and risk factors associated with interpersonal violence. *Source: The ecological framework: Examples of risk factors at each level.* https://www.who.int/groups/violence-prevention-alliance/approach: World Health Organization; 2022. Licence: CC BY-NC-SA 3.0 IGO.

Jenson and Fraser (2011) highlight common protective and risk factors that are associated with outcomes in adolescence and adulthood. *Common risk factors* include the following:

- Macro-level factors include poverty and lack of access to economic resources, social norms that favor antisocial behavior, availability of illegal drugs, access to guns, and neighborhood crime.
- Meso-level factors include family attitudes and behaviors favorable to negative behavior, strained family–child relationships, poor academic performance, and peer groups favorable to antisocial behavior.
- Micro-level factors include individual issues such as early behavior problems, impulsivity, poor attention, and other biological factors.

Protective factors foster self-reliance and include environmental influences such as physical safety and opportunities for education and employment. Protective factors also include social influences such as a high level of family commitment to education, and access to high-quality educational programs. At the individual level, protective factors include emotional resilience and a positive attitude.

Upstream and Downstream Interventions

The terms *upstream* and *downstream* are used to describe different types of interventions and strategies. Upstream interventions focus on improving core social and economic structures to decrease barriers and improve resources that allow people to achieve their full potential. Downstream interventions focus on increasing access to resources and services to mitigate the negative impacts of a disadvantaged environment or negative life situation (Cohen et al., 2010).

The upstream–downstream public health parable is quite a morbid one, but it also provides some hopeful solutions. The parable starts downstream on the banks of a picturesque river where a man stands fishing. The quiet of the day is broken by the sounds of a person drowning nearby. Of course, the fisherman jumps to the rescue. Once the rescue is complete, more sounds are heard—the sounds of more people struggling in the river and at risk of drowning. This parable juxtaposes two possible conditions. Condition 1 is focused on the immediate needs of the people in the river. The fisherman's role is fixed on jumping in and out of the river, bringing bodies to shore in hopes of survival. Condition 2 requires an alternative. This is called "moving upstream." This alternative moves the fisherman away from the shore to explore why people are falling into the river. A walk (or run) upstream may help solve the root cause of the problem and prevent more people from needing assistance downstream.

Prevention Science

Prevention science (described in Chapter 1) is aligned with moving upstream (National Collaborating Centre for Determinants of Health, 2014). A prevention science perspective offers a framework to address complex social problems that considers the dynamic interactions between individuals, families, communities, and social and political systems and how various levels of intervention may affect the development and persistence of the problems.

The prevention mindset can be applied to a broad range of problems. For example, early intervention may decrease the need for educational remediation in school. Regarding personal health, preventive screenings may catch early warning signs of disease. Intimate partner violence may be prevented through health education that considers healthy relationships.

Although prevention initiatives can be expensive, they are often associated with lower future costs. Prevention therefore has social and economic benefits for individuals and for society. One cost–benefit analysis highlighted long-term cost savings to society of approximately $10 for every $1 invested in high-quality preschool (Reynolds et al., 2011). Participation in preschool is associated with long-term benefits to the child and to society, such as reductions in spending on educational remediation and criminal justice, higher wages and employment, and lower welfare dependence (Heckman et al., 2010).

Prevention-oriented programs can be defined by their timing (before, during, or after a problem occurs) and targets (O'Connell et al., 2009):

- Primary prevention programs are targeted before the onset of the problem.
- Secondary prevention programs (often called intervention programs) are targeted at the onset of the problem or early in the development of the problem.
- Tertiary prevention programs (often called treatment programs) are targeted after the problem has already manifested.

- Universal prevention programs focus on all or most individuals or populations.
- Selective prevention programs focus on some individuals at risk of the problem.
- Indicated prevention programs focus on those who are most at risk or who are manifesting the problem.

Prevention science's ultimate application is in the dissemination of evidence-based practices, programs, and policies that can prevent, intervene, or treat social problems (Coie et al., 1993).

3.4 EVIDENCE-BASED PRACTICE AND PROCESSES

Evidence-based practice (EBP) is a term originally used in medicine. It is now applied in other disciplines, including education, mental health, and criminal justice. In the social work field, EBP is a process in which the practitioner combines well-researched interventions with professional experience, ethics, client preferences, and culture as the basis for the delivery of services. EBP is based on the knowledge of what works best, when, for whom, for what condition, and at what cost (Springer & Phillips, 2007). Although EBP provides a promising model to work with individuals, families, groups, and communities, the complexity and uniqueness of the human experience suggest that not all individuals respond to interventions the same way. Single best practices may work for some or even most people, but not all. Therefore, an EBP approach must consider the evidence as well as the client experience, and revisions to intervention and treatment plans may be necessary. For example, in our attempt to be culturally competent with clients of different backgrounds (see Chapter 7), we must be careful in evaluating the research on EBP to see how well it fits or must be adapted to the life circumstances of a client we encounter whose experience may not be represented well by the research.

What Works and When?

To bring about change at the individual, family, school, or community level, we must understand what type of practice, program, or policy will create the most positive change. High-quality research that uses experimental design is often considered the gold standard of evidence. In the social sciences, this method of investigation has been increasing, highlighting many successful interventions focused on education, health, and the environment.

Experimental design is not the only way to assess best practice or gain insights into effective and efficient interventions. For example, the Institute of Educational Sciences What Works Clearinghouse (https://ies.ed.gov/ncee/wwc/) considers quasi-experimental and non-experimental research designs in the field of education. The Campbell Collaboration (https://www.campbellcollaboration.org/) aggregates evidence into systematic research reviews in the fields of education, criminal justice, and social welfare. These resources highlight a wealth of information to form the basis for decisions about which practices, programs, and policies are associated with positive change.

As previously described, the timing of an intervention will influence its outcome. An intervention may occur before a problem starts (primary), at the onset of the problem (secondary), or after the problem has fully developed (tertiary).

For Whom?

Some programs and interventions are widely available (universal). Universal programs include public education and school-based substance abuse prevention programs. Public service announcements for safe driving and avoiding texting and other cellphone use while driving are widely distributed in the hope that all drivers will pay attention and increase road safety.

Selective programs are available only to those who meet specific eligibility criteria. Selective programs often target a specific risk or set of risk factors that are associated with the manifestation of the problem. Individuals are likely to be included in selective intervention programs if they have one or more risk factors. Risk factors can include poverty, academic delay, school failure, history of abuse, social maladjustment, or delinquency. In some cities, access to preschool for 3-year-olds is targeted to children with specific learning or developmental delays. Targeted preschool programs may also use poverty as a screening factor, prioritizing placements for low-income children (Barnett et al., 2004).

Indicated programs are most closely aligned to treatment services, and they seek to prevent further problems, consequences, or recidivism. Indicated programs target the highest risk individuals with known characteristics associated with the problem. For example, SUD treatment programs are available to individuals with a diagnosis. Criminal justice diversion programs are available to individuals who have been found guilty of committing crimes.

At What Cost?

Human services interventions need to consider both social and economic costs of implementation. In some cases, services may be necessary despite the costs to the individual or society. In other cases, the cost of services may serve as an investment that will result in future cost savings. For example, special education services often cost considerably more than educational services provided to students without disabilities. Cutting special education costs and limiting services may save a school district money in the short term, but it is likely that a reduction in services will be associated with future costs in the long term (Grant, 2005). High-quality educational services for students with disabilities may cost more, but these are likely to be associated with increased graduation and post-secondary employment rates. When interventions foster positive outcomes such as graduation and employment, fewer tax dollars are needed for social safety net programs.

Universal preschool has been highly debated. Investments in high-quality preschool programs are costly but have been associated with substantial social and economic benefits. Economist James Heckman (2012) has studied these benefits associated with early high-quality preschool. There is a high rate of return on these early childhood investments, including lower health care costs, higher levels of education, and lower rates of poverty and crime. Heckman's research suggests that investment in "early childhood education is a cost-effective strategy—even during a budget crisis" (Heckman, 2012, p. 2).

When deciding which social services to implement, practitioners and policymakers must assess the quality of the program and its impact on the intended outcome (Karoly, 2008). For example, does the program lower risk in one domain but increase risk in another, prompting unintended new costs? Is the program cost prohibitive, reducing the number of people who can be positively impacted? Does the policy lack stakeholder support, reducing the likelihood of proper implementation?

3.5 THE NEED FOR MULTISECTORAL COLLABORATION

There are many debates around who should conceptualize and implement solutions to social problems. Is it the role of government? Or is it the role of the business sector? Perhaps social problems are best dealt with by the individual or their family? What is the role of the nonprofit sector, faith communities, or other civil society organizations? We have seen that some of the most lasting changes are those that engage institutions and individuals across these various groups.

Triple Bottom Line

Social problems generally require a multisectoral response to create substantive and long-lasting social change. Multisectoral collaboration is sometimes referred to as the "triple bottom line" based on the idea that what is good for the community is good for business (Figure 3.3). Most businesses directly benefit from safe communities and a healthy, educated workforce. Partnerships involve active collaboration among government agencies, nongovernmental agencies (civil society), and the private sector (Health Policy Project, 2014). Solutions that include all three sectors are often necessary to impact structural change; the size of the role for each of them varies depending on the issue.

The business sector sometimes contributes to social problems but can also play a role in addressing them. Small and large businesses often support nonprofits through their

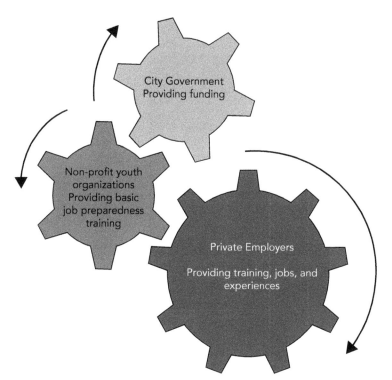

FIGURE 3.3   The triple bottom line refers to a three-pronged approach to addressing social problems that involves government, business, and the nonprofit sector.

TRY IT YOURSELF

Think of a social issue in your community. What institutions are engaging in solutions? What sectors are represented? Are there institutions that could be more engaged? High quality preschool is a financial investment. How can high quality preschool impact social and economic outcomes for schools and communities? Consider how local businesses and institutions may benefit from being in communities that implement high quality universal preschool?

corporate giving programs and can also be partners in implementing change. One such partnership is through targeted youth employment. Some cities experience a sharp increase in youth-related crime during the summer months when students are out of school. Cities such as Boston have applied a multisectoral response to expand youth employment opportunities, leveraging nonprofits to facilitate recruitment and training (Modestino, 2017). In Boston, the mayor's office provides the funding and leadership for the program, and the private sector creates employment opportunities for young people.

Coordinated Community Response: Intimate Partner Violence and the Duluth Model

The Centers for Disease Control and Prevention defines intimate partner violence (IPV) as a serious, preventable public health problem that affects millions of Americans. IPV describes physical, sexual, and/or psychological harm by a current or former partner or spouse. This type of violence occurs among both heterosexual and same-sex couples. The long history of legal, social, and religious tolerance of violence within intimate relationships made this issue particularly difficult for advocates to change. IPV is a complex problem due to psychological, emotional, social, and economic factors. After years of advocacy, nonfatal instances of IPV declined 63 percent from 1994 to 2012 (Truman & Morgan, 2014). So, how did this change take place?

One theory for the reduction in IPV frequency is that economic gains among women have contributed to increased independence and ability to avoid and/or detach more easily from abusive relationships. Changing societal norms about what is and is not acceptable within an intimate partner relationship have changed. This shift may also partially explain reduced rates of IPV.

Multipronged and multisectoral program structures were at the forefront of this change. In the early 1980s, advocates in Duluth, Minnesota, created a framework that is now referred to as the Duluth model (Domestic Abuse Intervention Programs, n.d.; Figure 3.4). This model established the importance of an effort that engaged all the institutions that respond to IPV, along with those working indirectly on the issue, applying a coordinated community response approach. Training was provided for members of law enforcement in the judicial and corrections systems, religious leaders, medical staff, and employers. Psychoeducational programs such as batterers' intervention were established to provide an intervention for perpetrators. The Duluth model provided a framework for changemakers to view social problems more holistically. It has been replicated throughout the country and is now seen as best practice. Clearly, the reduction in IPV was not impacted by one change but, rather, by many coordinated changes within and between many different systems.

The Duluth Model Approach

- A commitment to shift responsibility for victim safety from the victim to the community and state

- A shared collective mission and strategy regarding intervention that is based on a number of core philosophical agreements

- A shared understanding of how interventions are to be accountable to victim safety and offender accountability

- A shared understanding of how each agency's (practitioners') actions either support or undermine the collective goals and strategy of intervention

- Shared definitions of safety, battering, danger and risk, and accountability

- Prioritizes the voices and experiences of women who experience battering in the creation of those policies and procedures

Coordinated Community Response (CCR)

Developed and created by DAIP in collaboration with criminal and civil justice agencies, community members, advocates, and victims

- Written policies guiding each practitioner at each point of intervention that centralize victim safety and offender accountability and that coordinate an interagency intervention strategy.

- Protocols and procedures that link practitioners from different agencies and disciplines.

- An entity (preferably independent of the court) that tracks and monitors cases and assesses data.

- An interagency process that encourages practitioners to work together in a strategie manner to resolve problems.

- A process that allows for dialogue and problem-solving by focusing on systemic problems of an organization rather than on individual workers between criminal and civil justice agencies, community members and victims to close gaps and improve the community's response to battering.

- A central role for advocates and victims in defining and evaluating the interagency intervention model.

- A commitment to support each other's attempts to secure adequate resources to respond to these cases.

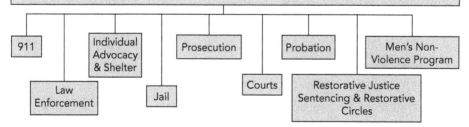

FIGURE 3.4   The Duluth model is a coordinated community response approach to intimate partner violence that is regarded as best practice in addressing this social problem. *Source*: Used with permission Domestic Abuse Prevention Programs, https://www .theduluthmodel.org.

Collective Impact

In many ways, the Duluth model was a precursor to the "collective impact" approach. Kania and Kramer (2011) explain that in order to address complex social problems, changemakers must engage in coordinated efforts among and between organizations grounded in clearly defined goals. Cities, nonprofits, and philanthropic organizations have continued to refine the principles of collective impact. Many identify the following five conditions as essential:

- *A common agenda*: The use of Population Results and Indicators provides a clear, practical, and measurable way of articulating a common agenda for a community.
- *Shared measurement system*: Defining performance measures for each community partner that clearly align with the common agenda (Population Results and Indicators) provides the information needed to make decisions and revise strategies going forward.
- *Mutually reinforcing activities*: Collecting data is only half the battle. Transparency in your planning can help you to use data to make decisions and guide your strategies to improve.
- *Continuous communication*: Communication, not just between partners but also with funders and the public, is a key component to any successful collective impact initiative.
- *Backbone support organization*: A backbone organization provides the supporting infrastructure for a collective impact effort and is a facilitator of a highly structured data-driven decision-making process. (Clear Impact, n.d.)

The collective impact approach of coordinating social change, using resources efficiently, and aligning goals and agendas has been identified as a best practice. The models and approaches in this chapter encourage us to acknowledge the complexity of social problems and the various players in the social change space.

SPOTLIGHT ON SERVICE-LEARNING

How does your organization fit within an ecological perspective? How is the organization impacted by micro, meso, and macro factors? How does the organization impact these systems? Reflecting on your service, consider the following:

1. What social problems does your service-learning site address?
2. What factors contribute to the issues that they are addressing?
3. How does your organization fit in within the larger scope of services?

Activity: Working independently or in small groups, create a visual to illustrate the networks, coalitions, and partnerships that your organization is part of.

SUMMARY

- A wicked problem is the idea that social problems differ from scientific problems given that they are not fully solvable. There is no one formula that can be applied and no precise criteria for when a solution has been reached.

- Often, social problems are broken down into what is worthy of investing resources in and what is less worthy. Groups such as children and elders often receive more societal support than post-incarcerated or undocumented individuals. Those that are perceived to be more responsible for their challenges (e.g., those with a history of substance abuse or criminal behavior) often receive less support.
- The just world belief is the concept that you get what you deserve, and you deserve what you get. However, life is more random than we would like, and working hard does not always result in success or victory. This belief may create bias that prevents us from being able to understand the perspectives and experiences of others.
- The medical model is based on assessment, diagnosis, and treatment of a problem, and it typically assumes the root causes are biological or genetic. The ecological model focuses on a more holistic approach by considering the context of both the individual and structural causes of a problem. It considers all the factors that may affect an individual's development and outcomes.
- Evidenced-based practice is the process of combining well-researched interventions with professional experience, ethics, client preferences, and culture as the basis for the delivery of services. In human services, this includes researching what works and when, programs with varying types of targeting (universal, selective, or indicated), and evaluating the social and economic cost of implementation.
- Multisectoral collaboration is based on the idea that what is good for the community is good for business. Most businesses directly benefit from safe communities and a healthy, educated workforce. Although the business sector may contribute to social problems, it can also play a role in the solution.

REVIEW QUESTIONS

Assessment Questions
1. What is an example of a wicked problem?
2. Why and how are the terms micro, meso, and macro relevant to the ecological model?
3. How is evidence-based practice applied? What knowledge is needed to apply it?
4. What strategies does collective impact apply?

Reflection Questions
1. Think about a social problem of interest to you, such as gang involvement. When have you seen a downstream solution applied? How might an upstream solution compare?
2. Consider a school district that is looking to increase graduation rates. How could you apply a prevention science mindset to implement prevention, intervention, and treatment programs or practices? How might the cost–benefit analysis be applied for this issue?
3. How can larger macro factors, such as the economy, impact the rate of Intimate Partner Violence?
4. When do you think social services might be necessary despite the cost to the individual or society? Are there any examples in your community?

REFERENCES

Barnett, W. S., Brown, K., & Shore, R. (2004). *The Universal vs. Targeted Debate: Should the United States Have Preschool for All?* National Institute for Early Education Research.

Barry, C. L., McGinty, E. E., Pescosolido, B. A., & Goldman, H. H. (2014). Stigma, discrimination, treatment effectiveness, and policy: Public views about drug addiction and mental illness. *Psychiatric Services, 65*(10), 1269–1272.

Bogenschneider, K. (1996). An ecological risk/protective theory for building prevention programs, policies, and community capacity to support youth. *Family Relations, 45*, 127–138.

Bronfenbrenner, U. (1977). Toward an experimental ecology of human development. *American Psychologist, 32*, 513–531.

Clear Impact. (n.d.). *5 conditions of collective impact.* https://clearimpact.com/achieving-collective-impact.

Cohen, L., Chavez, V., & Chehimi, S. (2010). *Prevention is primary: Strategies for community well being.* Wiley.

Coie, J. D., Watt, N. F., West, S. G., Hawkins, J. D., Asarnow, J. R., Markman, H. J., Ramey, S. L., Shure, M. B., & Long, B. (1993). The science of prevention: A conceptual framework and some directions for a national research agenda. *American Psychologist, 48*, 1013–1022.

Domestic Abuse Intervention Programs. (n.d.). *What is the Duluth model?.* Retrieved May 27, 2021, from https://www.theduluthmodel.org

Fraser, M. W. (1997). *Risk and resilience in childhood: An ecological perspective.* NASW Press.

Grant, R. (2005). State strategies to contain costs in the early intervention program: Policy and evidence. *Topics in Early Childhood Special Education, 25*(4), 243–250.

Health Policy Project. (2014). *Capacity development resource guide: Multisectoral coordination.* Futures Group, Health Policy Project.

Heckman, J. J. (2012). Invest in early childhood development: Reduce deficits, strengthen the economy. *Heckman Equation, 7*, 1–2.

Heckman, J. J., Moon, S. H., Pinto, R., Savelyev, P., & Yavitz, A. (2010). *A new cost–benefit and rate of return analysis for the Perry Preschool Program: A summary* (No. w16180). National Bureau of Economic Research.

Heine, S. J. (2020). *Cultural psychology* (4th ed.). Norton.

Jenson, J. M., & Fraser, M. W. (Eds.)., (2011). *Social policy for children and families: A risk and resilience perspective.* SAGE.

Kania, J., & Kramer, M. (2011, Winter). Collective impact [Web log post]. *Stanford Social Innovation Review.*

Karoly, L. A. (2008). *Valuing benefits in benefit–cost studies of social programs* [Technical report]. RAND Corporation.

Lerner, M. J., & Miller, D. T. (1978). Just world research and the attribution process: Looking back and ahead. *Psychological Bulletin, 85*(5), 1030–1051.

Modestino, A. S. (2017). *How do summer youth employment programs improve criminal justice outcomes, and for whom?* Federal Reserve Bank of Boston.

National Collaborating Centre for Determinants of Health. (2014). *Let's talk: Moving upstream.* National Collaborating Centre for Determinants of Health, St. Francis Xavier University.

O'Connell, M. E., Boat, T., Warner, K. E., & National Research Council. (2009). Defining the scope of prevention. In *Preventing mental, emotional, and behavioral disorders among young people: Progress and possibilities* (pp. 59–69). National Academies Press.

Reynolds, A. J., Temple, J. A., White, B. A., Ou, S. R., & Robertson, D. L. (2011). Age 26 cost–benefit analysis of the child–parent center early education program. *Child Development, 82*(1), 379–404.

Rittel, H. W., & Webber, M. M. (1973). Dilemmas in a general theory of planning. *Policy Sciences, 4*(2), 155–169.

Sidanius, J., & Pratto, F. (1999). *Social dominance: An intergroup theory of social hierarchy and oppression.* Cambridge University Press.

Springer, J. F., & Phillips, J. (2007). *The Institute of Medicine framework and its implication for the advancement of prevention policy, programs and practice.* Community Prevention Initiative.

Truman, J. L., & Morgan, R. E. (2014). *Nonfatal domestic violence 2003–2012.* Bureau of Justice Statistics, U.S. Department of Justice.

CHAPTER 4

Introduction to Direct Practice

Learning Objectives

After completing this chapter, you will be able to:

4.1. Define *direct practice*.

4.2. Describe the key aspects of professional helping relationships.

4.3. Explain the difference between counseling and psychotherapy.

4.4. Define *case management* and provide examples of the role played by the case manager.

4.5. List and describe the essential characteristics needed for direct practice.

4.6. Explain the importance of client confidentiality and name the legislation that established national standards for protecting the privacy of client information.

4.7. Define *advocacy* and explain how this process can result in improvements in the lives of clients.

Previous chapters in this book provide a framework for our historical and contemporary thinking and approaches to social issues. In this chapter, we take a deeper look at the essential features of direct practice human services work. You will gain an understanding of how a professional relationship differs from a social relationship. You will learn about key aspects of direct practice and client advocacy and become familiar with the tasks and responsibilities of practitioners who work as case managers. While reading this chapter, it will be useful to consider your own traits and goals and see how they may fit with the demands and rewards of direct practice in human services. It will also be useful for you to ask yourself how the value of social justice appears in direct practice work.

4.1 WHAT IS DIRECT PRACTICE?

Direct practice is defined as work in which a practitioner interacts directly with an individual, couple, family, or group (Figure 4.1). This type of practice occurs on a micro level (described in Chapter 1) because it involves direct human interactions and the

FIGURE 4.1   Direct practice involves direct human interactions and the forming of relationships. *Source*: Photo 195086110 © Prostockstudio|Dreamstime.com.

forming of relationships. For the sake of simplicity, we refer to "the client" as an individual unless otherwise indicated. Direct practice requires developing a helping relationship in which the practitioner provides assistance to the client. In this text, we use the term **helping relationship**, although elsewhere you may see it called a therapeutic or healing relationship. Ideally, the helping relationship empowers the client to make choices, changes, and actions to improve their life, but the term "helper" can also be construed as an imbalance of power in the relationship. Some clients or communities may not need "help" from a human service professional. How we refer to the relationship between a client or community and human services professional is not always straightforward.

A direct practice relationship can take on many attributes and forms. Some practitioners work with a person with psychiatric symptoms or a developmental disorder to help them find employment. Others work with clients who are unhoused or experiencing a housing crisis to help them locate or maintain stable, permanent housing. Some practitioners function as intake coordinators who ensure that people who qualify for a specific program are admitted to the program and that their most urgent needs are met. Professionals working at neighborhood centers may connect eligible people to benefits, entitlements, and other community resources. Some professionals work with clients who have been involved in the criminal justice system to ensure that they are integrated back into the community with housing, employment, and social supports. Some work to support recent immigrants by assisting with legal and language issues. Others work to improve the lives of senior citizens by helping them increase their activity, avoid social isolation, and become more engaged in their community.

At the associate's and bachelor's levels, the titles that direct practice human services practitioners hold vary, but they are often referred to as case managers, rehabilitation specialists, counselors, or mental health aides. At the master's level and higher, the direct practice roles retain a wide variety of titles but might be referred to again as case manager or as a social worker, counselor, therapist, or psychotherapist. Some direct practice roles, such as providing psychotherapy, require advanced training. However, all direct practice human services practitioners should have basic knowledge of how to effectively engage in a professional relationship. This chapter and the next provide an overview of that knowledge.

4.2 THE NATURE OF HELPING RELATIONSHIPS

Helping relationships differ from informal social relationships in several ways:

- The relationship lacks reciprocity.
- There is a power differential maintained by empathic, professional boundaries between the client and the practitioner. Because the client seeks help from the practitioner to address an identified problem, in a helping relationship, the practitioner has more power and influence than the client.
- The relationship is goal-oriented.

Nonreciprocity

The helping relationship is not reciprocal because it is expected that the client will benefit from it (not the practitioner). Although a human services practitioner may believe that they learn a great deal from helping relationships and benefit from the work, any benefit they experience is a secondary outcome, not the goal. The primary function and goal is always for the practitioner to help the client. In a direct-service relationship, there is always a goal. Examples of goals include healing from a traumatic experience, gaining employment, regaining custody of children, or becoming a better student.

Because of the special qualities of helping relationships, the ways we relate to another person in an informal relationship (e.g., with a friend or family member) are often inappropriate for a practitioner or client. A practitioner would not ask a client to do a favor for them because the client might feel obligated to say "yes." This sense of obligation could occur because the client needs the help provided by the practitioner or because they are grateful for help that has been provided in the past. Asking a favor of a client is considered an abuse of power.

Professional Boundaries

The professional relationship is governed by professional codes of conduct, state and federal laws, and agency policies, all of which require the practitioner to understand specific **professional boundaries** and to act accordingly. These boundaries preclude practitioners from treating a client as a close friend or confidant, dating a client, and being physically intimate with the client. Practitioners cannot yell at a client or cause them physical or emotional harm. Any of these behaviors are considered to be a **boundary violation**. Boundary violations are serious and in most cases will result in the practitioner losing their job. They can potentially lose their right to practice in the human services field and, in some cases, may be subject to criminal prosecution. Any type of boundary violation can hurt or traumatize the client. Supervision can help practitioners learn how to manage boundaries in healthy, positive ways.

There are also more subtle ways that professional boundaries come into play. For example, the type of personal information that is shared with clients differs from the information would be shared with family or friends. We might tell a friend about an issue that is troubling us, but we would not tell a client because the client is there to receive our help, not the other way around. Always keep in mind that professional boundaries apply in all instances of contact with clients.

The Goal-Oriented Nature of the Helping Relationship

In a direct practice professional relationship, there is always a goal. When we spend time with friends, we do not generally state the goals of the friendship, under what circumstances the goals will be met, or when the friendship will end. However, in a professional relationship, it is important to clearly state the goals and terms of work. These goals will be defined by the client's priorities and interests and can vary widely. Goal clarity ensures that the client and practitioner clearly understand and mutually agree on the relationship's purpose, stay focused, and do not waste time and resources. As you have already learned in this book, ethical behavior in the helping relationship is extremely important.

Interacting skillfully with a client ensures that the goals of the work will be met. A growing body of research demonstrates that the three most important elements of any direct practice intervention designed to help clients meet their goals are the practitioner's relationship building skills, the client–practitioner relationship (sometimes called the therapeutic alliance), and the client's hope about change, which can be enhanced by the practitioner's relationship-building approach (Drisko, 2004).

4.3 HOW DO COUNSELING AND PSYCHOTHERAPY DIFFER?

Counseling is commonly defined as providing assistance and guidance in resolving personal, social, or psychological problems, especially by a professional. Human services practitioners provide assistance to clients using psychotherapeutic techniques such as assessment, personal interviewing techniques, and sometimes testing for interests and strengths, but most direct practice human services professionals are not psychotherapists. The American Psychological Association (APA) Dictionary defines **psychotherapy** as "any psychological service provided by a trained professional that primarily uses forms of communication and interaction to assess, diagnose, and treat dysfunctional emotional reactions, ways of thinking, and behavior patterns" (APA, n.d., para 1). Psychotherapists require advanced training and licensure, the rules for which vary by profession and practice jurisdiction. Therefore, until one has an advanced degree (master's degree or higher) and license, human services counseling is limited in depth and scope, usually focused on technical aspects of supporting clients making changes and accessing resources.

Nonetheless, counseling skills are central to most human services direct practice positions. A human services practitioner is likely to use various counseling techniques to assist clients in achieving their goals. Counseling skills may be used to provide emotional and/or social support to someone seeking services, to communicate during a crisis, or in job coaching, to name a few examples. A great deal of human services work incorporates counseling into the interactions. In general, the more skillful a practitioner is in professional relationship building, the more they can inspire hope, and the stronger the therapeutic alliance, the more likely it is that the counseling will be effective (Drisko, 2004). Specific counseling techniques for human services practitioners are discussed in Chapter 5, and techniques for cultural competence are discussed in Chapter 7.

4.4 WHAT IS CASE MANAGEMENT?

Case management is a catchall term often used for human services practitioners in direct practice, although practitioners holding various titles often engage in much the same work. The Case Management Society of America (2017) defines case management as follows: "Case management is a collaborative process of assessment, planning, facilitation, care coordination, evaluation, and advocacy for options and services to meet an individual's and family's comprehensive … needs through communication and available resources to promote quality, cost-effective outcomes" (Para 1). Because of this broad definition and depending on the agency and the goal of the work, a case manager may or may not be involved in providing counseling to individuals or groups. A case manager with a bachelor's degree could be responsible for the following tasks as part of direct practice work:

- Completing a biopsychosocial assessment (Box 4.1) by considering risk and protective factors facing the client across multiple levels of systems
- Determining with the client the individual treatment and/or aftercare plans
- Connecting clients with community resources by making referrals and coordinating services with external providers
- Assisting clients in arranging essential appointments and accompanying clients to those appointments as needed
- Serving as an advocate and resource for the client, providing the client with information about available community support
- Promoting ongoing client participation in decisions involving plans, goals, and progress
- Supporting the client in employment and educational goal planning and attainment, including job coaching and skills training
- Coordinating discharge plans with multidisciplinary professionals
- Providing supportive counseling to help ensure a stable medical and psychological state during substance use detox/withdrawal or recovery from an acute episode of serious mental illness
- Providing other types of supportive and crisis counseling
- Leading educational, psychoeducational, therapeutic, and/or recovery client groups and/or facilitating social activities, discussion groups, and outings
- Participating as an active member of a multidisciplinary treatment team
- Assisting in multidisciplinary team efforts to handle crisis-oriented emergencies
- Conducting assessments, writing progress notes, entering data, and reviewing progress in accordance with agency and professional standards

Although the listed tasks and responsibilities vary, most require an ability to interact skillfully with an individual client or group in a variety of settings. The specific nature of the interactions will differ depending on the context, but some skills are essential to competent practice and will be identified in this chapter and the next.

BOX 4.1	Biopsychosocial Assessment

Framed by the ecological systems perspective, a biopsycho-social assessment, sometimes called a biopsychosocial–spiritual assessment, is a tool used to develop a full understanding of the client's life (Figure 4.2). This information helps the practitioner assess strengths and sources of resilience, experiences of adversity, and sources of risk across multiple systems levels. The assessment guides the practitioner in identifying needed interventions and referrals.

A biopsychosocial assessment typically includes the following components:

- The presenting or immediate problem for which the client is seeking services
- History of how the problem emerged

- Psychiatric and medical history and current issues
- Family history and current issues
- Housing history and current issues
- Social history and current issues
- Education and occupational history and current issues
- Military history and current status
- History of trauma and recent or ongoing trauma exposures
- History of and current substance use
- History of and current involvement with law enforcement/legal system
- Information on cultural factors, religion, and/or spirituality

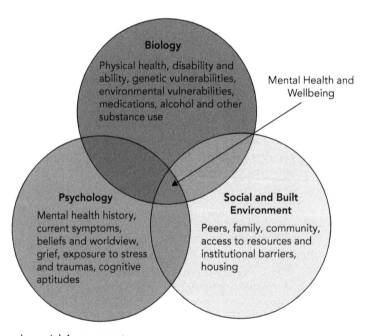

FIGURE 4.2   Biopsychosocial Assessments

4.5 ESSENTIAL CHARACTERISTICS FOR DIRECT PRACTICE

Amid the diversity of direct practice work, a number of essential characteristics, rooted in mainstream practice theories, are important to consistently incorporate into practice. Scientific evidence supports direct practice using a **person-centered** approach in which the practitioner views the client with unconditional positive regard, believes in their ability to change, and conveys authenticity and empathy (Farber & Doolin, 2011; Thomas, 2006).

Unconditional Positive Regard

The concept of unconditional positive regard is especially important. When a client seeks help from a human services practitioner, they often feel vulnerable and sometimes even ashamed. The more the client is able to share the full nature of their challenges, the more the practitioner can help. An attitude of **unconditional positive regard** on the part of the practitioner helps the client feel more comfortable. This is different from condoning the negative behaviors of a client, who may have behaved in destructive or violent ways. Being able to cognitively separate behaviors from the person is essential to this work. In order to be truly helpful, the practitioner must avoid conveying any negative judgments or feelings toward the client. Instead, they must identify and focus on the inherent value of the person and communicate this sense of value and worth to the client. Carl Rogers (Figure 4.3), a noted psychologist and theorist, wrote extensively about this concept beginning in the 1950s, and 21st-century research continues to validate it (Drisko, 2004; Farber & Doolin, 2011; Thomas, 2006).

Person-Centered Approach

A person-centered approach, formalized in the work of Carl Rogers, is essential for direct services practitioners. Rogers coined the term **humanistic** to describe a person-centered approach, which emphasizes the importance of conveying empathy and

FIGURE 4.3   Carl Rogers (1902–1987). Rogers is known as one of the founders of humanistic psychology. *Source*: Bob Van Doren, circa 1980.

unconditional positive regard with the expectation that humans can grow the fullest in a supportive relationship and environment (Rogers, 1957, 1958). This humanistic approach to psychotherapy is often considered an orienting theoretical perspective for direct practice human services work. Although there are many other scientifically sound ways to engage in direct practice, ranging from cognitive–behavioral and narrative theories and practices to motivational interviewing and solutions-focused work, it is best practice to use a humanistic theoretical perspective as the basis for interactions with clients in order to build the foundation for strong and respectful relationships.

In a person-centered approach, the practitioner's focus is on helping the client in the way they wish to be helped, often referred to as "meeting a client where they are." This is trickier than it sounds. Practitioners might not always have the same priorities or even define the client's needs and challenges in the same way as their clients do. Despite these differences, the practitioner must always take the perspective of the client, rather than forcing their own perspective, values, and beliefs onto the client. In short, the practitioner must practice with cultural competence and humility, considering each client to represent a culture of one. The humanity of the client and their dignity and worth must always be prioritized in the work. In that way, direct practice work is consistent with the social justice value underlying the human services professions.

Person-Centered Language

A logical outgrowth of the person-centered approach is the use of person-centered language. This means using language to describe clients without labeling them. For example, in the past, the term "schizophrenic" was used to describe a person with a diagnosis of schizophrenia. This term emphasized the diagnosis over the person and centered the person's social identity in severe psychopathology. Person-centered language focuses on the person. In the example of schizophrenia, one might now say instead, "an individual living with symptoms of schizophrenia." By avoiding a judgmental tone and not defining people by their diagnoses or problems, person-centered language individualizes, humanizes, and empowers. Once again, this is consistent with the social justice values of human service professions.

Empathy

Unconditional positive regard, person-centered and empowering/collaborative approaches, and person-centered language are all rooted in the need to respond empathically to clients. **Empathy** is the ability to understand and share the feelings of another person. Although its centrality to good direct practice is now well defined and supported by research (Moyers & Miller, 2013), the importance of empathy in helping relationships was first described by Carl Rogers (1957). Being able to experience and convey empathy for a client is absolutely essential. Lack of empathy can be harmful to a helping relationship (Moyers & Miller, 2013). Knowing how to express empathy is considered a key skill in direct practice human services work.

Empowering and Collaborative Approach

Taking an empowering and collaborative approach means that the practitioner and the client are viewed as equal partners in the direct practice relationship. The professional has expertise in some areas, and the client has expertise in others—most important, their own lived experiences. Working together, the practitioner and client determine the nature of the challenges the client is facing, as well as the strengths and sources of resilience the client brings to the table. They work collaboratively to find the best resolution to the identified problem(s) and increase the client's identified strengths. Empowerment becomes part of the process when practitioners encourage and support clients' use of self-determination to make decisions and changes. You cannot give empowerment to another person, but you can support their self-empowering actions throughout the process of the helping relationship. Using an empowering and collaborative approach ensures that the client's culture, values, and beliefs are centered, supporting practice that is culturally competent and oriented toward social justice.

Cultural Competence and Cultural Humility in Direct Practice

In direct practice, the work toward becoming a culturally competent practitioner is done by acknowledging to oneself and perhaps even to the client that one does not have knowledge of every possible human experience. Furthermore, one must be open to learning from the client and to valuing the client's experience and interpretation of their experience. The direct practice human services practitioner must have the self-awareness to understand the limits of their own life experience and their own potential for bias. They must also be able to regulate their thoughts and feelings in a way that manages the influence of personal biases and personal (rather than professional) values when working with clients. In the lifelong effort of working toward cultural competence, and in taking a stance of cultural humility toward working with diversity and difference, direct practice human services practitioners become proactive in fighting discrimination and bias, including their own, and promote understanding of what makes people unique. Engaging in direct practice with cultural humility means one acknowledges that understanding difference is an ongoing process that must be engaged in with a growth mindset, ongoing and honest self-appraisal, flexibility, and willingness to be corrected and educated by clients.

4.6 CLIENT CONFIDENTIALITY

As discussed in Chapter 6, maintaining **client confidentiality** refers to keeping all information received from a client private. The need to maintain confidentiality is governed by both ethical guidelines and federal and state laws. In direct practice, maintaining client confidentiality is also important for reasons related to the helping relationship. It is central to establishing and maintaining trust, without which it is impossible to have a truly helpful direct practice relationship. You can imagine how it would feel to share very personal information with someone you thought you could trust only to learn that they told others about it. Maintaining client confidentiality is therefore central to direct practice work. Across all direct practice human services settings, it is vital that practitioners understand the ethics of confidentiality and obey all laws and regulations regarding confidentiality of client information.

Health Insurance Portability and Accountability Act

The U.S. Health Insurance Portability and Accountability Act (HIPAA), passed in 2003, created standards to protect patient and client personal health information. Whenever a patient visits a health care practitioner, the practitioner is required to provide information about HIPAA protections. Patients are required to sign a release form stating that they have read the information and understand their rights regarding the confidentiality of their personal information.

The most important thing to know is that HIPAA protects one's privacy as a human services practitioner and the client's privacy as well. Identifying information about clients cannot be shared with anyone—not family members nor other treatment providers—without the client's written consent. It also means that clients have a right to see their records, and in the case of minors, parents or guardians have the right to review their child's record.

The Harm Principle

Rarely, a situation arises when confidentiality must be broken. One circumstance is when a client becomes a danger to themself or others—this is called the **harm principle**. A client who is actively suicidal or talking about hurting or killing another person must receive a special evaluation from two physicians to determine if they need to be admitted to a psychiatric hospital. The other situation is in cases of child or elder abuse. If a practitioner suspects that a child (younger than age 18 years) or older adult (older than age 65 years) is being physically, emotionally, or financially abused, they must call their local hotline and report it. This also applies if the practitioner discovers that the client is abusing another person.

Proof is not needed to report suspected abuse. The agency to which the concern is reported will conduct an investigation, often within 24 hours. In most states, the information can be reported confidentially. However, in some cases, it is appropriate for the practitioner to let the client know when a report has been made on their behalf. Although human services practitioners are often concerned about potentially damaging the helping relationship by breaking confidentiality, it is legally and ethically required to do so to prevent harm to others. The physical safety of the client and others comes first; the helping relationship can be repaired as needed.

4.7 CLIENT ADVOCACY

Although direct practice involves working directly with the client, the social justice mission of human services determines that the work cannot stop there (Freddolino et al., 2004). **Advocacy** entails work performed to change policies, practices, and conditions of clients served by human services professionals. It traditionally includes activities with goals of "protecting the vulnerable, creating supports to enhance functioning, protecting and advancing claims or appeals, and fostering identity and control" (Freddolino et al., 2004, p. 121). When a human services practitioner engages in advocacy, it means they support, recommend, or take a stand for something on behalf of the client or on behalf of a group to which the client belongs. Through advocacy, resources, institutions, policies, and laws are changed to better serve populations with previously unmet needs.

In practice, advocacy can be as focused as working with vocational programs to ensure that the client has needed disability accommodations, or it can be as broad as presenting information to lawmakers to advocate for a client's right to use a public

CASE STUDY 4.1 Melinda

Melinda's job with a community agency involved bringing children to visit their mothers in prison. The goal of the program was to help the mothers and children strengthen their relationships and decrease the stress of separation caused by imprisonment. Melinda's role included many case management tasks. First, she met with the children and their legal guardians and completed a biopsychosocial assessment of each child. The assessment helped Melinda understand the child and the family, determine how the prison visit program could help, and identify other referrals needed to improve the children's and families' lives. Melinda explained how the prison visits worked and made sure that both the child and the guardian were comfortable with the program. This meeting marked the beginning of the case management relationship.

Melinda put her personal feelings about crime aside and consistently conveyed unconditional positive regard because she knew the mothers and children would benefit more from their work together if they felt understood rather than judged. Elsewhere in prison, the mothers were referred to as "inmates," but Melinda and her program referred to the women as "mothers" because it was more humanizing and positive, and accurately reflected their identities.

Melinda designed and facilitated fun educational programs for the mothers and children that conformed to prison-visit rules. She also led a parenting support group within the prison, where the mothers could speak confidentially about their situation and learn new parenting strategies. Although Melinda shared a cultural background with some of the mothers, the group was diverse, and even the mothers who seemed similar to her had experienced different life chances. As the support group facilitator, Melinda put her own values and beliefs aside and took an attitude of trying to learn from and understand the mothers, and serve as a connector between them, rather than taking center stage and imposing her own values and beliefs. In that way, she acted with cultural humility.

During the prison visit educational programs, when it was time to leave their mothers, sometimes a child would act out. On one occasion, a 6-year-old girl named Lilly refused to move when it was time to leave. Melinda advocated with the prison guards, asking them to allow Lilly to stay a few more minutes after the mothers and other children had left the visiting room. She sat quietly next to Lilly. Once the room was empty and her mother was gone, it no longer seemed like a fun place, and Lilly was ready to go home to her grandmother.

Considering Lilly's immediate and longer term needs was more effective than punishment or scolding would have been. Melinda later advocated on Lilly's behalf, asking her grandmother's permission so Lilly could receive additional therapy to help her cope with her mother's imprisonment. After a few sessions, Lilly was able to better manage saying goodbye to her mother after a visit.

Melinda joined a local advocacy group to petition lawmakers to set aside resources for women leaving prison. To obtain their support, she shared stories of ways children were affected by their mother's imprisonment, making sure to change the names and other identifying information. Melinda's individual advocacy for Lilly and systems advocacy for women leaving the prison were two ways she enacted the social justice value of a human services practitioner.

Although Melinda's primary job description was simply to "bring children to visit their mothers in prison," knowledge, skills, attitudes, and professionalism informed her work to ensure that it was both effective and compassionate. The role of cultural humility and the value of social justice were central features of her work.

Think About . . .

1. Which essential characteristics of direct practice do Melinda's actions demonstrate?
2. How did Melinda show empathy for her clients?
3. What professional approach did Melinda demonstrate by including both the children and their guardians in the decision to participate in the prison-visit program?
4. How did Melinda advocate for Lilly specifically?
5. How did Melinda advocate for all the mothers and families that were her clients?
6. Where did you see Melinda acting on the value of social justice in this case study?
7. In what way(s) did Melinda act with cultural humility?

restroom for the gender with which they identify. Engaging in advocacy actively demonstrates concern for clients and is central to fulfilling the social justice mission of human services professions. Advocacy becomes a tool of empowerment when practitioners support clients' efforts to stand up for their own rights.

SPOTLIGHT ON SERVICE-LEARNING

Although not all service-learning placements involve engaging in direct practice, most human services agencies have some direct interface with the people they were created to serve. As you look at your service-learning setting and engage in self-reflection, consider the following questions:

1. What types of direct practice services are offered in your organization?
2. What are your organization's policies on confidentiality?
3. How do you use person-centered language?
4. What challenges to conveying empathy or authenticity have you faced? How have you coped with it in the moment? How have you coped with it afterward?
5. When would you decide to advocate on behalf of a client or group of clients?
6. Do you have any personal values or beliefs that would be difficult to put aside to engage in successful and ethical direct practice work? What about fears or concerns that could get in your way?

SUMMARY

- Direct practice is defined as work in which a human services practitioner interacts directly with an individual, couple, family, or group.
- The key aspects of professional helping relationships include a power differential (the practitioner has more power than the client), nonreciprocity (the relationship exists to benefit the client, not the practitioner), the relationship is goal-oriented, and the practitioner maintains professional boundaries in interacting with the client.
- Counseling is defined as providing assistance and guidance in resolving personal, social, or psychological problems, especially by a professional.
- Psychotherapy is therapy provided by a licensed and trained professional that relies on forms of communication and interaction to assess, diagnose, and treat dysfunctional emotional reactions, ways of thinking, and behavior patterns. It requires an advanced degree and licensure.
- Case management is a collaborative process of assessment, planning, facilitation, care coordination, evaluation, and advocacy for options and services to meet a client's comprehensive health needs through communication and available resources to promote quality, cost-effective outcomes. Case managers play many roles within human services organizations.
- The essential elements of direct practice work are unconditional positive regard, a person-centered approach and person-centered language, an empowering and collaborative approach, empathy, and cultural competence and humility.
- An empowering and collaborative approach to direct practice work ensures you are practicing with cultural competence and humility, and supporting the value of social justice.
- Maintaining client confidentiality is important to respect the client's privacy and safeguard their personal information.
- HIPAA created standards to protect patient and client personal health information.
- According to the harm principle, a practitioner can reveal a client's personal information only if it is necessary to do so to protect the client or others from harm.

- Advocacy describes a wide spectrum of work aimed at changing policies, practices, and conditions to improve the lives of clients or meet the needs of specific populations. It can link direct practice work with the value of social justice.

REVIEW QUESTIONS

Assessment Questions
1. What are some of the differences between an informal helping relationship and a professional human services relationship?
2. What are the central characteristics of counseling in direct practice human services work?
3. What are the legal and ethical considerations one needs to make when considering the sharing of client information?
4. What is the role of advocacy in direct practice human services?

Reflection Questions
1. If there were not professional boundaries established in helping relationships, what kinds of problems could emerge?
2. Many people hesitate to report suspected child or elder abuse when they do not have proof, even though suspicion requires a report. What would help or hinder you fulfilling your duty to report?
3. Completing a biopsychosocial assessment requires a direct service provider to ask many questions. What topics would be most interesting to you? What topics, if any, would make you uncomfortable to ask about?
4. Are there any client problems with which you would have difficulty empathizing? If so, what might you do to address that problem?

REFERENCES

American Psychological Association. (n.d.). *APA Dictionary of Psychology.* American Psychological Association. Retrieved April 5, 2023, from https://dictionary.apa.org/psychotherapy?_ga=2.148723902.821157151.1680706665-1161793241.1680706660

Case Management Society of America. (2017). *What is a case manager?* https://cmsa.org/who-we-are/what-is-a-case-manager/

Drisko, J. W. (2004). Common factors in psychotherapy outcome: Meta-analytic findings and their implications for practice and research. *Families in Society, 85,* 81–90.

Farber, B. A., & Doolin, E. M. (2011). Positive regard. *Psychotherapy, 48*(1), 58–64. doi:10.1037/a0022141

Freddolino, P. P., Moxley, D. P., & Hyduk, C. A. (2004). A differential model of advocacy in social work practice. *Families in Society, 85*(1), 119–128.

Moyers, T. B., & Miller, W. R. (2013). Is low therapist empathy toxic? *Psychology of Addictive Behaviors, 27*(3), 878–884. doi:10.1037/a0030274

Rogers, C. R. (1957). The necessary and sufficient conditions of therapeutic personality change. *Journal of Consulting Psychology, 21*(2), 95–103. doi:10.1037/h0045357

Rogers, C. R. (1958). The characteristics of a helping relationship. *Personnel & Guidance Journal, 37*(1), 6–16.

Thomas, M. L. (2006). The contributing factors of change in a therapeutic process. *Contemporary Family Therapy, 28,* 201–210. doi:10.1007/s10591-006-9000-4

CHAPTER 5

Direct Practice Techniques

Learning Objectives

After completing this chapter, you will be able to:

5.1. Describe the humanistic approach to direct practice.

5.2. List foundational counseling skills in the areas of nonverbal and verbal communication and explain how these skills influence the helping relationship.

5.3. Explain theoretical frameworks for counseling and related techniques.

5.4. Describe how direct practice works in group settings.

5.5. Explore the increasing popularity of telebehavioral health.

In this chapter, we continue our examination of human services practice at the micro level by providing an overview of the complex interaction of skills, knowledge, and attitudes that inform ethical human services counseling. There are many ways to engage and counsel clients. Critically evaluating the available evidence-based practices for a specific client problem helps determine which techniques make the most sense for a particular client and situation. Practitioners must also assess their own competency to provide any given intervention and determine what type of referrals should be made (if any) to address issues that cannot be addressed by the practitioner. In this chapter, we discuss the theory and techniques used in various approaches to practice, along with the nature of group work. In Chapter 4, we discussed how cultural competence and humility, along with the value of social justice, are embedded in direct practice social work. As you read, notice where those elements appear in counseling more specifically.

5.1 HUMANISTIC APPROACH TO DIRECT PRACTICE

In Chapter 4, we discussed the humanistic approach of Carl Rogers, which incorporates empathy and authenticity, a person-centered approach, and belief in the client's ability to change. These elements build a central framework for your direct work with clients.

If you keep these key concepts in mind when you work with people, chances are you will be able to help them. However, this general framework is just the beginning.

The Rogerian, humanistic perspective can be considered a lens through which to see other more specific intervention strategies. From this perspective, the practitioner acknowledges that each person is unique and has value (Hutchison, 2012). This may seem obvious at first, but practitioners often work with people who have done things or believe things that are difficult to imagine. For example, clients may have a history of substance abuse or child abuse or neglect. At times, it can be difficult to see the humanity and worth of a person, but the humanistic perspective, and indeed the ability to be helpful at all, demands that the practitioner do so.

A key premise of the humanistic perspective is that people have the capacity to change themselves, even to make radical changes, because all people have vast internal resources for self-understanding and self-directed behavior. They may not have tapped into those resources in the past, and it is often the practitioner's job to help them learn how to do it. Needed resources (and barriers to resources) might be internal or external, occurring at various systems levels. The social justice value of human services demands that even in counseling, the practitioner is aware of the multiple systems at play in an individual's life and works with and on behalf of the client to address and marshal them.

The practitioner must try to develop a deep understanding of each client. Understanding the internal frames of reference of individual clients is important to be able to help them. Knowing the client well prevents the practitioner from making mistaken assumptions about them, promoting culturally competent practice.

Another important concept is that of the true self and the ideal self (Hutchison, 2012). This concept suggests that everyone has two images of the self: the person who we are (true self) and the image of the ideal self we would like to be. When the distance between the two is too great, pathology enters. Behaving in ways that are not consistent with the true self causes problems. Helping clients close that gap is an important element of direct practice.

It is also important to consider why humans behave as they do. From the humanistic perspective, all human behavior is driven by a desire for growth, personal meaning, and competence and by a need to experience a bond with others (Hutchison, 2012).

Counseling Across Differences

Clients will have important aspects of their identities that are different from those of the practitioner and that come into play in the helping relationship. Differences in race or ethnicity, gender identity and expression, sexuality, immigration status, and socioeconomic status are just a few that will affect a client's response to counseling and to an individual practitioner—and vice versa. The concepts of cultural competence and humility are thus central to working effectively across differences in the counseling relationship.

Furthermore, practitioners must understand how different communities, institutions, and broader systems may be contributing to the challenges faced by a client (Box 5.1). The traumatic effects of racism, homophobia, transphobia, and other biases, as well as living in the economic margins, affect individuals, families, and groups in various ways. Guides for working with clients experiencing these types of traumas and

BOX 5.1	Advocacy

In direct practice, the human services practitioner is doing just that—providing services to the client. However, human services professions consider social justice to be an important part of the work. Often, merely providing counseling techniques such as the ones described here will only alleviate a small part of a client's challenges. Advocating on behalf of the individual client, as well as on behalf of any oppressed or marginalized group to which a client belongs, is an integral part of being an effective practitioner.

challenges are beginning to emerge. For example, Comas-Díaz et al. (2019) provide an important special issue of *American Psychologist* to promote understanding and working with racial trauma, and Ferguson-Colvin and Maccio (2012) provide a toolkit for practitioners working with lesbian, gay, bisexual, transgender, and queer/questioning (LGBTQ+) runaway and homeless youth. The most important first step in this kind of work is acknowledging and validating the reality of the lived experience of bias and oppression. Questioning the reality of their personal experiences would be yet another experience of oppression for the client. This is a case in which cultural humility can go a long way, and lack of cultural competence can do real harm.

Stages of the Helping Relationship

When providing human services in a counseling setting, it is important to think of the process of the helping relationship (Figure 5.1). The structure of this process is quite simple. It has a beginning, middle, and end:

- *The beginning* involves developing rapport and making a treatment plan. Treatment planning involves an intake process, during which a biopsychosocial interview is held with the client and comprehensive, holistic information regarding the client's past and present life (including strengths, protective factors, challenges, stressors, and traumas) is collected. This information forms the biopsychosocial assessment, which is used to guide initial treatment plans and understanding of the client and the challenges they face. The information-gathering process may take place over one session or several, throughout which the client and practitioner are getting to know each other and developing a therapeutic rapport. During this beginning phase, practitioners and clients identify goals for their work together. The practitioner also considers what referrals should be made (if any) to best address the client's needs.

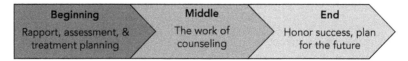

FIGURE 5.1 The Helping Relationship Process

- *The middle* phase is when the work of counseling is done. Counseling might involve the use of more complex therapeutic tools and strategies. It can include supportive and motivating talk along with information about referrals and connections to needed resources, such as childcare, food, transportation, housing support, and employment services. During this phase, the professional relationship continues, and work done in the sessions contributes to the client's growth and healing.
- The *end* of the counseling relationship, sometimes referred to as "termination," occurs when the therapeutic goal has been reached or, in some cases, it ends due to other factors. The last meeting(s) can be used to honor success, note areas for further growth, identify a plan of action should similar problems emerge in the future, and make any needed safety plans. Occasionally, clients will regress or become distraught at the termination of counseling treatment. Often, when treatment goals have been clearly identified at the beginning, and the clients agree with the treatment plan and the probable length of treatment, clients will leave counseling with a sense of accomplishment. They understand that moving on to an improved life has been an underlying goal throughout the counseling process.

Short-Term Direct Practice Work

Many agencies engage in short-term work with clients, in which clients meet with a human services practitioner as few as one or two times. Although this chapter focuses on longer term direct practice relationships, many of the skills discussed are transferable to even the shortest treatment relationships. The beginning, middle, and end processes still apply. Practitioners in short-term settings may do a more focused intake interview, directing questions specifically around services that their agency provides. Treatment will often focus on connection with important resources and referrals. The helping relationship ends with the final meeting with the client when all the client's needs that can be addressed by the agency have been addressed and referrals have been made.

Documentation

Documentation is an important part of the counseling process. Documentation holds practitioners accountable by creating a medical–legal record and serves as a form of communication across practitioners, within the confines of patient privacy laws. Commonly used formats for documentation are SOAP notes or SOAP-D notes (NYC Department of Youth and Community Development, 2011). Generally, one or two sentences are written for each of the following categories:

S = Strengths observed
O = Objective account of the interaction
A = Assessment of the situation/individual
P = Plan (progress toward specific goal)
D = Data/new information gathered

Good documentation allows a colleague to easily determine the next step with a client. It also demonstrates respect for the client. If the client were to read the notes, as they are usually legally entitled to do, they would feel respected and agree with the objective account of the interaction (NYC Department of Youth and Community Development, 2011).

5.2 FOUNDATIONAL COUNSELING SKILLS

Certain skills are considered foundational counseling skills because they are used in just about every counseling setting. These foundational skills can be divided broadly into nonverbal and verbal communication categories.

Nonverbal Communication

Nonverbal skills relate to physical appearance, movements, and behaviors. Both the client and the practitioner will engage in nonverbal communication during their interaction. Paying attention to and asking about the client's nonverbal cues will help you understand the individual and contribute to building the helping relationship. Managing your own nonverbal behavior effectively can help you gain trust and avoid misunderstandings. Because different cultures have different expectations of nonverbal behaviors, and because nonverbal behaviors can be interpreted differently across cultures and individuals, considering these behaviors through the lens of cultural humility is essential. Neukrug and Schwitzer (2006) delineate several categories of nonverbal communication as central to developing the helping relationship (p.91). These are presented and elaborated upon next.

Attire

Attire requirements vary from agency to agency, and it is important that practitioners follow the dress codes of their agencies to ensure that their appearance is professional. Attire can convey messages about the level of professionalism and the activities the practitioner expects to engage in. Appropriate attire demonstrates respect for the client.

Eye Contact

Maintaining good eye contact in a counseling session is important because it signals interest and active listening. However, be careful to avoid staring at a client, as this can make the person uncomfortable. Some clients may not return your eye contact, and this can mean many things. A client with poor eye contact may feel defiant of any authority you have or feel reluctant to be meeting with you, or the client may feel shy, ashamed of the conversation topic or the situation they are in. As you will learn more about in Chapter 7, it is important to recognize that direct eye contact is viewed positively in most Western cultures but not in all cultures. The client may have been raised in a culture in which norms around eye contact are different. In some cultures, direct, sustained eye contact is considered rude, disrespectful, or even aggressive.

Posture and Body Position

Your posture and how you position your body can convey messages about you and about the nature of your meeting with the client. An open body position is sitting with your arms and legs uncrossed, facing the client, and slightly leaning toward them as they speak. When in doubt, this is a good body position to fall back on. Crossing your arms can convey that you are not receptive to what the person is saying. It can also be interpreted as expressing your authority at a time when it is not necessary, and openness is desired.

Personal Space
Use of personal space will be dictated by cross-cultural expectations and your comfort level, along with that of your client. Before you meet with a client for the first time in an office, it can be helpful to arrange chairs in various configurations to see what distance is most comfortable to you. Do not be surprised if a client moves their chair farther away or closer to you. Unless you feel that your physical boundaries are being violated, it is important to respect the client's comfort level and need for personal space.

Facial Expressions
It is incredibly important to monitor your facial expressions when counseling clients. If your expression conveys negative judgment, for example, then words that try to convey other sentiments, such as unconditional positive regard, will be useless. Facial expressions communicate how a practitioner feels about the client and what they are saying (Figure 5.2). It is important to be able to control these effectively. In trauma work in particular, it is important to let clients know that you can tolerate hearing about the painful things they have experienced. Wincing or cringing can be counterproductive. A good way to practice is by watching TV shows or movies. Try watching something you know is funny or sad, and monitor your facial expressions and other body language as you watch.

Nonverbal and Minimal Verbal Responses
There are times when a client is speaking, and wanting them to know that they are heard and understood is important for building rapport. Nonverbal responses such as facial expressions or head nodding can be effective in helping the client feel heard. Sometimes

FIGURE 5.2   Facial expressions can communicate how a practitioner feels. *Source*: Photo 2563463 © Lisa F. Young|Dreamstime.com.

minimal verbal responses such as "mmhmm," "yeah," and "oh wow" can let the client know you are following them and can convey empathy just as effectively as full sentences (De Jong & Berg, 2013).

Silence

In the United States, we rarely sit together in silence with others. Long periods of quiet time might start to feel awkward and uncomfortable. However, in a counseling session, silence can be very useful. Silence allows a client to reflect on what they have been saying. A practitioner can use silence to process and interpret what a client has said and formulate the best possible response. Periods of silence can push the conversation forward and increase the depth of attention to a given topic. By not rushing to fill every moment with words, a counselor encourages the client to do the talking and exploring, which is the process through which growth occurs in this model. The use of silence offers the client the opportunity to learn more about nonverbal communication. Furthermore, words are sometimes used to divert attention from feelings. Of course, silence can in itself be a problem, such as when a client refuses to respond to the practitioner. Too much silence in a session can also backfire if a client feels so uncomfortable that the session is intolerable. Thus, silence is an important tool that should be carefully considered and used only when appropriate. Note that there might be cultural implications and personal interpretations of silence that vary among clients. As always, be aware of such potential differences and willing to explain your choices, including the choice to sit in silence.

A Note About Touch

Most agencies have specific rules around touching. Some may forbid it entirely, and in other agencies, touch might be part of the work. For example, practitioners working in applied behavioral analysis with small children will need to use gentle touch to indicate what a child should be doing as they learn various tasks. Those working in prisons might be forbidden from any touch, even a handshake. Touch can mean different things to different people, depending on a wide range of variables that include cultural background, personal history (including trauma history), individual preferences, and what a person wants at a given time. When the rules of touch in an agency are not clear, a good rule of thumb is to keep any touch potentially public (in an office with an open door or in the hallway), minimal, and professional. In general, "professional" means handshakes, although in some cultures a different physical greeting is preferable. Whereas some might think a quick, light touch on the shoulder or arm is harmless, for others this can feel like a boundary violation. It is best to proceed with caution. Any kind of sexual or violent touch between a client and practitioner is strictly forbidden.

Verbal Communication

We all know that it's not only what you say that matters, it's how you say it. This is an important consideration when speaking with clients. You should not only attend to your words but also be aware of the tone and volume of your voice. Your intonation can add or detract from the impact of what you are saying.

Communicating empathy and establishing a connection with the client are important aspects of counseling. Several foundational techniques are used in almost every counseling practice: open-ended questions, summarizing statements, and expressions of empathy.

Types of Questions

There are many types of questions you might ask a client. Two major types are closed-ended and open-ended. Closed-ended questions have a specific answer, often a binary like, "yes" or "no." They are important for fact-finding and clarifying information. Closed-ended questions a practitioner might ask in an initial client meeting could include the following:

- "Who do you live with?"
- "Did you graduate from high school?"
- "Do you sometimes drink beer, wine, or other alcoholic beverages?"
- "Have you ever been involved in the criminal justice system?"

The responses to such questions may be things you want to ask about in a more nuanced way. Open-ended questions can help you do that.

Asking Open-Ended Questions

Questions are open-ended when they can yield many possible answers and encourage a client to go into some depth as they respond. Compare these open-ended questions to the closed-ended questions in the previous section:

- "How do you feel about living with your mother?"
- "What happened that led you to leave high school before you graduated?"
- "Can you tell me a bit about the role of alcohol in your life?"
- "What were the circumstances that led to your criminal justice involvement?"

These questions yield a different, more specific, and more complete type of response, even though they cover the same general topics. Remember to use the important nonverbal skills when a client is responding to an open-ended question. Doing so ensures clients know the practitioner cares, is listening, and is ready to help them.

Summarizing

Summarizing is another skill a practitioner can use to help a client feel heard. There are several ways to summarize what a client has said, but it is simplest to remember that after a client has shared a good deal of information on a topic, it is important to summarize in your own words the key points the client has made. This helps them feel heard, lets them know you have been paying attention, can serve to quickly resolve any misunderstandings, and helps you convey empathy.

Expressing Empathy

There are many ways to express empathy, ranging from facial expression to minimal verbal responses to summaries. The practitioner should also consciously construct empathetic statements throughout a counseling session so that the empathy is explicit. The simplest way to express empathy explicitly is to use this format: You feel_____about_____because_____(Neukrug & Schwitzer, 2006). The first blank contains a word that expresses the client's feelings. In the second blank, you summarize

Tyler is a 21-year-old man who has problems with hearing voices and often feels very down. He is meeting with a new case manager for the first time. The case manager's role is to provide supportive counseling in a treatment program that Tyler has been attending daily for a few months. The foundational counseling skill being demonstrated is noted in brackets following each practitioner statement.

HUMAN SERVICES PRACTITIONER: Tyler, who are you living with now? [closed-ended question]

TYLER: My mother. (*He makes a face.*)

PRACTITIONER: I see you're making a face [responding to nonverbal cues]. What about living with your mother makes you make that face? [open-ended question]

TYLER: Oh well, you know, I'm 21. I should have graduated college, I should be starting my career, living on my own or with some really cool roommates who are my best friends.

PRACTITIONER: (*Nods with a concerned facial expression*) [nonverbal behavior to communicate understanding]

TYLER: But no, I've just been in and out of the hospital and coming to this day program and I don't get anything done, I failed college, and I live with my mother like I'm a child. How can I feel like an adult when I live like a child?

PRACTITIONER: So, for you, living with your mom is a reminder that you aren't where you want to be in life yet, and you have things you would have liked to have accomplished by now that you haven't been able to because you've been in and out of the hospital so much. [summary]

TYLER: Yeah, and, no offense, but I don't see the point of coming to this program every day. What am I doing with my life here? I want to be an orchestra conductor, not just a patient. I'm not achieving my potential.

PRACTITIONER: It sounds like you feel disheartened because you have big dreams and coming to this program hasn't helped you reach them yet. [empathic statement]

TYLER: I do feel disheartened! I feel like I am being squeezed into this box that I don't want to be in.

Think About ...

We can see that through skillful communication a client will open up about their feelings rather quickly, instead of staying on more surface topics. Notably, Tyler does this even though he does not want to be going to the program every day anymore.

---

what the client has those feelings about. The third blank contains the client's reasons why. Empathetic statements can also be used to help clients expand their emotional vocabulary, something from which most people can benefit. Case Study 5.1 provides an example of a conversation where many communication skills were used by the practitioner.

5.3 THEORETICAL FRAMEWORKS FOR COUNSELING

In human services, a theoretical framework is a group of ideas and hypotheses that explain human behavior under various circumstances. Counseling theories aim to explain what helps a person change in the ways that they want to. There are a multitude of such theories and related practices. We have already discussed the humanistic perspective a great deal. Now we focus on two more theories and related practices that have a strong evidence base: (a) cognitive–behavioral theory and treatment and (b) motivational interviewing.

Cognitive–Behavioral Theory and Techniques
Cognitive–behavioral theory suggests that conscious thoughts and observable behaviors are the best predictors of a client's emotional state and therefore the key areas to address in a psychotherapeutic process. In this theory, thoughts, feelings, and behaviors

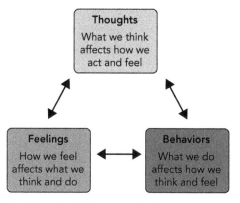

FIGURE 5.3   The Cognitive-Behavioral Therapy Triangle

all affect and build upon one another in reciprocal processes. The emphasis is on the conscious and observable. This theory is often depicted as the cognitive–behavioral triangle (Figure 5.3). Interventions based on this theory are described as cognitive-behavioral therapy (CBT).

Scientific evidence supports CBT interventions in the treatment of a wide range of issues, from childhood sexual trauma to depression and eating disorders. Because CBT interventions tend to be time-limited and supported by strong scientific evidence, insurance companies are more willing to pay for these interventions versus longer-term interventions. For this reason, CBT interventions are commonly used in human services direct practice settings such as community mental health clinics. There are several core concepts and skills in CBT that can be quick to learn but that take time, practice, and supervision to master. Although it is best to use the scientifically validated manuals and protocols as a whole, there are pieces common across many CBT protocols that can be useful on their own.

Psychoeducation

The first CBT session involves orienting a client to what CBT is, as well as identifying the problems and goals of the client, from their perspective. The CBT triangle is shown to the client, and the targets of conscious thoughts and observable behaviors are explained in a simple manner, using as little jargon as possible. This process is called **psychoeducation**, and even just learning this initial information can be therapeutic for a client.

SMART Goals

The SMART acronym stands for specific, measurable, assignable (or attainable), realistic, and timely (Wilding, 2015). It is used for effective goal setting in counseling that uses CBT, and SMART goals are often seen in case management work:

- *Specific*: Goals should identify precisely what is supposed to improve or the problem to be resolved or eliminated.
- *Measurable*: Goals must be measurable. This can be done using something as simple as a subjective scale. For example, a practitioner asks, "On a scale from 0 to 10, with 0 being the least severe and 10 being the most severe, how severe is

your problem today?" The goal is for the client's experience of the problem to decrease with treatment over time and their experience of strengths or success to increase with treatment over time. Such a measure is specific to the client and relies on client self-awareness.

- *Assignable/attainable*: Goals must be attainable because if they seem too out of reach, taking any steps toward them will seem pointless. It can help to start small and move toward larger goals.
- *Realistic*: It is helpful to have goals that are realistic. Setting a goal that says someone will "never" or "always" do something in the future is often impossible. For example, when people are trying to lose weight, they often say they will "never" eat desserts or chips again, when a more realistic approach would be to identify the boundaries and circumstances in which one would eat those things. Many small, attainable steps make larger goals seem achievable and realistic. Sometimes a goal does need to have a "never" attached to it, of course. Drinking and driving or leaving small children home alone are two examples that come to mind.
- *Timely*: It is human nature to need specific time frames for achieving goals. Without a specific time frame, there is no urgency to act (Wilding, 2015). However, time frames must also be realistic.

Finally, best practices suggest that counseling goals should be strengths-based, whenever possible focusing on what can be done more rather than on what should not be done. The person's strengths and resources, including their culture(s) and communities, should all be considered in developing the goals, objectives, and tasks.

Cognitive Restructuring

Conscious thoughts are a primary target of CBT, based on the idea that negative thought patterns lead to negative emotional states, and positive thought patterns lead to positive emotional states. Cognitive restructuring is a multistep process that involves assessing a client's pattern of thinking that leads to negative feeling states, determining with the client that some of their thoughts or thought patterns are ineffective for managing important life challenges, and using discussion and exercises with the client to promote goal attainment (Wilding, 2015). For example, sometimes an event occurs that leads to an automatic thought and then a feeling state, sometimes happening so quickly that a client does not recognize what is happening. Identifying and addressing these thoughts and thought patterns is the work of "cognitive restructuring."

TRY IT YOURSELF

Think of something that happened that perhaps did not go well, left you feeling disappointed, or was just in some way unpleasant for you. Try to remember the details and really go into the moment. Then, reflect on how you feel. Probably not that great. Next, think of the last time you felt really good. What was happening? Can you mentally relive that moment? Reflect on how you feel again—most people will feel much better thinking about something positive. As simple as it seems, that is what the cognitive piece of CBT is all about—consciously managing one's thoughts so that positive thoughts are more dominant and positive emotions can emerge.

Cognitive restructuring focuses just on the cognitive/thinking part of CBT, but behavior plays an important role in one's emotional life as well. Behaviors can serve to create and sustain negative emotional feeling states. For example, when people begin to feel depressed, they often lose their energy and stop engaging in pleasurable activities. (In fact, they might not even view activities they enjoyed in the past as pleasurable anymore. That is a cognitive part of the nature of depression.) As a result of engaging in fewer pleasurable activities, their depressed mood increases, creating a vicious cycle. Behavioral interventions are often designed to break vicious cycles, such as the inactivity of depression, among many others.

Third-Wave Interventions

Identifying and working to decrease thoughts and behaviors that evoke or sustain a negative feeling state or, more important, increasing those that evoke or sustain a positive feeling state is part of the original focus of CBT. In what is now known as third-wave CBT, clients learn various strategies to deal with their thoughts and feelings in the moment, with an emphasis on mindfulness, emotions, acceptance, values, goals, and metacognition (Hayes & Hofmann, 2017). A central idea in third-wave approaches is that often when a person is trying not to think of something, or not to feel or act in certain ways, it is difficult to think of, feel, or do anything else but that thing one is avoiding.

Some people have thoughts and images in their minds that are so intense that trying to avoid them only makes them more prominent. People who have experienced trauma often find this to be true. For those and others, learning to cope with and accept unpleasant thoughts and images, rather than struggle to avoid them, is the most productive strategy. Mindfulness meditation can help people identify the difficult or unpleasant thoughts, feelings, and physical sensations and learn to tolerate those phenomena by focusing on the here and now. Grounding exercises can help people stay safe and focused on the present moment, despite intrusive thoughts. These strategies are often connected with other CBT techniques that include core cognitive restructuring and behavioral change strategies.

For many clients, changing thoughts or behaviors is not so simple. Indeed, these new skills require practice and support. Changes to feelings, thoughts, and behaviors do not often come simply from evoking a simple cause–effect reward system. There are in fact many factors that underlie why a person will or will not change. Factors relating to a person's physical and social environment, including ongoing exposure to traumatic experiences, housing or food insecurity, and/or other important unmet needs, can make individual-level change more difficult. Nonetheless, even people who are struggling to have their basic needs met will also strive toward self-actualization, meaning, and purpose.

TRY IT YOURSELF

Right now, whatever you do, do not think of elephants. Don't think about how they look, or what they sound like, or what their trunks do. Think of anything else except elephants.

For most people, it is pretty difficult to not think of elephants right now.

Motivational Interviewing Theory and Techniques

Motivational interviewing is a behavioral change–enhancing approach that stems from a humanistic, Rogerian perspective, with which you have already been familiarized. Motivational interviewing is a type of counseling that defines the "motivation" as motivation to change problematic behavior. This differentiates it from cognitive approaches that seek to change thought patterns. In this model, behavior change requires *self-efficacy*, which is the belief a person has that they can do something. Sometimes self-efficacy is innate, but it is often built through practice and episodes of trial and error. Although a client may be motivated to change a behavior, the change will not take place until the client has self-efficacy.

According to its developers, "Motivational interviewing is a client-centered, directive method for enhancing intrinsic motivation to change by exploring and resolving ambivalence" (Miller & Rollnick, 2013, p.25):

- *Client-centered* means the focus is on the goals prioritized by the client, not problem areas that a practitioner views as most important.
- Motivational interviewing is *directive*. This does not mean that the practitioner tells the client what to do—quite the opposite. The practitioner gently guides the client to talk more about the ways they want to change and can change.
- This method *enhances intrinsic motivation to change*. The humanistic psychological perspective tells us that all people are motivated for change; in motivational interviewing, the practitioner must discover what exactly the person is motivated for.
- Motivational interviewing helps clients *explore and resolve ambivalence*. People commonly experience ambivalence, or mixed feelings and contradictory ideas, around the very things they say they want to change. For example, most people do not keep their New Year's resolutions. This is not pathological, but merely human nature. Motivational interviewing presents a way to explore what the ambivalence is around a specific change and to resolve it in a way that will propel people toward the change.

The theory of how motivational interviewing works is a set of hypotheses (Miller & Rose, 2009), which can be summarized as follows:

- The practitioner receives training in motivational interviewing.
- The practitioner engages with empathy while simultaneously using techniques that are consistent with motivational interviewing practice.
- This leads to the client engaging in preparatory change talk and increased motivation to change, which in turn leads to a commitment to behavior change and, ultimately, the behavior change itself.

It has been noted that merely practicing with empathy and in the spirit of motivational interviewing can lead to behavior change, without any of the intermediary steps, which highlights the importance of developing empathy-related skills (Miller & Rose, 2009).

Autonomy support is another important feature of motivational interviewing, wherein the practitioner is tasked with respecting and supporting a client's irrevocable right of self-direction, even when the practitioner sees that the client is making a mistake, believes the client is prioritizing the wrong behavior to change, or believes the client is headed for a relapse. Except in cases of imminent danger to self or others, the practitioner must accept the client's self-determination and support their acting with autonomy.

Motivational Interviewing Techniques

The four central techniques of motivational interviewing are abbreviated with the acronym OARS, which stands for open-ended questions, affirmations, reflective listening, and summaries (Miller & Rollnick, 2013).

Open-ended questions and summaries have already been discussed as foundational techniques. Affirmations involve the practitioner seeking and verbalizing the virtues, strengths, and successes they see in the client. These compliments must be genuine and can serve to promote self-efficacy and validate client thoughts and feelings. They can also acknowledge the difficulties a client has faced, and perhaps their resilience in the face of adversity, bolstering self-efficacy and readiness to face future obstacles. Affirmations can evoke powerful responses because many people have not received abundant acknowledgment of their positive attributes and actions.

Reflective listening is a key component of motivational interviewing. Reflecting back to a client what they have said is done to emphasize the value of the statement or to let the client know their words were heard and understood. It allows the client to hear what they have said and clarify, revise, or affirm their statement. Simple reflection involves merely repeating what a client has said. Paraphrasing involves putting what a client has said into one's own words. Reflections of feelings are the deepest type, reflecting the emotions behind what someone has said. Metaphors are often useful in reflection of feelings. A reflection is shorter than a summary, and in its many forms it can be interspersed throughout counseling dialogues.

Because motivational interviewing is all about working with clients to enhance their motivation to change, understanding the phases of change is central to that work. Prochaska and DiClemente (1984) identified the stages of client change. These are precontemplation, contemplation, preparation, action, maintenance, and relapse:

- *Precontemplation* is the stage when a client does not believe there is a problem or see a need for change. The practitioner's goal is to develop a trusting relationship and raise awareness. This term is used instead of the more judgmental word "denial."
- *Contemplation* is the stage when the client sees possibility of change but is uncertain and has unresolved ambivalence about it. The practitioner's goal then is to work with the client to address the ambivalence, build self-efficacy, and, ultimately, build motivation to change.
- *Preparation* is the stage when the client has begun to make plans for change and set goals, and the practitioner's concurrent goal is to support self-efficacy and motivation, negotiate a plan, and facilitate decision-making.
- *Action* is when the client begins implementing a plan, and the practitioner provides support.
- *Maintenance* is the stage when a client continues the behavior change and, to the extent that the practitioner remains involved, the role of the practitioner is to identify strategies to prevent relapse. Although relapse is considered an expected part of the change process, work to prevent relapse is nonetheless important. The longer a change can be sustained, the more self-efficacy the client will have, enabling their recovery from relapse.

- *Relapse* refers to going back or between any of the previous stages. It is considered an integral part of the change process, as the client builds self-efficacy through trial periods of change and can go from any stage back to any other. Most people do not sustain changes, especially major ones, on the first effort, but instead learn through trial and error. So, while one works to prevent relapse, one also accepts and learns from it when it happens.

Knowing which stage of change a client is in helps guide a practitioner's responses and actions and helps explain why and how a client is acting (or not acting) to make important changes.

Effectiveness of Motivational Interviewing

Motivational interviewing works especially well in short-term work, when clients may need to do a lot of follow-through on their own. It is widely used and has a strong empirical foundation for work with multiple populations. According to the Campbell Collaboration (2016), it has proven effectiveness in helping people recover from substance use disorders, including those who have not benefitted from prior treatments; smoking cessation; decreasing pathological and problem gambling; enhancing psychiatric and medical treatment adherence; supporting housing interventions for people who have been homeless; decreasing HIV risk behavior; increasing effective contraception use; improving diet, exercise, and health behaviors; improving outcomes in youth living with HIV and AIDS; and youth substance use prevention. Of note, using CBT and motivational interviewing skills together is another common practice among counselors. This approach to counseling is called "motivation-enhanced CBT" and again has a substantial evidence base.

As someone who provides counseling in the human services, it would make sense to consider motivational interviewing as a key tool in your toolbox because you can use it to work with clients facing many issues. As with CBT, it is important to realize that although motivational interviewing techniques appear easy to learn, using this method effectively requires practice, reflection, and, ideally, expert guidance from a supervisor or mentor.

You must also be aware that motivational interviewing is not a one-size-fits-all approach to direct practice work. Many challenges that people face, such as eating disorders, recovery from trauma, and coping with long-term losses, are not effectively helped using motivational interviewing. Exploring the research to examine which approaches work best with various problems and client groups is the ethical way to ensure clients with whom you work are being served in the best possible way and through a lens of cultural humility. If you do not have the skills to deliver the needed intervention, it is best to refer out to someone who does.

5.4 COUNSELING WITH GROUPS

An increasing amount of direct practice work, including counseling, occurs in groups (Figure 5.4). Groups are a cost-effective means of providing services, and they also offer unique value that individual counseling cannot. This unique value lies in the opportunity for group members to provide each other mutual support. Group members with the same or similar challenges can offer unique insights and support that comes from shared experiences. Such support also decreases social isolation caused by the individual's challenges.

FIGURE 5.4   Group Counseling *Source:* Photo 55895343 © Monkey Business Images|Dreamstime.com

Most types of counseling can be conducted in groups. The same foundational techniques used in individual counseling can be applied in groups, but group leaders have to make additional considerations (Center for Substance Abuse Treatment, 2005). Group leaders might sometimes use evidence-based treatment manuals to guide groups through a series of psychoeducational lessons, exercises, and discussions. A clear sense of the purpose of the group is important, as is confidence in their own group leadership abilities. Group leaders need to both state and model behavior they expect from group members, and they must also regulate their emotions. Group leaders need to apply rules and guidelines for the group consistently so that impressions of favoritism do not emerge and derail the group functioning. Flexibility is also important for group leaders because groups may have different needs at different times, and group members may provide different challenges. Keeping group members feeling emotionally safe with each other, especially when conflicts between group members have emerged, and protecting the confidentiality of group members are unique challenges that do not present themselves in individual practice.

5.5 TELEBEHAVIORAL HEALTH

Telebehavioral health has emerged in the past decade, especially since the COVID-19 pandemic, as an increasingly popular mode for counseling (Figure 5.5). Current data suggest that counseling through online video chats is effective and equitable (Mochari-Greenberger & Pande, 2021). By removing constraints of time, need to travel, need for child care, the barriers of stigma, and increasing the flexibility of office hours, telebehavioral health has made mental health counseling available to a far wider range of the population, including those made vulnerable by social determinants of health who are likely to have more barriers to accessing quality mental health care. Therefore, counseling online can be seen as a way to practice within a social justice frame. However, this form of counseling is relatively recent and the evidence remains emergent. It is not yet clear which techniques and skills translate best and for whom in online settings, and under what circumstances telecounseling should not be done.

FIGURE 5.5   Telebehavioral Health *Source*: Photo 215534255 © Valerii Honcharuk|Dreamstime.com

CASE STUDY 5.2   Nathaniel

Nathaniel is a 45-year-old gay White man who had recovered from a moderate alcohol use disorder in his late 20s. For many years, he was in the maintenance phase of the behavioral change of recovery from a substance use disorder. Although he had used psychotherapy to help stop drinking, he no longer saw a therapist. He regularly attended Alcoholic Anonymous meetings and had a strong network of friendships that arose from the meetings. Since becoming sober, his career as a graphic designer soared, and he even had a contract to illustrate a children's book, one of his lifelong dreams. His relationship with his 15-year-old son, once estranged, was also back on track. He felt his life was better than he had imagined it would ever be. He maintained his sobriety even during the stresses of the COVID-19 pandemic.

After the pandemic ended, he increasingly found himself at social events where alcohol was served. One night at a dinner party to celebrate the end of the pandemic, he decided to have a glass of wine so he could feel like he was more a part of the celebration. Although he was worried he might lose control as he had in the past, he found he enjoyed the glass of wine with the meal and did not suffer from any severe consequences that night or the next day. He therefore moved from the maintenance phase, through relapse, to the precontemplation stage of change, as he decided that he was able to enjoy wine with dinner "like an adult" and without undesirable consequences. Over the next few months, he found himself drinking more and more,

and he realized he was waking up with headaches, groggy, annoyed with his son, and unable to focus on his work. One morning, he arose with a particularly bad headache and decided that he was not in fact an adult who enjoyed wine with dinner and that he "was better as an adult who didn't drink." He gave up alcohol again, moving from precontemplation back to the maintenance phase, as his many years of sobriety gave him self-efficacy that enabled him to do so with relative ease.

Think about . . .

1. This case illustrates how a client can move between stages of change in a nonlinear fashion. When people move from maintenance to active use, often their human service practitioners can feel like they have failed. What in motivational interviewing and the stages of change can help you recognize that this is not a failure on your part, nor on the client's?

2. If you were working with Nathaniel when he started drinking again, knowing his problematic history with alcohol, what would you do?

3. Nathaniel decided he no longer wanted to attend Alcoholic Anonymous meetings after he stopped drinking the second time. How would you respond to that decision?

4. If you met with Nathaniel for counseling after his relapse, what specific techniques might you apply?

SPOTLIGHT ON SERVICE-LEARNING

Using one of the approaches covered in this chapter, discuss how you or another professional in your organization might apply the techniques.

SUMMARY

- There are many different techniques and skills used in direct practice human services work. This chapter has provided an overview of two that are ubiquitous in the field and can be effectively applied to clients across multiple practice areas.
- Motivational interviewing and cognitive–behavioral techniques can be helpful for counselors in a wide variety of settings.
- Although many of the skills that are applied appear relatively simple on paper, they are in fact quite challenging to apply consistently. Advanced training with adequate supervision is necessary for anyone who wishes to provide psychotherapy.
- Group counseling and telebehavioral health counseling use some of the same skills as in-person, individual strategies, but they vary in important ways.
- Using any set of specific counseling skills alone is not enough. One must also consider the evidence base, relevance for the specific client, practice through the lens of cultural competence and humility, and carefully consider any social justice issues affecting one's client.

REVIEW QUESTIONS

Assessment Questions

1. What are the core elements of the humanistic approach to direct practice?
2. What is the first step in working with clients who have had negative experiences, including trauma, due to bias?
3. How would you define the stages of the helping relationship?
4. What is the purpose of documentation in direct practice?

Reflection Questions

1. Consider a time when something was conveyed to you in nonverbal language. What did you notice about the person's body language and other nonverbal communication that made their message come across?
2. If you made a SMART goal for yourself, what would it look like? What would you need to do to make it happen?
3. When you think about relapse as a normal part of change, how does that alter how you think about changes you or people you know have tried to make over time?
4. In what circumstances do you think a client should receive counseling in person instead of via telehealth?

REFERENCES

Campbell Collaboration. (2016). https://www.campbellcollaboration.org

Center for Substance Abuse Treatment. (2005). Group leadership, concepts, and techniques. In *Substance abuse treatment: Group therapy* (Treatment Improvement Protocol Series No. 41). Substance Abuse and Mental Health Services Administration. https://www.ncbi.nlm.nih.gov/books/NBK64211

Comas-Díaz, L., Hall, G. N., & Neville, H. A. (2019). Racial trauma: Theory, research, and healing: Introduction to the special issue. *American Psychologist, 74*(1), 1.

De Jong, P., & Berg, I. (2013). *Interviewing for solutions* (4th ed.). Brooks/Cole.

Ferguson-Colvin, K. M., & Maccio, E. M. (2012). *Toolkit for practitioners/researchers working with lesbian, gay, bisexual, transgender, and queer/questioning (LGBTQ) runaway and homeless youth (RHY)*. National Resource Center for Permanency and Family Connections, Silberman School of Social Work. http://www.hunter.cuny.edu/socwork/nrcfcpp/info_services/download/LGBTQ%20HRY%20Toolkit%20September%202012.pdf

Hayes, S. C., & Hofmann, S. G. (2017). The third wave of cognitive behavioral therapy and the rise of process-based care. *World Psychiatry, 16*(3), 245–246. http://doi.org/10.1002/wps.20442

Hutchison, E. D. (2012). *Essentials of human behavior: Integrating person, environment, and the life course.* SAGE.

Miller, W. R., & Rollnick, S. (2013). *Motivational interviewing: Helping people change* (3rd ed.). Guilford.

Miller, W. R., & Rose, G. S. (2009). Toward a theory of motivational interviewing. *American Psychologist, 64*(6), 527–537.

Mochari-Greenberger, H., & Pande, R. L. (2021). Behavioral health in America during the COVID-19 pandemic: Meeting increased needs through access to high quality virtual care. *American Journal of Health Promotion, 35*(2), 312–317. https://doi.org/10.1177/0890117120983982d

Neukrug, E. S., & Schwitzer, A. M. (2006). *Skills and tools for today's counselors and psychotherapists: From natural helping to professional counseling.* Thomson Brooks/Cole.

NYC Department of Youth and Community Development. (2011). *Case management toolkit.* https://www.hecma.org/wp-content/uploads/2019/05/NYC_DYCD_Case_Management_Toolkit-2011.pdf

Prochaska, J. O., & DiClemente, C. C. (1984). *The transtheoretical approach: Crossing traditional boundaries of therapy.* Dow Jones-Irwin.

Wilding, C. (2015). *Cognitive behavioural therapy (CBT): Evidence-based, goal-oriented self-help techniques: A practical CBT primer.* Teach Yourself.

CHAPTER 6

Values and Ethics in Human Services Practice

Learning Objectives

After completing this chapter, you will be able to:

6.1. Define *ethics* and explain the concepts of relativism and positivism.

6.2. Name professional organizations whose codes of ethics apply to the work of human services practitioners and describe the consequences of violating these ethical codes.

6.3. List ethical issues involved in working with multicultural populations.

6.4. Explain the importance of informed consent and confidentiality in human services practice.

6.5. Describe how the strengths perspective relates to ethical decision-making and behavior.

6.6. Name and describe key principles that apply to conducting research with human subjects in an ethical manner.

The field of human services is not value neutral. Many people are drawn to the profession because they believe that we can do better as a society. Some enter the field because they believe that society's current structures limit opportunities for certain individuals, families, and communities while providing unfair advantages to others. Members of our profession seek to create services, institutions, and policies that foster human potential, especially for those who have been historically underrepresented or marginalized. How we turn these aspirations into practice is complicated because we must function within broken and discriminatory social systems and often with limited funding. Our society is pluralistic, with divergent values, and people do not always agree on how to interpret and respond to social issues. Themes throughout this textbook ask you to reflect on issues of ethical practice. The location of this chapter is an intentional bridge between direct practice, meso, and macro approaches.

As human services professionals, how do we practice ethically when we come to this field with our own experiences, beliefs, and biases? What are the specific ethics delineated by human service professions? In this chapter, we consider the significance of ethical practice, but your understanding and application of ethical practice do not end with this chapter. Ethics involve complex issues that you will reflect on and revisit throughout your personal and professional life.

6.1 DEFINING ETHICS

Simply stated, **ethics** can be defined as the moral principles that guide a person's or organization's decision-making and actions. **Values** are fundamental beliefs that guide or motivate attitudes and actions. Ethical decisions are based on an individual's moral code—what they believe to be right or good in a given situation. Ethical decisions favor virtue over vice. Examples of ethical principles that might guide an organization's thinking could be justice, equity, and doing no harm to others. Some of the values often seen in human services practice include being antiracist, ending sexism and homophobia, being active allies and accomplices against ableism, and more.

Applying ethics in practice can get complicated, however, because people may disagree over what is right and wrong, or competing values demand that we take on more than one perspective to understand a situation. In human services, it is particularly difficult because we do not always agree on what constitutes a social problem (as discussed in Chapter 3). In addition, when there is agreement that an intervention is warranted, individuals and organizations do not always agree on when or how the intervention should occur, or who should be involved.

Relativism

Relativism is a theory that highlights the context of human experience and history and suggests that perspectives of right and wrong may differ based on one's relative position in society. Race, religion, culture, and context may shift our interpretation of events and create distinct ideas about the most ethical approach to decision-making (Box 6.1).

Female genital mutilation or cutting (FGM/C) is a frequently discussed topic in regard to relativism. Deeply rooted in religious and cultural beliefs in many areas of the world, FGM/C is accepted among many cultures. Despite historical and local justifications, FGM/C has no health benefits, can cause short- and long-term health complications, and is often a traumatic experience. UNICEF notes that more than 200 million women and girls have undergone some form of FGM/C, and more than half of that number are in Egypt, Indonesia, and Ethiopia. Some argue that the Western fight against FGM/C (e.g., Krása, 2010) is a case of cultural imperialism (e.g., Oba, 2008), in which Western values and culture, which generally deems FGM/C as inappropriate, are viewed as superior to others. In fact, many advocacy efforts to eliminate FGM/C come from the West and not from the countries where the practice occurs, further complicating the relativistic view one takes on the issue.

Positivism

Are there universal truths that apply to everyone, regardless of race, religion, or culture? **Positivism** is a theory that holds that singular truths *are* attainable and objective

BOX 6.1   Eugenics

Throughout history, powerful individuals in various societies put forward social change efforts that would now be described as immoral or unethical. One of the most troubling examples in U.S. history is the eugenics movement. During the early 1900s, people became interested in "good breeding," and the American Eugenics Society was established. Early on, "better baby" competitions were held throughout the country, and activities promoted a baby's "ideal" traits, such as height, hair, or eye color. The movement later shifted to focus on eliminating traits perceived as negative. Leaders in the eugenics movement advocated for the creation of sterilization policies, resulting in programs in most states (Figure 6.1). The aim of these policies was to prohibit the reproductive abilities of individuals who were deemed inferior due to criminality, "feeble-mindedness," and "sexual deviance" (Ko, 2016). People, mostly women, were coerced or forced to undergo sterilizations, and many did not understand that the procedures were permanent. The majority of the procedures were tubal ligations. Not surprisingly, these sterilization practices were disproportionately performed on women of color by eugenicist White

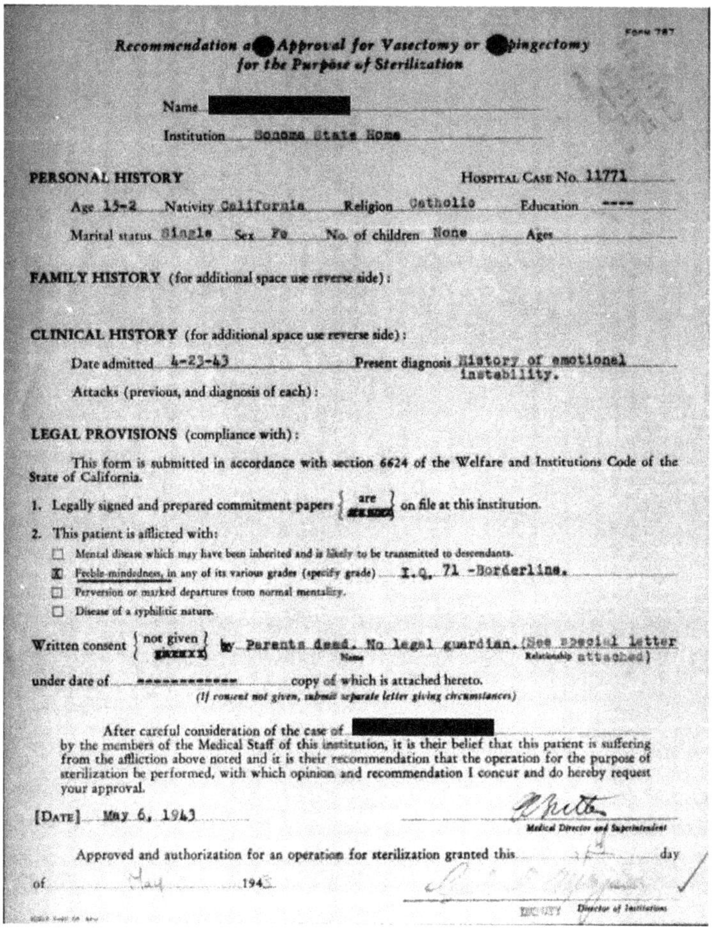

FIGURE 6.1   Sample sterilization form for a 15-year-old female in California
Source: Sterilization and Social Justice Lab, University of Michigan (CC BY-SA 4.0)

Continued

physicians who harbored dangerous and negative views toward people of color and prevailing beliefs that the "fittest" people were White. Approximately 60,000 sterilization procedures were performed according to official reports, although many believe that the actual number is much higher. Most states overturned their sterilization laws during the 1970s. Chillingly, eugenics policies and practices were widely accepted by many people in power, including academics, policymakers, and many in the medical establishment.

When Puerto Rico became a U.S. territory in 1917, leaders cited concerns about its overpopulation and economic viability as the rationale for implementing an aggressive eugenics program there. During this time, approximately one-third of Puerto Rican women in their reproductive years underwent sterilization (Krase, 2014). A door-to-door outreach approach was used in which health workers would provide women with incentives to undergo sterilization. In addition, women seeking admission to a hospital for childbirth were admitted under the condition that they would undergo sterilization after giving birth.

standards exist for making moral decisions. Positivism favors scientific processes for determining outcomes. Through methodological rigor, testing, and assessment, positivism seeks to make logical decisions about best practices. Assessing the outcomes of best practices and replicating positive findings across cultures and contexts can help build upon the theory of positivism.

6.2 PROFESSIONAL CODES OF ETHICS

Human services practice is inherently complex, as individuals who access services have complex histories, varying degrees of wellness, and live within complex systems. Human services professionals are grounded in social justice while emphasizing respect for the inherent worth and dignity of people and respecting and honoring individual self-determination. These values align with their professional code of ethics.

Many professions have established codes of ethics to guide practice, including the medical, legal, and human services fields. Professionals possess their own unique life experiences, beliefs, and biases that influence how they perceive individuals and situations. Grounding principles serve an important function to guide your own professional conduct and to provide knowledge of what to expect from colleagues. Many of these principles are articulated in professional codes of ethical conduct. Although codes of conduct are not "recipes" with specific instructions that can be applied to specific interactions, they can help guide your thinking and inform practice. Examples of these professional codes include those of the National Association of Social Workers (NASW), the National Organization for Human Services, and the American Psychological Association.

National Association of Social Workers

The NASW Code of Ethics (https://www.socialworkers.org/About/Ethics/Code-of-Ethics) is one of the most established frameworks that addresses many areas of practice and is useful to understand many of the key concepts and ethical questions named in this chapter. According to NASW, the code of ethics serves six major purposes:

- Identifies core values on which social work's mission is based
- Summarizes broad ethical principles that reflect the profession's core values and establishes a set of specific ethical standards that should be used to guide social work practice

- Helps social workers identify relevant considerations when professional obligations conflict or ethical uncertainties arise
- Provides ethical standards to which the general public can hold the social work profession accountable
- Socializes practitioners new to the field to social work's mission, values, ethical principles, and ethical standards
- Articulates standards the profession can use to assess whether social workers have engaged in unethical conduct

National Organization for Human Services

The National Organization for Human Services established a set of ethical standards (https://www.nationalhumanservices.org/ethical-standards-for-hs-professionals) that highlight the areas of responsibility for human services practitioners to engage in ethical practice. Practitioners often must balance these responsibilities amid complex and challenging circumstances. These areas include responsibility to the following:

- Clients
- Employers and colleagues
- Students
- Self
- The public and society
- The profession

Mandatory Versus Aspirational Ethics

Mandatory ethics refer to the minimum legal professional practice required, whereas **aspirational ethics** refer to the personal and professional behaviors required to engage in the best practice possible to provide services to clients and communities. Aspirational ethics afford a practitioner more leeway in interpreting practice and policy to benefit clients. For example, a client whose symptoms do not closely match a standard diagnostic case might still be deemed worthy of assessment and treatment because the professional is motivated by their duty to provide services and avoid harming the client by denying services; this would be an application of aspirational ethics. In the very same situation, a strict interpretation of diagnosable symptoms might warrant the practitioner to deny a treatment known to be overprescribed; this could be an application of mandatory ethics because the practitioner performed their job of making a diagnosis. Because the field of human services is value-laden, we might question whether the second practitioner was behaving in the client's best interest.

Another example would be a practitioner administering a job inventory with a foreign-born client, acknowledging that the instrument was not normed to an international sample. The practitioner must interpret the results with as culturally congruent a lens as possible. In this case, the professional is thinking in relativistic terms and understands that tools for assessment and case management might not always be culturally universal.

Preventive Ethics

Preventive ethics have been applied to the human services field as a way of further engaging practitioners in ethical decision-making. Beyond the foundational code of ethics, preventive ethics consider when and how ethical conflicts can be reduced or eliminated.

The objective of a preventive ethics paradigm is to consider how the practitioner can best meet their ethical obligations in serving individuals, families, and communities (National Center for Ethics in Health Care, 2014).

Imagine working with a deeply religious client seeking help for a substance use disorder. Such a client might benefit from membership in a local church, given many parishes offer educational and rehabilitation services to reduce the likelihood of relapse. Having strong partnerships with local community leaders can be both preventive and ethical to help address a client's religious identity and meet their needs for treatment.

Virtue Ethics

Another way of thinking about human services practice is through the lens of **virtue ethics**. Virtue ethics do not separate the individual self from the professional self. Adams (2009) explains that virtues are stable personal dispositions or character traits to do good. Chamiec-Case (2013) further explains:

> The virtues that form our character enable us to effectively carry out the practices that we have chosen to engage in because of what is most important to us (what we value) as defined and shaped by the tradition(s) of which we are a part. Said another way, values are crucial in that they inspire and drive us to pursue certain practices, but virtues and character traits are crucial as well because they form who we are in ways that enable us to effectively meet the goals of the practices we have chosen. As such, both values and virtues—in addition to knowledge and skills—are critical components of competency. (p. 259)

Ethical Violations

The NASW has formal procedures to adjudicate ethics complaints filed against its members. In subscribing to this code, social workers are required to cooperate in its implementation, participate in NASW adjudication proceedings, and abide by any NASW disciplinary rulings or sanctions based on it. When unethical conduct has occurred, a report can be filed with state licensing boards. In extreme cases, practitioners can lose their license.

6.3 ETHICS AND MULTICULTURAL POPULATIONS

For work with specific populations, many organizations offer guidelines from dedicated divisions, task forces, or workgroups. For example, the American Psychological Association has a number of divisions that publish research and guidelines on practice for women (Division 35), incorporating religion and spirituality (Division 36), working with couples and families (Division 43), LGBTQ+ issues (Division 44), and ethnic and racial minorities (Division 45). In Chapter 7, you will learn more specific microskills and techniques for becoming more culturally competent.

Some students read this fictional case (see Case Study 6.1 on page 89) and think, "I absolutely cannot take this client because I don't have the same worldview and their life is so different from mine." Imagine, however, how the client would feel in this situation, to take time out of their overwhelming situation to seek help. Could the attitude about not identifying with the client endanger the client's well-being? A practitioner who is not

CASE STUDY 6.1	Manuel

Manuel is 34 years old, HIV-positive, and has recently emigrated from Brazil to the United States. In Brazil, he was a doctor. While there, he witnessed a hate crime and believes that he is suffering from post-traumatic stress disorder. He is currently underemployed (working in a restaurant) because he does not have a license to practice medicine in the United States. Manuel's only form of social support is his partner, another immigrant from Brazil, with whom he shares a one-bedroom apartment in an area of town with high rates of community violence. He is seeking mental health services for being in an "overwhelming situation."

Think About . . .

1. What would be the difference in applying mandatory or aspirational ethics? Mandatory ethics would require us to provide services that all clients would receive, such as conducting an intake interview to collect information and to determine if a psychiatric evaluation is warranted, conceptualizing the case to optimize treatment, and developing a treatment plan.

2. How could it help to develop strong rapport with the client by paying attention to international news and adjusting your assessment and treatment plan to be culturally competent?

3. If you were the therapist, what other ethical guidelines could be followed to foster the therapeutic alliance between practitioner and the client and ultimately improve the client's outcome?

culturally competent or aware of their ethical responsibility would not serve this client in the best way possible. So how can trainees broaden their worldview to become more competent and feel more confident in serving everyone in their community and not just those with whom they share an obvious common background? One route is to turn to applying aspirational ethics to know when and how to make certain decisions in relationships in which sensitivity and **nonmaleficence** (avoiding causing harm) are warranted.

Appropriate supervision is essential for cases such as this. Practitioners have an opportunity to ask questions and receive feedback and advice from their supervisor about best practices for any particular case. A trainee practitioner might feel like they could understand Manuel's pain but, in order to agree to take the case and help provide Manuel some much needed support, want supervision over parts of the case in which they feel inadequate. In many agencies, practitioners do not function alone; they have access to a team of other practitioners who are available for peer supervision or professional advice. Many accrediting agencies require that practitioners engage in continuing education on an annual basis to keep up with current knowledge and the latest innovations in treatment and practice.

6.4 ETHICS IN PRACTICE

Human services professionals function as individual practitioners and also as representatives of the institutions and agencies that employ them. Developing one's own sense of ethical practice can be a lifelong endeavor that involves gaining knowledge and building skills in communication and empathy that enable effective interactions with clients in a number of practice domains, including intake, assessment, case conceptualization, treatment planning, and outreach.

Your ethical decisions will be made based partly on the country and/or state in which you are licensed to practice and also on your clinical insight and intuition for a case. Consider, for example, working with an underage client who reports self-injurious cutting behavior. Under what conditions can an underage client describe trauma, substance use, or suicidality before a practitioner needs to function as a mandated reporter to call a local family support agency or police officer? Perhaps this client tells their counselor that they are not suicidal but that they engage in self-harm to "remember what emotion feels like"; the counselor may document this in their clinical notes and reporting about the case but may judge the client to not be suicidal. Depending on the rules of the agency, state, and country in which you work, the underage client might also need to ask their caregiver or parent to provide informed consent.

The age of the client is a cultural demographic variable that requires us to know how to respond effectively and appropriately given their ability to understand what is happening in treatment and the limits of confidentiality. Consider also working with a significantly older client who demonstrates symptoms of dementia: Will they be able to understand and provide informed consent, and under what conditions should their legally designated caregiver be called in to help make this decision?

Let's consider one more client, this time a low-income individual in the United States who does not have health insurance but who wants to pursue mental health treatment. This person also cannot afford to pay out-of-pocket for treatment at the standard rate. Is it ethical to turn this person away from helpful and potentially life-changing support? Is it ethical for a practitioner to take cases pro bono (for free) or use a reduced fee or **sliding-scale fee** model for clients who demonstrate financial need? If so, what is the appropriate balance? With a sliding-scale fee, practitioners or agencies offer a reduced cost for services than the standard rate. Individual practitioners and agencies usually negotiate what these fees are so that the most destitute clients receive the least burdensome payments, whereas clients who can afford treatment or have insurance pay the standard rate. Note that in some countries in which community mental health and social work programming is fully funded by the government, these ethical questions are less aspirational because no client has to pay out-of-pocket for services.

"Gray Areas" and Changing Environments

Practitioners may encounter "gray areas" of decision-making when existing practices do not have a specific mandate on what to do in a given situation. When this occurs, they can make use of ongoing supervision, peer supervision, and continuing education opportunities to improve their ethical reasoning skills and consider new pathways for engaging in ethical and culturally competent practice. Applying a code of ethics does not mean simply following a formula in which guidelines of the profession are implemented in identical ways with all clients. Instead, it requires intentional thought and consideration of the client's safety and needs, along with understanding the client's cultural background and demographic characteristics.

The shift to telehealth for the provision of mental health services during the COVID-19 pandemic forced mental health professionals to reconsider the ethical guidelines of how to conduct therapy online. They had to make adjustments to allow for privacy during sessions when others present in the home could potentially hear the conversation. Consider for example, a client with no child care who has a 6-month-old infant with them in the room during a Zoom therapy session; a practitioner might agree with the client that given the circumstances, mental health services can still ethically be provided. Many practitioners to figure out how to accommodate clients who needed to care for children, older adults, or pets during sessions. Individuals and institutions had to collaborate and rethink recording procedures for session notes; providing supervision to trainees also seeing clients; and how to continue engaging in couples, group, and family therapy using an online format.

Dual Relationships

The relationship between a service provider and client should be held to a different standard than a potential nonprofessional relationship between the practitioner and client. Kagle and Giebelhausen (1994) describe how social workers might engage in more than one kind of relationship with their clients—for example, they might attend the same church or share a friend in common. Although there is a possibility of romantic interest between a practitioner and client, the code of ethics from NASW states that pursuing such a relationship would violate professional boundaries. In contrast, the code of ethics from the American Psychological Association allows such a relationship to be pursued ethically after a significant amount of time has passed. Practitioners should be familiar with the code of ethics from the accreditation body or professional organization related to their field. Some codes of ethics are stricter and discourage any type of extraprofessional activities with clients, whereas other codes allow for more leeway, with certain types of social interaction being permitted.

Experienced practitioners will talk with their clients about potential dual relationships. For example, they may ask their client about potentially running into each other at the grocery store. Should they stop and say hello? What if they happen to be friends with the same person? Should they negotiate activities to avoid contact, or can practitioner and client separate their sense of self in treatment versus their sense of self in a completely different social context? What about dual relationships in the online space and social media? Should clients be able to follow practitioners and vice versa? In many cases, some practitioners have a personal, private account only accessible to friends and family and a separate, public-facing account to promote their professional career and work. In some circumstances, such as working in a small town or being members of a close-knit ethnic or religious community locally or online, the likelihood of a dual relationship might be higher and would warrant a detailed discussion between practitioner and client.

Other social interactions might be deemed ethical and appropriate given the nature of the nonprofessional contact taking place. For example, when working in a prison context, social workers are trained to avoid all outside social contact with incarcerated people they meet in the prison, whereas when working in a school context, a school social worker is likely expected to engage with clients, families, and other community members in a socially appropriate manner.

Informed Consent

The process of obtaining informed consent to receive services is straightforward when the client is aged 18 years or older, not incapacitated, and can fully understand the context of receiving aid from a social worker or counselor (Ingelfinger, 1979). In this process, when a client provides their **informed consent**, they acknowledge that they can ask questions about the services they are receiving and can terminate at any time. They are consenting to the services and signing a document stating that they have been informed about the nature of the services.

Consent forms can either be signed or unsigned, such as a consent form for an online survey where the consent text introduces the participant to the study (see the discussion of research ethics below).

For minors (younger than age 18 years), from whom does the practitioner obtain informed consent? According to a paper published by the National Center for Biotechnology Information, minors in some states may provide informed consent when no parent or guardian is present (McNary, 2014); therefore, practitioners need to know the laws regarding consent in the geographic location where they are practicing. It may complicate issues if one party (a teenage client) consents but another party (the teenage client's parent) does not. A practitioner may need to clarify parental or legal guardian status before obtaining informed consent from the correct parties. McNary (2014) further advises seeking supervision and consulting with an attorney for more complicated cases.

Careful weighing of client confidentiality can be managed in many cases in which adolescent clients have the right to pursue counseling or health-related services on their own; however, in many parts of the US, a parent is required to be notified in the case of an adolescent client pursuing an abortion. White et al. (2022) found that sometimes when parent involvement has been unsupportive, counseling and administrative staff feel more of a duty to protect the rights of the client.

A client who has dementia may at times lack the cognitive ability to fully comprehend their environment, but they might still be able to provide consent. A practitioner may spend more time explaining consent or may ask a caregiver to accompany the client and sign an informed consent and confidentiality agreement. Practitioners frequently work with underserved populations (e.g., those for whom English is not their primary language) and may engage clients in thorough discussions of informed consent to build rapport and ensure that clients understand their rights and the services to be provided.

Confidentiality

Human services professionals respect the confidentiality of their clients to ensure personal privacy. Protecting **confidentiality** ensures that personal details and information about a client or their experience are not shared with others. Human services professionals should be clear with their clients about confidentiality and exceptions to confidentiality. To be sure, practitioners generally ask clients to sign a confidentiality agreement in which the client acknowledges an understanding of confidentiality and agrees to collaborate with their practitioner in the services described. This agreement to continue the collaborative relationship constitutes a type of informed consent, wherein the client also has the right to ask for information about treatment goals and theory, or even change the practitioner with whom they are working. Although protecting confidentiality is a key component to develop trust between a client and a human services professional, there are times when confidentiality must be broken. If a client discloses imminent harm to themselves or others, or if information about abuse or neglect is shared, the practitioner will need to take necessary steps to intervene and protect the health and safety of the client or those at risk of harm.

6.5 STRENGTHS PERSPECTIVE

Chapter 2 discussed many of the philosophies that guided practice throughout the history of the field, including approaches that viewed individual challenges as moral failings. During the past several decades, the field has committed to a strengths perspective, challenging the prevailing notions of problem-centered practice and offering an alternative grounded in building on the client's existing strengths and resources (Dybicz, 2011). Problem-centered practice identifies and focuses on client deficits; a strengths perspective, however, is a fundamental and ethical way of practicing that rests on the critical belief that people are greater than the sum of their "deficits." Believing in the capacity for change in people, institutions, and systems is foundational for successful and meaningful practice. Embracing a strengths perspective based on believing in the inherent "dignity and worth of the person" as articulated in the NASW code of ethics is fundamental to practice:

- Social workers treat each person in a caring and respectful fashion, mindful of individual differences and cultural and ethnic diversity.
- Social workers promote clients' socially responsible self-determination.
- Social workers seek to enhance clients' capacity and opportunity to change and to address their own needs.

Elements of Ethics in Professional Life

Banks (2009) suggests that there are more holistic ways of viewing ethical practice and encourages us to shift from "professional ethics" to "ethics in professional life." Using this approach, Banks (2009) identifies three elements of ethics in professional life:

- *Commitment*: This involves paying attention to the value commitments of practitioners, seeing them as having commitments to a range of values, including personal and political, as well as professional and societal. It entails taking account of a person's motivations for doing the work, including the role of passion and vocation in their professional life.

TRY IT YOURSELF

Spend a few minutes considering the scenarios below and complete the chart to show how you would behave in each situation and share your ideas with a partner or small group. Spend some time discussing the issues as a class.

	Never	Sometimes	Always
Accept a gift from a client/program participant (less than $20)			
Accept a gift from a client/program participant (more than $50)			
Initiate a conversation with a client/program participant when you see them out in public			
Accept a request on social media			
Invite a client/program participant to a fundraiser			
Exchange services for something other than a fee with a client/program participant			
Give a client/program participant your personal phone number			
Share a personal story with a client/program participant			

- *Character*: Considering the importance of a practitioner's moral qualities leads to a focus on the person rather than their actions or conduct. Important questions include the following: How should I live? What kind of person should I be? How can I be caring and courageous as a person and practitioner?
- *Context*: This involves acknowledging that practitioners work in particular contexts in which politics, policy, the profession, and employing agency define what is relevant. It entails a holistic approach, situating the practitioner in webs of relationships and responsibilities, taking into account the importance of moral orientation, perception, imagination, and emotion work.

6.6 KEY PRINCIPLES OF ETHICS IN HUMAN RESEARCH

Human services practitioners produce and use research in many ways. **Primary research** refers to data that are collected and analyzed directly by the person or organization, or someone they hire, to better understand people's beliefs and actions, community needs, or the impacts of programs and services on client outcomes. Practitioners also use **secondary research**, which refers to existing data that have been collected by someone else, to learn how best to address individual, family, or community needs. Research can inform best practice, how to develop and implement successful programs, and how to advocate for policies that maximize benefits and reduce harm. A practitioner might review past research on depression in older adults, for example, to develop ideas that might best work with an individual older adult client. **Empirically supported treatment** research, an example of empirically-based practice, is extremely helpful to practitioners because it consists of study data that show that there are effective treatment or intervention strategies for a specific population with a specific condition.

Most human services research involves collecting data from people. This information can be collected directly through in-person interviews or surveys or using telephone or online methods. Human subject research has a long and difficult history, and the rights of individual participants have not always been the priority. In some cases, human subjects have been harmed by their participation in research.

Unethical Research

One of the most infamous cases of unethical research is the Tuskegee Syphilis Study (1932–1972). This study sought to examine the effects of untreated syphilis in 400 poor African American men. Research subjects were recruited and followed over time to better understand the course of syphilis. Although the goals of the study may have been to better understand the impacts of syphilis and develop medical interventions to treat the disease, the way in which the study was developed and conducted placed the burdens and risks of the research on one vulnerable community. Treatment was withheld from study participants, even after penicillin was known to cure the disease. In fact, it took decades after the discovery of penicillin for the study to end (1972) and more than two decades later for an official national apology to be issued to the men and their families (White House Office of the Press Secretary, 1997).

National Research Act

In response to the unethical practices of the Tuskegee study, several changes were made in the research process and the recruitment and treatment of human subjects. In 1974, the National Research Act created the National Commission for the Protection of Human Subjects of Biomedical and Behavioral Research and established standards for ethical research practice with human subjects (Corbie-Smith, 1999). Specifically, the act required researchers to obtain voluntary informed consent from all study participants. Informed consent in research means that a person agrees to participate in the study, and they are also made aware of all the possible known benefits and risks associated with participation. Institutional review boards (IRBs) were developed to review research protocols and ensure the protection of vulnerable populations. The IRBs' primary service is to ensure that researchers are meeting their ethical obligations—for example, maximizing social benefits and minimizing harm to participants in research.

The *Belmont Report*, written by the National Commission, summarizes the ethical principles upheld in the National Research Act (https://www.hhs.gov/ohrp/regulations-and-policy/belmont-report/index.html). The report highlighted three basic ethical principles and three applications of those principles (Table 6.1).

Respect for Persons

This principle requires that each person should be valued and treated fairly and that vulnerable populations are entitled to protections. For example, children, pregnant individuals, racial and ethnic minorities, and persons with disabilities are among the protected populations.

Informed consent in research mandates that researchers provide all necessary information to allow a research subject to understand the balance of risks and benefits before making a decision about participation (Table 6.2). Informed consent assumes that the research subject has received ample and appropriate information about the goals and objectives of the research and any known risks and benefits associated with participation. Each research subject should enter into a research study voluntarily and without coercion. Coercion may come from those in a position of power or authority or may be associated with excessive monetary rewards or other favors for participation. For example, IRB protections are extended to prisoners who may feel coerced to participate in research if they think they will receive benefits or favors for participation or have benefits retracted for a lack of participation.

Beneficence

Beneficence seeks to reduce potential harm associated with research and maximize possible benefits. Beneficence builds upon the Hippocratic oath to "do no harm" by considering what are appropriate risks that may be necessary to foster benefits.

TABLE 6.1 Ethical Principles of the National Research Act

Ethical Principle	Application
Respect for persons	Informed consent
Beneficence	Assessment of risks and benefits
Justice	Selection of human subjects

TABLE 6.2   Basic Elements of Informed Consent with Human Subjects

Who?	Name of researchers, study name, funding source of sponsor
What?	What is the study about? This should include a statement of voluntary participation and the right to terminate participation. No one should be forced or coerced to participate.
	Statement about what the participant will do in the study: This should include the time commitment, location of the study, and number of meetings or sessions. The basic procedures of the study should be included.
Why?	Why is the participant being asked to participate in the study? Does it have to do with their age, gender, health status, experience, etc.?
Risks	What are the known or anticipated risks of participation? What is the likelihood of these risks occurring in the study?
Benefits	What are the anticipated benefits? There may not be a direct benefit to the participant. Incentives to participate, including financial payments, are not considered a direct benefit.
Access to information or data	Who will have access to the data or personal information associated with the data? How is personal information shared and protected? Issues of confidentiality and anonymity should be clear.
Incentives	Will there be payment for study participants or reimbursements for travel? The incentives should be reasonable to pay for the time of the participant but not excessive.
Researcher contact	Clearly identify the researcher's contact information or other professional who can answer questions and address complaints.
Consent	Placement of names and signatures of the research staff and participant to show written consent. Alternatives to signed consent may include verbal consent or waived consent.

This ethical principle does not rule out all risk but balances the possibility for some risk with the opportunity to provide benefits.

An assessment of risks and benefits provides the researcher an opportunity to consider the design and scope of the study and if the research meets the requirements to proceed. This assessment also provides the IRB review committee an opportunity to determine if the research is warranted and should be available for human subject recruitment. These processes consider if any risks may occur, the likelihood of risk, and the magnitude of the risk.

Justice

Justice considers who takes on the burden of the risks and benefits associated with the research process. In the case of the Tuskegee study, only poor African American men were selected as research subjects, even though syphilis was not limited to this population. In this case, only one group of people bore the burdens of risk. The ethical principle of justice considers who benefits and who is put at risk by the research.

The selection of human subjects focuses on individual and social justice. At the individual level, research that provides benefits or risks should be distributed fairly within and between populations, with special attention for vulnerable populations. Social justice considers not only the individual but also the role of benefiting or burdening social classes or groups with opportunities or lack of opportunities to participate in research.

Research and the Community

Ethical research is more than the development and implementation of ethical research protocols. Ethical research must also focus on the needs and best interests of communities. Researchers should be working with and for the communities they study, engaging in communication and collaboration. Culturally competent research should highlight the researchers' awareness of and sensitivity to the community they study. This awareness can and should inform the research questions and processes.

Researchers in all human services fields should consider if and how their work addresses community needs and involves the stakeholders within communities. "Parachute research" should be avoided. This is research conducted by individuals from outside of a community who "parachute in," research a phenomenon, and then leave as soon as the data have been collected. Members of communities that are the subject of this type of research may be marginalized in the process of the research and its analysis and conclusions.

In the late 1990s, Children Requiring a Caring Kommunity (CRACK) emerged as an organization in the United States seeking to reduce the number of babies born to mothers who used drugs while pregnant. The founder had personal experience as an adoptive mother of children who were born with signs of withdrawal. Now named Project Prevention, based in Harrisburg, North Carolina, the organization is best known for its controversial practice of incentivizing long-term birth control or sterilization for individuals living with substance use disorders. Program participants received $300 if they agreed to receive an intrauterine device, contraceptive implant or injection, or sterilization (tubal ligation or vasectomy). The organizational premise was based on the idea of preventing future costs to systems such as health care, criminal justice, and child welfare by preventing pregnancies among individuals living with substance abuse challenges. This program highlights many concerns around ethical practice. What are some of the ethical concerns?

SPOTLIGHT ON SERVICE-LEARNING

In your organization, what are some of the values or ethical principles you can observe? Are there frameworks that appear to guide the practice of the staff? Here are some questions to consider:

1. How can you apply a strengths perspective to the work that is being done within your service-learning?
2. Does your organization have a policy about social media and consent?
3. Can you identify two or more of the ethical principles discussed in this chapter and apply them to experiences or observations in your service-learning?

SUMMARY

- Ethics are the moral principles that guide a person's or an organization's decision-making and actions. Ethics are informed by values and the beliefs that guide or motivate attitudes and actions. Ethics are impacted by people's history, experiences, and perspectives. Ethical standards, however, rely on shared objective standards for making moral decisions.

- According to relativism, perspectives of right and wrong may differ based on one's relative position in society. In contrast, positivism is a theory which holds that singular truths *are* attainable and objective standards exist for making moral decisions.
- Most professional organizations, including social work and human services organizations, have developed a set of standards, or code of ethics. When violations of ethical standards are suspected, a complaint can be filed with a state licensing board. Formal procedures consider the complaint and findings of unethical practice may lead to a loss of professional licensure and/or termination.
- When working with multicultural populations, human service professionals should support the client to ensure that all relevant services and supports are received. Human services professionals should apply aspirational ethics, engaging in the best practice possible, to support every client. Supervision and ongoing professional development around culturally sensitive practice are two methods to foster career-long ethical practice.
- Informed consent is the process of getting permission from a client or research participant to participate in services or research. The process involves the individual knowing and understanding all the possible benefits and harms of the service or study. Informed consent requires the human services professional to clearly explain key issues and the client or participant to understand and agree to the terms and conditions.
- Confidentiality in the professional relationship between the client and the practitioner fosters trust. Confidentiality ensures that information between the client and the practitioner remains private and is not shared with others outside of the relationship. The exception to confidentiality is if a client shares information about harm to themself or others. In this case, a human services professional may need to disrupt confidentiality to ensure the safety or well-being of the person at risk.
- A strengths perspective provides a powerful lens to view clients as capable of change and reform. Believing in the capacity to change suggests that the focus of a client relationship is to support the positive growth and development of each person and believe in the inherent dignity and worth of all people.
- Key principles of ethics in research were developed in the *Belmont Report*, focusing on the respect for persons to be treated fairly, a clear assessment of the risks and benefits of research, and equity and justice with regard to who is selected to participate in research and how research subjects benefit from research findings.

REVIEW QUESTIONS

Assessment Questions

1. What is the difference between values and ethics?
2. Define relativism and positivism. How do they apply to the field of human services?
3. Compare and contrast a deficit perspective and strengths perspective. How might a human services professional use a strengths model?
4. What is informed consent and why is it needed?

Reflection Questions

1. What ethics and values do you live by? How might this affect your actions as a human services professional?
2. Are there areas of practice that would challenge your ethical perspectives?
3. Brainstorm something you might be interested in researching about your community. How can you ensure your research would be ethical and respectful and also benefit the community?
4. What is your opinion of the approach that Project Prevention developed? Consider issues related to informed consent, the worth and dignity of each person, strength perspectives, and nonmaleficence.

REFERENCES

Adams, P. (2009). Ethics with character: Virtues and the ethical social worker. *Journal of Sociology & Social Welfare, 36*(3), Article 5.

Banks, S. (2009). Ethics that work? A critical review of ethics and values in teaching and practice—Papers from the *Ethics & Social Welfare* Conference, London, 10 November 2008: Editorial Introduction. *Ethics & Social Welfare, 3*(1), 54–76.

Chamiec-Case, R. (2013). The contribution of virtue ethics to a richer understanding of social work competencies. *Social Work and Christianity, 40*(3), 251–270.

Corbie-Smith, G. (1999). The continuing legacy of the Tuskegee Syphilis Study: considerations for clinical investigation. *The American Journal of the Medical Sciences, 317*(1), 5–8.

Dybicz, P. (2011). Interpreting the strengths perspective through narrative theory. *Families in Society, 92*(3), 247–253.

Ingelfinger, F. J. (1979). Informed (but uneducated) consent. In J. M. Humber & R. F. Almeder (Eds.), *Biomedical ethics and the law* (pp. 265–267). Springer.

Kagle, J. D., & Giebelhausen, P. N. (1994). Dual relationships and professional boundaries, *Social Work, 39*(2), 213–220.

Ko, L. (2016, Jan 29). Unwanted sterilization and eugenics programs in the United States. *PBS Independent Lens.* https://www.pbs.org/independentlens/blog/unwanted-sterilization-and-eugenics-programs-in-the-united-states/

Krása, K. (2010). Human rights for women: The ethical and legal discussion about female genital mutilation in Germany in comparison with other Western European countries. *Medicine, Health Care and Philosophy, 13*(3), 269–278.

Krase, K. (2014, October 1). *The history of forced sterilization in the United States.* https://www.ourbodiesourselves.org/book-excerpts/health-article/forced-sterilization

McNary, A. (2014). Consent to treatment of minors. *Innovations in Clinical Neuroscience, 11*(3-4), 43–45.

National Center for Ethics in Health Care (2014). Preventive Ethics: Addressing Ethics Quality Gaps on a Systems Level. 2nd ed. Washington, DC: U.S. Department of Veterans Affairs.

Oba, A. A. (2008). Female circumcision as female genital mutilation: Human rights or cultural imperialism? *Global Jurist, 8*(3).

White, K., Narasimhan, S., Hartwig, S. A., Carroll, E., McBrayer, A., Hubbard, S., Rebouché, R., Kottke, M., & Stidham Hall, K. (2022). Parental involvement policies for minors seeking abortion in the Southeast and quality of care. *Sexuality Research and Social Policy, 19,* 264–272. https://doi.org/10.1007/s13178-021-00539-0

White House Office of the Press Secretary, Remarks by the President in apology for study done in Tuskegee (1997, May) Retrieved from http://clinton4.nara.gov/New/Remarks/Fri/19970516-898.html

CHAPTER 7

Diversity and Multiculturalism in Human Services Practice

Learning Objectives

After completing this chapter, you will be able to:

7.1. Define *culture* and explain how it is relevant to providing services to a client.

7.2. Describe two models of cultural identity and explain the importance of intersectionality.

7.3. Provide a brief historical background on cultural competence in the helping profession.

7.4. Name four categories of microskills for cultural competence and describe what each entails.

7.5. Explain how culturally informed assessment and service planning contributes to improved client outcomes.

Imagine being a counselor meeting a client for the first time. The client is wearing clothing rarely seen in your community, speaks with an unfamiliar accent, and describes experiences from an immigrant perspective that you only know about from news reports. How can you be an effective listener and understand their situation? How could you empathize with their experience of engaging in an unfamiliar community? How would you serve as a competent advocate for this client? How would you assist the client in developing capacities or accessing local resources? This scenario is likely to be a common experience for human services practitioners as they seek to be culturally competent service providers. As ethical practitioners, it is critical that we effectively serve *all* our clients. However, there can be challenges in being able to fully understand and advocate for the needs of clients with cultural backgrounds and perspectives that are unfamiliar to us. In our role as client advocate, it is incumbent upon us to develop the tools and skills necessary to effectively serve all our clients.

This chapter explores theories for understanding cultural diversity and identity, along with themes and skills needed to engage across difference. We examine different types of cultural identities and discuss contemporary approaches to effective communication and attitudes for working effectively in a multicultural society.

7.1 CULTURE AND MODELS OF IDENTITY

The concept of **culture** has widely been understood by social scientists to have a few different meanings. The term culture can refer to the set of customs, traditions, lore, behaviors, and beliefs that are typically passed down from one generation to another (Heine, 2020). For example, Ethiopian culture might include the practice of making and eating the spongy flatbread called injera; knowledge of Orthodox Christian norms, which are quite prevalent within the Ethiopian community; and understanding the traditional forms of telling time, which use sunrise as a standard and a 13-month calendar. The term culture can also be used to refer to people from a particular geographic region or regions where certain customs and traditions are shared. For example, Spanish-speaking culture could refer to any of the Spanish-speaking populations in the Americas and Spain. Polish culture can describe ethnic Polish people living in Poland as well as Polish individuals who left their country of origin and now live in other countries. Techie culture is a term that refers to people employed in information technology careers and individuals who are highly engaged in the use of new and developing technologies.

Culture can also refer to information about a particular group. In this sense, Spanish-speaking culture might refer to the grammatical norms of conjugating verbs and knowing which cultures use *vosotros* and which prefer *ustedes*, both of which mean "you" in the plural sense, or to the slang particular to subcultures within the main group. For example, *janguear*, which means "to hang out," is popular among some Boricua (people of Puerto Rican descent) and other Spanish-speaking populations in the New York City area, but not among all Spanish speakers.

Cultural Identity

Culture is often used as a lens through which one can outline patterns of similarities and differences in the identities we as human services providers share with our clients. Reflecting on these patterns helps illuminate the kinds of attitudes, knowledge, skills, and actions that practitioners can take on to be able to work effectively with people from different populations (Sue et al., 1992). Understanding how identity matters in the helping relationship can clarify potential power dynamics and expectations with our clients, inform our assessment and treatment strategies, and optimize our role within the human services profession.

Many training exercises encourage students to engage in active self-reflection of cultural identity to be more attuned to their own experiences and how they may be similar or dissimilar to those of their clients.

Cultural identity refers to the level of affiliation, membership, and/or identification with being part of a particular cultural group (Tajfel & Turner, 1979). You might identify very strongly with being a psychology, social work, or human services major because you are passionate about training for a career that will make a difference in the world.

TRY IT YOURSELF

Take a moment to reflect on how your income level has led you to where you are now, how you came to be in this class at this school reading this textbook. How has your access to financial resources affected your ability to gain an education? To what extent must you rely on family or loans to stay in school? Now imagine you are a human services professional working with a client who did not have the same access to higher education. Their daily experiences, especially those related to finances and economic status, may be completely different from yours. How can you relate to this client to create an effective partnership?

For many people, having a cultural identity based on being a member of a minority group is very salient, meaning that this part of their identity is significant and noteworthy to their sense of self (Tatum, 2017). The term **minority** denotes a cultural group that is subordinate, less privileged, underresourced, and sometimes fewer in number than those in the majority (Kirk & Okazawa-Rey, 2018). Being from a minority culture contrasts with membership in one or more dominant or majority cultural identities. A dominant cultural identity in the context where you live and work could be racial, such as White, and thus in that context, a subordinate racial or cultural identity could be Black, Asian/Pacific Islander, Latinx or Latine, or Indigenous, based on the demographics and resources available in that context. Minority and majority cultural identities define more than just race and ethnicity; they can define linguistic, religious, gender, sexual orientation, and socioeconomic groupings, along with others. Imagine a predominantly White institution, in which the majority of university counseling center staff are White. How might a student of color seeking mental health treatment feel about navigating the system to receive the services they need?

Awareness of clients' cultural identities and empathizing with their situation allows us to better understand their needs and behavior and how confident and comfortable they will be in the helping relationship. Imagine a multilingual Haitian immigrant seeking help at an agency that has no Haitian, darker skinned, or Haitian Creole-speaking staff. Being Haitian, Black, or Creole-speaking may be very salient parts of this client's identity and may impact what information the client chooses to disclose, how comfortable the client feels, and what cues the client is looking for from service providers. An effective practitioner knows how to create an interpersonal dynamic that fosters empathy and the client's ability to share and trust that what they share will be understood and validated.

People vary tremendously with regard to how much they think about any one facet of their identity and how relevant that part of their identity might be to their symptoms and way that they communicate. Many people find a part of their cultural identity to be very salient and quite relevant to who they are, how they are seen and socialized, and what they think about, whereas others do not (Mitchell & Boyle, 2015). The time period in which a person may be thinking about their cultural identity can also have an influence on how they behave when seeking services. Many people in the United States may not think about their U.S. or "American" identity very often; however, research shows that in a particular historical context—for example, in the years following the September 11, 2001, terrorist attacks—many people in the United States more strongly identify with the country or being "American" as a major part of their identity, compared to during other time periods (Schildkraut, 2002).

7.2 MODELS OF IDENTITY AND INTERSECTIONALITY

Several models from the field of counseling psychology serve to outline specific dimensions or facets of cultural identity to acknowledge how every individual possesses different cultural norms and traditions as part of their sense of self. In general, inclusive models that help us understand ourselves and the cultural backgrounds of our clients cover categories such as race and ethnicity, nationality and citizenship, phenotype/appearance, linguistic capabilities, socioeconomic status and education level, sex and gender, sexual orientation, religious/spiritual identity, ability status (including physical or mental health-related disabilities), age, and professional identity.

RESPECTFUL Model

An established model used to capture different facets of our cultural identities is the RESPECTFUL model, developed by D'Andrea and Daniels (2001). This model encompasses 10 dimensions:

> Religion/spirituality
> Economic/social class background
> Sexual identity
> Personal style and education
> Ethnic/racial identity
> Chronological/life span status and challenges
> Trauma/crisis
> Family background and history
> Unique physical characteristics (including pertinent skills or disabilities)
> Location of residence and language spoken

In practice, we would also add gender identity to this model such that when thinking about "S," a practitioner would seek to understand a person's sexual orientation and gender, which are two distinct aspects of a person's identity.

ADDRESSING Model

A valuable alternative model in the field that describes various aspects of cultural identity is Pamela Hays's (2008) ADDRESSING framework:

> Age
> Developmental and acquired disabilities
> Religion
> Ethnicity
> Socioeconomic status
> Sexual orientation
> Indigenous heritage
> National origin
> Gender

Intersectionality

It is important to understand the extent to which each individual category of cultural identity has an impact on our own life and our clients' lives and also the extent to which the intersectional categories of certain identities can play a role. Legal scholar Kimberlé Crenshaw's (1990) landmark work on the concept of **intersectionality** has increasingly been studied by social scientists and practitioners so as to fully grasp the impact of inhabiting specific identities that are often associated with experiences of privilege, discrimination, and oppression (Figure 7.1). Crenshaw found that businesses that hired women or Black employees only hired White women for some administrative positions and Black men for physical labor-related positions. As a result, the "double-bind" of being a Black woman seeking employment at this type of business led to workplace discrimination at the point of applying for a job. Tools such as the RESPECTFUL model may help us understand and outline *individual* parts of a client's identity, but thinking *intersectionally* helps us understand more of the client's actual experience and lived worldview, particularly if the client incurs a unique experience of occupying more than one cultural identity that could be oppressed.

Recall the immigrant Haitian client previously discussed. If we applied our knowledge about immigrant culture, Haitian culture, or understanding of femininity and womanhood as independent bodies of information, we would very likely overlook the unique interplay of the experience of inhabiting multiple dominant and subordinate culture identities. Understanding variations in cultural identities can help us develop the set of skills necessary for working effectively with people from different cultural backgrounds and traditions.

FIGURE 7.1 Kimberlé Crenshaw *Source*: lev radin/Shutterstock

TRY IT YOURSELF

Using the grid shown in Table 7.1, consider what your identities are and note if they are part of a dominant or subordinate/minority culture where you live and work. Answer the reflection questions that follow.

Why is it important to be self-aware of your identity and if it is dominant or subordinate? What experiences have you had that have been affected by a dominant identity you hold? What about subordinate identity? How might a dominant identity of yours affect a client whose identity is subordinate? What kind of power dynamic could this create? What could happen if a client from multiple subordinate identities works with a counselor from multiple dominant identities? What can they do to make the client feel as comfortable and safe as possible?

Adapted from Ivey et al., (2016).

TABLE 7.1   Understanding Your Own Identity and Status in Society

10 Dimensions	Identity	Dominant/Subordinate
Religion/spirituality		
Economic background		
Sexual identity and gender identity		
Personal style and education		
Ethnic/racial identity		
Chronological/life span status and challenges		
Trauma/crisis		
Family background and history		
Unique physical characteristics		
Location of residence, language ability		

7.3 THE HISTORY OF CULTURAL COMPETENCE IN THE HELPING PROFESSIONS

In the United States, desegregation of the public school system officially occurred in 1954 with a Supreme Court decision, but it took decades for this process to actually be enforced. During this time, clinical practice and research began to blossom with increasing numbers of scholars, theorists, and practitioners being female, of color, and from international backgrounds.

The prevailing belief among many practitioners up to this point had been that human services' capabilities were "one size fits all," meaning that services should be provided to all clients in the exact same manner, without concern for clients' cultural identities or worldviews. This represented a culturally "colorblind" approach. Scholars of color began to challenge this notion, arguing that assessment and treatment or services would not always be effective if a critical aspect of a person's identity was ignored in the client–practitioner relationship. Ignoring the unique histories and characteristics of clients in favor of a colorblind or culture-neutral approach is more limiting in practice in part because it disregards the harmful past where distrust of health and human services programming among many minority groups (Suite, La Bril, Primm, & Harrison-Ross, 2007) was created due to harmful and unethical policies often permitted without clients' consent Instead, a more culturally responsive and inclusive professional style is warranted.

The majority of research published to date examining the incorporation of cultural skills and knowledge has focused on including race and ethnicity into the analysis of effective relationship building, communication, case conceptualization, and provision of services. Psychologists Janet Helms (1993) and Jean Phinney (1990) are credited with understanding the differences in ethnic and racial identity development such that practitioners should understand that any individual could have a strong or weak affiliation with either part of their identity, rather than assume that if a client has a strong ethnic identity, then their race is also salient to them (Ponterotto & Park-Taylor, 2007). For example, a client who is ethnically Korean and a newly arrived first-generation immigrant might feel much more tied to her Korean identity than to an Asian or Asian American identity. Effective practitioners know how to ask about immigration and acculturation in a way that helps the client feel understood.

Psychologists Derald Wing Sue, Patricia Arredondo, and Roderick J. McDavis (1992) summarized a trajectory of how a person can learn to become a more culturally competent service provider (Sue & Sue, 1990):

1. Becoming more aware of their assumptions about human behaviors, values, and biases
2. Understanding the worldviews of clients without judgment
3. Engaging in a process to further develop sensitivities, knowledge, and skills to be able to work effectively with different populations

Note that cultural competence is not an end goal. A person does not simply participate in some seminars, get experience with different clients, read book chapters like this, and then—voila!—suddenly become a culturally competent service provider. Cultural competence requires constant vigilance, education, supervision, and self-awareness to continue to learn more about different cultures and identities, keep current with emerging treatment studies and behavior management plans, and learn about local resources and stay connected to professional networks that can help develop further competencies.

Just as one's own sense of personal and professional ethics can shift, evolve, and change over time (see Chapter 6), cultural competence is a set of skills and awarenesses that are part of an ongoing process of change and growth. In fact, licensed practitioners are usually required to earn continuing education units on a regular basis to retain their licensure. This allows practitioners to gain exposure to new knowledge and practices. Many practitioners do not use the phrase "cultural competence" to refer to this skill set because the term *competence* might imply finality or sufficiency, with no need to continue training or developing. Instead, some practitioners prefer the terms cultural sensitivity, cultural awareness, or cultural agility to imply a variable skill set and awareness that can continue to develop over one's career.

We cannot just assume that because we share a set of cultural identities with our clients, we are automatically going to be culturally competent—no one culture is monolithically the same. For example, a licensed therapist might be fluent in Spanish, but if the Spanish-speaking client explains symptoms from a **culture-bound syndrome** or disorder whose presentation, explanation, or characteristics are more endemic to a particular cultural group or geographic area using a different Spanish dialect than that of the therapist, the practitioner might need to study these concepts to allow for true understanding of the client's experience. We can also not assume that because a client is from a particular cultural background, the specific demographics that are part of who they are present a major lens for that client's symptoms or situation. For example, not every trans client seeking help is looking for trans-supportive resources. Not every client of color seeking treatment will describe racism or their racial identity as being a major factor related to their symptoms.

To become a more culturally competent practitioner, it is important to have a flexible mindset, a cohort of like-minded colleagues who are also learning to develop their sensitivities and skills, and to take advantage of culturally relevant supervision and training opportunities. In addition, once established in a position, the practitioner can advocate for more cultural diversity in terms of organization staff, translations of materials, and outreach to the local community.

Professional Development Opportunities

Currently, many human services practitioners continue to gain exposure to new theories and practices regarding culturally competent service provision by becoming members of professional organizations focusing on a particular population or cultural identity, such as the National Association of Social Workers' National Committee on Women's Issues; the National Association of Social Workers' National Committee on Lesbian, Gay, Bisexual, and Transgender Issues; the Association of Black Psychologists; the National Latinx Psychological Association; the Asian American Psychological Association; and the Society of Indian Psychologists. These organizations offer networking meetings, continuing education credits, and a professional home for like-minded people seeking to learn about and advocate for particular populations. Professional development gives practitioners an opportunity to create more equity and access to quality services in the health care and human services system (McDaniel, Woods, Pratt, & Simms, 2017).

Practitioners also engage in peer supervision and often have their own supervisors in which issues of cultural competence and awareness can be discussed. Many organizations also provide research time built into the workday schedule so that practitioners can increase their awareness of cultural norms and beliefs around mental health and well-being.

7.4 ESSENTIAL MICROSKILLS FOR CULTURAL COMPETENCE

Microskills are defined as specific competencies required to communicate effectively with others. Effective and empathetic communication involves a wide range of interpersonal skills. In this section, we discuss some key microskills that are important to develop in becoming a more culturally competent practitioner. These skills are grouped into four categories:

- Attending to verbal and nonverbal behavior
- Avoiding discriminatory thoughts and behavior
- Validating cultural identities and experiences
- Developing greater self-awareness and humility

Attending to Verbal and Nonverbal Behavior

Paying attention to the spoken word and verbal cues given by clients allows us to under-stand both what a person is talking about and their emotional status. Many people also rely on nonverbal cues, such as rate of breathing, sighing, eye contact or aversion, facial expressions, and gestures, as part of how they communicate. Nonverbal cues may also have culturally implicit meanings that can be valuable to understanding the client's situation and needs. For example, many clients from Asian, Latin, and Arabic cultures rely on **soma-tization**, expressing psychological distress through physical symptoms (Heine, 2020). A person might describe somatic complaints such as headaches, trouble sleeping, difficulty concentrating, or say something such as "my heart beats so fast when I think about it" to illustrate a problem or situation (Koss, 1990; Maffini & Wong, 2014). Clients from European cultures tend to prefer **psychologization**, using psychological terminology to describe their feelings or behavior, such as "everything about that situation causes me anxiety" (Heine, 2020).

Moreover, we cannot assume that the meaning of a word or symbol is the same to every culture. For example, imagine an Indigenous Choctaw client complaining of dis-turbing visions of seeing herself more like a "turkey" instead of a "terrapin." It would help to review the symbolic meaning of these ideas in Choctaw culture by doing your own research—for example, reading a children's book centered on a Choctaw folk tale (e.g., Tingle, 2006)—and demonstrating cultural curiosity as to your client's experience. Cul-turally competent practitioners will not dismiss clients who prefer one way of verbally communicating about their symptoms, and they should stay open to idioms of distress. Your Choctaw client might be conveying how she acts too quickly ("turkey") rather than take things slowly to consider her behavior ("terrapin"), without mentioning all of the cultural meaning behind the terms. Asking questions to draw out more cultural defini-tions and context (i.e., "What significance does the turkey or terrapin have to you, and how do you think they reflect on your behavior?") can facilitate the therapeutic relation-ship and shared understanding of the vocabulary.

It is helpful to understand the client's communication style, in terms of it being high-context or low-context (Heine, 2020). **High-context communication** relies less on specific spoken words and more on tone, implicit meaning, and the relationship between speaker and listener. **Low-context communication** tends to rely much more on explicit words and their meanings.

Many languages, such as Chinese, do not have specific tenses to indicate past, pres-ent, or future, or plurals to indicate the quantity of an object. Spoken aloud, the gender of the subject of a sentence might not be explicitly stated. To best understand a client who uses implicit communication, it helps to think of the relationship you have with them and concentrate on the cues that help indicate the temporal or spatial manner in which the person speaks. In some cases, you might already understand what a client is describ-ing by observing nonverbal cues such as an eyebrow raise, downward gaze, or a shift in posture. It is often helpful to check in with the client to validate their expression with a confirming question or statement. Keep in mind that the vocabulary used by the client is influenced by the person's cultural, economic, and educational background.

Several communication practices can be helpful in establishing connections with clients, especially those with backgrounds that are very different from that of the practi-tioner. **Validation** is when a listener affirms, supports, and understands a client's perspective and identity. Validation uses supportive, empathic vocabulary to address difficult experiences (e.g., discrimination and trauma), and it helps the client understand that the practitioner sees them for who they are and respects their willingness to open up. Validation acknowledges pain and trauma in a way that is uplifting, empathic, and encouraging. If a client of color talks about a painful experience of racism, an effective counselor might say "I can understand, from your experiences, that those types of encounters happen all too often, and are quite a burden. I would feel drained too if I were in your situation." Validation can help form bonds when a practitioner and client come from different cultural identities. Effective counselors understand the limits of validation, however, in that they generally would not validate clients' harmful thoughts, emotions, or behaviors.

Empathetic feedback reflects back what the client has said by paraphrasing and showing understanding of a client's lived experience (Ivey et al., 2016). For example, an empathetic response to a client's account of sexual assault might be, "What happened to you is terrible, yet I am glad you feel comfortable opening up about it and that you are taking steps to heal. I'm here to help you find the services you need." Another example would be a White practitioner working with a Black client who reports painful experiences of discrimination. An empathic response could be, "Your anger is very justified in that situation. I would feel that too if I were in your shoes." Such a statement is validating and focuses on conveying emotional connection and understanding. A nonempathic response could be a microaggression and disservice, such as a White practitioner saying, "I cannot relate to the experience you are sharing because we are different racially" and then declining to empathize with or understand the pain that client feels:

Empathic confrontation is designed to shed light on a potential mismatch in client motivation and behavior in a way that is constructive to the client by highlighting and naming the concrete ideas (Ivey et al., 2016). Not all confrontation is a negative experience; it is often critical to help a client gain insight on their problem by understanding the obstacles in their way. For example, let's say you are working with a mother receiving drug rehabilitation services who has been relapsing lately but knows she must stay off drugs to re-earn custody of her children. Pointing out the discrepancy in the behavior can lead to an "aha" moment that their behavior is moving in the opposite direction of their goals: "On the one hand, I see that you are motivated to be a good parent and take care of your children by staying off drugs, but on the other hand, I see a difficult struggle in the temptation of using when you feel the need." Notice this summary is not judgmental but instead is meant to help the client clarify the decisions and behaviors they can commit to in order to accomplish real change.

Empathic self-disclosure is when a professional uses information, feelings, or ideas from their own life or cultural background to convey empathy and understanding. For example, an Asian therapist might tell his Latinx client, "I can really understand how excluded you felt in that moment, because I've been there too, some people in my family behave the same way." It is often enough to point out similarity in cultural identity and experience to help build rapport. Be aware, however, that some clients from Asian backgrounds prefer fewer personal stories from a practitioner to preserve their perception of them as an expert and professional (e.g., Kim et al., 2003).

Avoiding Discriminatory Attitudes and Behavior

Some clients feel uncomfortable, on guard, or concerned that their service provider will not fully understand their worldview. Clients from underrepresented groups are often concerned about the level of reliability and accuracy of their practitioner's practice. At times, practitioners themselves are overly concerned about appearing incompetent or unable to fully understand their clients (Cummings & O'Donohue, 2018). Unfortunately, it is relatively common for clients to experience invalidating interactions with human services professionals. Table 7.2 lists some types of discrimination and their potential impact on the client–practitioner relationship.

Microaggressions are unintentional yet demeaning slights, behaviors, and comments that undermine, undervalue, and depreciate the identities and experiences of members of marginalized groups (Sue, 2018). For example, a practitioner working with an older client may assume that the client is cognitively unable to understand the concept of confidentiality, but how would the practitioner know that? Could she be making an assumption that contributes to a dismissive and demeaning atmosphere? In fact, the practitioner is likely committing a microaggression. Holding discriminatory, ageist beliefs can create an uncomfortable power dynamic between a younger service provider and an older client whereby the client's actual identity and functional capabilities are dismissed, overlooked, and discounted.

Practitioners often enroll in training experiences designed to understand their own discriminatory attitudes and potential microaggressions and learn how to identify them

TABLE 7.2   Discriminatory Attitudes and Behavior and Effects on the Client–Practitioner Relationship

Type of Discrimination	Definition	Potential Effect on the Client–Practitioner Relationship
Age	Unfair treatment due to an individual's age	Practitioner may make incorrect assumptions about an individual's skills, interests, or capabilities
Disability	Unfair treatment due to an individual's disability or physical/mental impairment	Practitioner may treat an individual as limited or "less than"
Sexual orientation	Unfair treatment due to an individual's gender identity or sexual orientation	Practitioner may make assumptions about an individual's behavior or make comments implying that there is a problem with the individual's gender identity or sexual orientation
Status as a spouse/parent	Unfair treatment due to an individual's marital or parental status	Practitioner may make negative comments about an individual's status as married, separated, divorced, or as a parent or make assumptions about the individual's behavior related to these roles
Religion or spiritual beliefs/practices	Unfair treatment due to an individual's religious affiliation or religious/spiritual practices/beliefs	Practitioner may make comments that invalidate or disrespect an individual's religion or beliefs/practices
National origin	Unfair treatment due to an individual's birthplace, ancestry, cultural background, or linguistic characteristics	Practitioner may make assumptions based on an individual's accent, language, dialect, or culture

Adapted from the Centers for Disease Control and Prevention (2021).

and come up with ways to avoid them in interactions with clients and also how to address them should they occur. Some professional organizations offer online training and seminars, such as the American Counseling Association's anti-racism toolkit (2020), to help broaden practitioners' awareness and skillsets around bias and effective therapeutic engagement. Being able to recognize patterns of discrimination and systems of oppression can help practitioners take a more subjective and intersectional view of clients that is more accurate to their lived experiences.

Validating Cultural Identities and Experiences

A wide body of research suggests that validating clients' cultural identities and experiences of racialized trauma (e.g., Carter, 2007), gender or sex-related trauma (Madsen & Abell, 2010), minority sexual orientation identities (Shelton & Delgado-Romero, 2013) and more can help clients of different minority backgrounds feel safe and understood. One major way practitioners can validate minority clients' experiences is to avoid committing microaggressions.

Validation is particularly important when developing rapport with a client with whom there might be potential **power dynamics** at play (Boyd, 1996), in which there is a perceived or real difference in relative status in the client–practitioner relationship due to a difference in cultural identity between the client and the practitioner (Figure 7.2). For example, research has shown (a) that many ethnic minority clients do not feel comfortable sharing experiences of pain or racism with White professionals because government and human services institutions have not always adequately trained staff to behave in a culturally competent manner and (b) that bias is embedded in both individuals and institutions. Racism and other forms of oppression (e.g., sexism, heterosexism, and classism) have pervaded the human services sector for decades. Carten et al. (2016) provide a useful overview to explain the importance of both individuals and institutions behaving ethically and in a more anti-racist and anti-discriminatory manner.

FIGURE 7.2 Counselors engaged in couples therapy pay attention to power dynamics and verbal and nonverbal body language. *Source*: Prostock-studio/Shutterstock.

For example, when an HIV-positive Black male client from a large city speaks to a social worker about finding services in the suburban town where he now lives, if the practitioner, who is White and heterosexual, is unaware of racial privilege and heterosexual privilege, and also lacks access to information about local sexual health resources specific to Black men, or is ignorant about HIV-related medications, procedures, and resources in the area, what might result? At worst, the client might be unlikely to obtain appropriate services and might incur microaggressions from the social worker about race, gender, or sexuality. At best, the client might end up taking more time in meetings with their social worker than needed to educate the practitioner about their own cultural identities or experiences. An institution instead could provide more training opportunities to their staff to know how to center Black men's mental and physical health and to avoid bias in their encounters with clients.

Boyd (1996) recommends that practitioners openly point out potential power dynamics in ways that can be empowering to the client and that practitioners continue to get training on cultural competence after licensure. With the HIV-positive client just described, the practitioner could read about culturally and racially specific terminology and effective treatment strategies and resources to assist Black HIV-positive individuals. Certainly, the realm of cultural competence is not limited to responding to power dynamics about race in a binary context (e.g., White and non-White); non-Black counselors of color may also possess biases about Black clients or HIV-positive individuals and can also mediate power dynamics to work effectively across differences.

Developing Greater Self-Awareness and Humility

We as practitioners cannot know every fact about every culture and be entirely competent every time we work with a client. It is okay to demonstrate curiosity by asking clients to describe their upbringing and cultural background to underscore how they are the experts in their own lives. If assumptions have been made or microaggressions inadvertently committed, the practitioner should admit to the misunderstanding or potentially offensive behavior and make an effort to do better in the future.

Cultural humility refers to the ability to maintain an interpersonal stance that is "other-oriented . . . in relation to aspects of cultural identity that are most important to the client. Cultural humility is especially apparent when a practitioner is able to express respect for the client and a lack of superiority" (Hook et al., 2013, p. 3). Developing a sense of cultural humility takes time. Some White counselors, for example, may need to acknowledge some of their own blind spots due to racial privilege or being unable to comprehend the realities of clients of color (e.g., Kendall, 2013); this "self-work" to acknowledge how one's experience can be shaped by relative privilege can help practitioners be more humble and less presumptive. Being more sensitive to gender norms, for example, might mean a practitioner adapts techniques from **feminist therapy** (Corey, 2017) that help clients understand patterns in their expression of emotion and coping behavior due to gender socialization. Such a counselor might also investigate how sexist or patriarchal policies and structures in society make it more difficult to pursue behaviors and programs that can help clients overcome their problems. In fact, many new models of treatment incorporate an understanding of systemic factors that contribute to the lack of access to mental health services and other types of resources and the structural biases built within the education and health care systems (Box 7.1).

BOX 7.1	From Theory to Action

Imagine you are a practitioner who identifies as atheist, and you are working with a client who strongly identifies with the Jewish faith. You want to demonstrate cultural competence but lack training that would allow you to understand how Jewish culture might influence your client's problems, presentation, or communication. After an initial meeting, you feel like the client did not easily open up and that you may have made too many assumptions. You feel a bit resigned but want to remain hopeful that the client will be more forthcoming the next time you meet.

1. What are three things you can do to prepare for your next meeting?
2. What are three things you can do during your next meeting to improve the client–practitioner relationship?

7.5 CULTURALLY INFORMED ASSESSMENT AND SERVICE PLANNING

Effective human services practitioners provide services that adequately incorporate information about clients' cultural identities and backgrounds and require evaluation skills that adapt to the needs of the people and contexts in which practitioners work. This section describes some examples of proper culturally informed assessment and service provision.

Assessment Tools and Potential Bias

Assessment refers to the overall evaluation of a client's symptoms and functioning (Cowger, 1994). It is common practice to assess and evaluate the impact of a client's family background and environment on their experience of stress, as well as the client's goals and needs. Thorough, culturally informed assessment may include asking the client questions about their immigration status, legal status, language background, spiritual and religious beliefs, how they understand mental and physical health, their understanding of treatment, and past experiences in treatment (Center for Substance Abuse Treatment, 2014). More in-depth cultural knowledge might ask about tribal or elder status and birth order, family and gender roles, intergenerational trauma, and even more. It is important to also ask about relative strengths, coping strategies, and cultural wisdom. For some clients, a concrete strengths-based approach is quite motivating, allowing them to describe and focus on the resources they have in their own lives as well as those of their extended family and community (e.g., Padesky & Mooney, 2012).

Formal assessment procedures might include the use of responses to a well-established questionnaire on anxiety or depression, in-home or classroom observations, information from legal documents or medical charts, references to a diagnostic index, and more. Such procedures usually are standardized to some extent to different populations, and offer training and guidance on how to score and interpret responses, which can be important when using instruments for which your client populations might not have been originally tested. Expert judgment of how to interpret client responses and data when engaging in such formal assessment procedures is essential.

If the assessment tools used by your agency were normed on a mostly White, *edu*cated, *i*ndustrialized, *r*ich, *d*emocratic population, it is possible that they have what is referred to in the social sciences as the **WEIRD bias** (Henrich et al., 2010). This means that there are far too many studies and diagnostic tools focusing on these populations, rather than on the majority of the rest of the world. However, a score on an assessment tool from a client from any particular culture may be a good indication of their actual level of distress or need, but to know this with some accuracy requires the practitioner to be engaged in vigilant and culturally sound attunement to clients' experiences.

Another example is the overreliance on the *Diagnostic and Statistical Manual of Mental Disorders* (DSM), published by the American Psychiatric Association (2013), which lists categories and criteria for psychiatric and psychological conditions accepted in U.S. practice. Some client populations' cultural idioms for distress and experiences of culture-bound syndromes—psychological conditions whose prevalence or symptomology are significantly more common among a specific culture or group of cultures (Heine, 2020)—are not fully addressed by the DSM (Figure 7.3). Although the DSM provides a useful scientific standard for understanding mental illness, some practitioners might use a broader and more holistic assessment procedure that incorporates both physical and mental health. In practice, a human services practitioner might incorporate information from the DSM and the *International Classification of Diseases* (World Health Organization, 2019), a diagnostic compendium that is translated into more than 30 languages, used in many more countries internationally, and includes both mental disorders and health-related disorders.

Informal assessment requires attention to the client's verbal and nonverbal behavior and interpretation of aspects of the client's emotional and behavioral style. For example, a client who shows up 5 minutes late for every meeting might be interpreted as difficult or unconscientious, but this pattern of behavior could also be due to anxiety, transportation challenges, or an accepted cultural norm that promptness is not a priority. Consider, for example, how some Asian and Asian American clients are not comfortable with continued direct eye contact, particularly with authority figures, because in many Asian cultures this behavior is regarded as disrespectful (Leong & Lee, 2006). There is no formal test or procedure to know how to interpret all the possible

FIGURE 7.3   A client born outside of the United States describes symptoms that do not entirely fit diagnostic criteria in the DSM. *Source*: wavebreakmedia/Shutterstock.

behavioral patterns that may have cultural determinants, but as a professional gains experience and works with clients from varied backgrounds, their intuition and judgment will continue to improve.

Service Planning

Engaging in culturally responsive treatment or service planning requires the practitioner to understand the extent to which different cultural experiences and identities can impact the selection and provision of appropriate services and how outcomes are evaluated. It is the practitioner's job to gather and understand culturally relevant information, conceptualize how the client views their situation and needs, and select an approach to providing services that will most likely result in the best outcome for the client.

Historically, many theoretical approaches included in the counseling process (see Chapter 4) were normed on primarily White and/or European clients and therefore may not be universally applicable to clients of other cultural backgrounds. The psychoanalytic approach, for example, although influential in inspiring an understanding of how unconscious forces might relate to clients' present-day experience of resistance and conflict, particularly tied to early childhood experiences of shame, guilt, and punishment, was a theory developed by Sigmund Freud based on observations of his mostly upper income European clients (Corey, 2017).

Given some of the limitations of our theoretical historical understanding of mental distress, how can a counselor engage in culturally responsive treatment planning? Let's practice by examining the case below (adapted from Center for Substance Abuse Treatment, 2014).

Refer back to Sue et al.'s (1992) model of cultural competence by focusing on facts and knowledge about the different cultural identities and experiences of the client, as well as skills, activities, and interventions that have been known to work with members of those populations. In this particular client case study, the therapist realizes that by understanding the client's acculturation level as well as how the client's marriage to an

---

| CASE STUDY 7.1 | Zhang Min |

Zhang Min, a 25-year-old first-generation Chinese woman, was referred to a counselor by her primary care physician because she reported having episodes of depression. The counselor who conducted the intake interview had received training in cultural competence and was mindful of cultural factors in evaluating Zhang Min. The referral noted that Zhang Min was born in Hong Kong, so the counselor expected hesitance to discuss problems, given the stigma attached to mental illness and substance abuse in Chinese culture. During the evaluation, however, the therapist was surprised to find that Zhang Min was quite forthcoming. Zhang Min mentioned missing deadlines at work and calling in sick at least once a week, and also noted that her

co-workers had expressed concern after finding a bottle of wine in her desk. She admitted that she had been drinking heavily, which she linked to work stress and recent discord with her Irish American spouse.

Think About ...

1. If you were this person's practitioner, how would you form rapport with this client?
2. What stereotypes might come to mind and how would you mitigate them when working with this client?
3. How could you maintain humility while understanding this client's worldview?

Irish American spouse has influenced her beliefs, some factual knowledge the therapist knows about Asian Americans, immigrants, or people from collectivist cultures does not apply accurately to this specific client. The counselor was surprised that her client behaved in ways counterstereotypical to what she had learned about Asian culture and that her client was relatively verbal and forthcoming and not submissive, as she had expected. From further conversation about the client's perspective, the counselor also discovered that the coping mechanism of drinking alcohol was relatively normalized by her husband and also that taboos around alcohol use are not as widespread in Hong Kong as they are in mainland China.

Notice this particular client has turned more inward and has resorted less to social coping strategies and instead to use alcohol to manage depressive symptoms. Because the client sees the source of her depression as being somewhat relational in nature, a counselor might consider introducing couples or family therapy, cognitive therapy that focuses on changing thoughts about the client's family history and behaviors, or a behavioral approach that focuses on learning new techniques to reduce intense emotional outbursts and communicate more effectively with other family members.

A counselor practicing cultural humility may recognize a power differential in their therapist–client relationship. Their own awareness of a potential lack of culturally specific information for that particular client's background and identities might lead the counselor to engage in a further consultation with a community elder or leader, rabbi, priest, other religious informant, or even some other advocate or academic expert on the particular cultural bodies of knowledge that help explain the client's lived experience.

SPOTLIGHT ON SERVICE-LEARNING

Service-learning activities offer an extremely valuable opportunity for students to gain hands-on experience in local communities, engaging in projects in which they provide services, educate, and collaborate on programming designed to empower members of underresourced groups. These experiences help students learn more of the day-to-day realities of people with vastly different backgrounds and identities. How can a practitioner who does not identify as a member of the targeted local community population effectively act as an ally and collaborator?

SUMMARY

- Culture is the set of customs, traditions, and beliefs that is handed down generation to generation via cultural transmission. Understanding how and why cultural identity matters in the helping relationship can illuminate and clarify potential power dynamics and expectations with clients, inform assessment and treatment strategies, and optimize the practitioner's role within the human services profession.
- Certain aspects of a client's cultural identity may be salient and thus shape their experience and worldview. It may also influence how they behave when seeking services and the treatment or services that are most effective for them.
- The RESPECTFUL model and the ADDRESSING model are inclusive models that help us understand ourselves and the cultural backgrounds of our clients in

regard to race and ethnicity, nationality and citizenship, phenotype/appearance, linguistic capabilities, socioeconomic status and education level, sex and gender, sexual orientation, religious/spiritual identity, ability status (including physical or mental health-related disabilities), age, and professional identity.

- Historically, the prevailing belief among many practitioners was that human services' capabilities were "one size fits all." What that typically meant was to provide services without incorporating the cultural identities or worldviews of clients. However, this proved problematic because treatment and services were not optimal or effective when critical parts of a person's identity were ignored.

- Attending to verbal and nonverbal behavior is a microskill that includes paying attention to both spoken words and nonverbal cues a client provides to better understand their situation and needs. Culturally competent practitioners develop a wide range of communication skills that allow them to effectively communicate with and serve clients representing a wide range of communication styles.

- A second microskill is validating cultural identities and experiences. This is significant in developing rapport with a client, especially when there are potential power dynamics at play.

- A third microskill encourages an understanding of microaggressions, what they are, and how to avoid them.

- A fourth microskill focuses on developing greater self-awareness and humility, which includes demonstrating curiosity about the client's cultural background and acknowledging that practitioners cannot know everything about every culture and may occasionally make mistakes.

- Formal assessment and service planning must be done in a manner that is sensitive to the client's cultural identity and unique experiences. It is the practitioner's job to gather and understand culturally relevant information and provide appropriate services or treatment in alignment with this information.

REVIEW QUESTIONS

Assessment Questions

1. What is the definition of culture? How is culture useful to understand when working with clients?
2. What is intersectionality? How do intersectional experiences impact clients' well-being and the client–therapist relationship?
3. What are microaggressions and how can microaggressions toward clients impact the client–practitioner relationship?
4. How can assessment methods and service planning be improved in a culturally informed manner to address the needs of all populations?

Reflection Questions

1. Which power dynamics would cause the most difficulty or tension between you and clients from a different cultural background? How would you better communicate in order to have a more productive relationship?
2. What forces have shaped your cultural identity? How do theories of identity apply to the community in which your organization operates?

3. Which microskills could you use most effectively to work with clients from different cultural backgrounds? What skills and areas of awareness would you need to develop to increase the range of different clients with whom you would be able to work?

4. Imagine a client who is experiencing some difficulty in feeling being heard by their therapist because the therapist has committed an unintentional microaggression. How might the client behave in this situation? How might the therapist recover from this mistake? (This scenario could also be done as a classroom role-play.)

REFERENCES

American Counseling Association. (2020). *Anti-racism toolkit.* https://www.counseling.org/docs/default-source/resources-for-counselors/anti-racism-toolkit.pdf

American Psychiatric Association. (2013). *Diagnostic and statistical manual of mental disorders* (5th ed.). American Psychiatric Publishing.

Boyd, K. K. (1996). Power imbalances and therapy. *Focus, 11,* 1–4.

Carten, A. J., Siskind, A., & Greene, M.P. (Eds.). (2016). *Strategies for deconstructing racism in the health and human services sector.* Oxford University Press.

Carter, R. T. (2007). Racism and psychological and emotional injury: Recognizing and assessing race-based traumatic stress. *The Counseling Psychologist, 35,* 13–105. https://doi.org/10.1177/0011000006292033

Center for Substance Abuse Treatment. (2014). *Culturally responsive evaluation and treatment planning* (Treatment Improvement Protocol Series, No. 59). Substance Abuse and Mental Health Services Administration. https://www.ncbi.nlm.nih.gov/books/NBK248423

Centers for Disease Control and Prevention. (2021). *Types of discrimination.* https://www.cdc.gov/oeeowe/faqs/discrimination.htm

Corey, G. (2017). *Theory and practice of counseling and psychotherapy* (10th ed.). Cengage.

Cowger, C. D. (1994). Assessing client strengths: Clinical assessment for client empowerment. *Social Work, 39,* 262–268.

Crenshaw, K. (1990). Mapping the margins: Intersectionality, identity politics, and violence against women of color. *Stanford Law Review, 43,* 1241–1299. https://doi.org/10.2307/1229039

Cummings, C., & O'Donohue, W. (2018). Psychological reactions and cultural competence. In C. Frisby & W. O'Donohue (Eds.), *Cultural competence in applied psychology* (pp. 139–153). Springer.

D'Andrea, M., & Daniels, J. (2001). RESPECTFUL counseling: An integrative model for counselors. In D. Pope-Davis & H. Coleman (Eds.), *The interface of class, culture and gender in counseling* (pp. 417–466). SAGE.

Hays, P. A. (2008). *Addressing cultural complexities in practice: Assessment, diagnosis, and therapy* (2nd ed.). American Psychological Association.

Heine, S. J. (2020). *Cultural psychology* (4th ed.). Norton.

Helms, J. E. (1993). Introduction: Review of racial identity terminology. In J. E. Helms (Ed.), *Black and White racial identity: Theory, research and practice* (pp. 3–7). Praeger.

Henrich, J., Heine, S. J., & Norenzayan, A. (2010). Most people are not WEIRD. *Nature, 466*(7302), 29.

Hook, J. N., Davis, D. E., Owen, J., Worthington, E. L., Jr., & Utsey, S. O. (2013). Cultural humility: Measuring openness to culturally diverse clients. *Journal of Counseling Psychology, 60,* 353–366. doi:10.1037/a0032595

Ivey, A. E., Ivey, M. B., & Zalaquett, C. P. (2016). *Essentials of intentional interviewing: Counseling in a multicultural world* (3rd ed.). Cengage.

Kendall, F. (2013). *Understanding White privilege: Creating pathways to authentic relationships across race* (2nd ed.). Routledge.

Kim, B. S. K., Hill, C., Gelso, C. J., & Goates, M. K. (2003). Counselor self-disclosure, East Asian American client adherence to Asian cultural values, and counseling process. *Journal of Counseling Psychology, 50,* 324–332. doi:10.1037/0022-0167.50.3.324

Kirk, G., & Okazawa-Rey, M. (2018). Identities and social locations: Who am I? Who are my people? In M. Adams, W. J. Blumenfeld,

D. C. J. Catalano, K. S. DeJong, H. W. Hackman, L. E. Hopkins, B. J. Love, M. L. Peters, D. Shlasko, & X. Zúñiga (Eds.), *Readings for diversity and social justice* (4th ed., pp. 10–15). Routledge.

Koss, J. D. (1990). Somatization and somatic complaint syndromes among Hispanics: Overview and ethnopsychological perspectives. *Transcultural Psychiatric Research Review*, *27*, 5–29. https://doi.org/10.1177/136346159002700101

Leong, F. T., & Lee, S.-H. (2006). A cultural accommodation model for cross-cultural psychotherapy: Illustrated with the case of Asian Americans. *Psychotherapy: Theory, Research, Practice, Training*, *43*, 410–423. https://doi.org/10.1037/0033-3204.43.4.410

Madsen, M. D., & Abell, N. (2010). Trauma Resilience Scale: Validation of protective factors associated with adaptation following violence. *Research on Social Work Practice*, *20*, 223–233. https://doi.org/10.1177/1049731509347853

Maffini, C. S., & Wong, Y. J. (2014). Assessing somatization with Asian American clients. In L. Benuto, N. Thaler, & B. Leany (Eds.), *Guide to psychological assessment with Asians* (pp. 347–360). Springer. https://doi.org/10.1007/978-1-4939-0796-0_22

McDaniel, M., Woods, T., Pratt, E., & Simms, M. (2017, November 28). *Identifying racial and ethnic disparities in human services: A conceptual framework and review* (OPRE Report No. 2017–69). Urban Institute. https://www.urban.org/research/publication/identifying-racial-and-ethnic-disparities-human-services

Mitchell, R., & Boyle, B. (2015). Professional diversity, identity salience and team innovation: The moderating role of open-mindedness norms. *Journal of Organizational Behavior*, *36*(6), 873–894.

Padesky, C. A., & Mooney, K. A. (2012). Strengths-based cognitive–behavioural therapy: A four-step model to build resilience. *Clinical Psychology & Psychotherapy*, *19*, 283–290.

Phinney, J. S. (1990). Ethnic identity in adolescents and adults: Review of the research. *Psychological Bulletin*, *108*, 499–514.

Ponterotto, J. G., & Park-Taylor, J. (2007). Racial and ethnic identity theory, measurement, and research in counseling psychology: Present status and future directions. *Journal of Counseling Psychology*, *54*(3), 282–294.

Schildkraut, D. J. (2002). The more things change … American identity and mass and elite responses to 9/11. *Political Psychology*, *23*(3), 511–535.

Shelton, K., & Delgado-Romero, E. A. (2013). Sexual orientation microaggressions: The experience of lesbian, gay, bisexual, and queer clients in psychotherapy. *Psychology of Sexual Orientation and Gender Diversity*, *1*, 59–70. https://doi.org/10.1037/2329-0382.1.S.59

Sue, D. W. (2018). Microaggressions, marginality, and oppression: An introduction. In M. Adams, W. J. Blumenfeld, D. C. J. Catalano, K. S. DeJong, H. W. Hackman, L. E. Hopkins, B. J. Love, M. L. Peters, D. Shlasko, & X. Zúñiga (Eds.), *Readings for diversity and social justice* (4th ed., pp. 22–26). Routledge.

Sue, D. W., Arrendondo, P., & McDavis, R. J. (1992). Multicultural counseling competencies and standards: A call to the profession. *Journal of Multicultural Counseling and Development*, *20*, 64–88. https://doi.org/10.1002/j.2161-1912.1992.tb00563.x

Sue, D. W., & Sue, D. (1990). *Counseling the culturally different: Theory and practice*. Wiley.

Suite, D. H., La Bril, R., Primm, A., & Harrison-Ross, P. (2007). Beyond misdiagnosis, misunderstanding and mistrust: Relevance of the historical perspective in the medical and mental health treatment of people of color. *Journal of the National Medical Association*, *99*, 879–885.

Tajfel, H., & Turner, J. C. (1979). An integrative theory of intergroup conflict. In W. G. Austin & S. Worchel (Eds.), *The social psychology of intergroup relations* (pp. 33–47). Brooks/Cole.

Tatum, B. D. (2017). *Why are all the Black kids sitting together in the cafeteria? And other conversations about race* (20th anniversary ed.). Basic Books.

Tingle, T. (2006). *When Turtle grew feathers: A tale from the Choctaw Nation*. BirchBark.

World Health Organization. (2019). *International Statistical Classification of Diseases and Related Health Problems* (11th ed.).

CHAPTER 8

Managing Human Services Organizations

Learning Objectives

After completing this chapter, you will be able to:

8.1. Define the role of government-managed and -funded human services programs.

8.2. Explain the role and tax status of nonprofit organizations.

8.3. Describe various nonprofit funding models.

8.4. Explain the governance role of a nonprofit organization's board of directors.

8.5. Explain how nonprofit programs are developed and evaluated.

8.6. Outline various ways that human services organizations can be structured and managed.

8.7. Define *mutual aid organization* and describe the role these groups have played in U.S. history.

8.8. Explain why many local human services organizations join state, regional, and national networks.

Social services are provided by formal entities such as government agencies, private for-profit businesses, and **nonprofit organizations**, along with informal organizations such as mutual aid networks. To address social issues and effect social change, these organizations must focus on external realities—the environment in which they operate—and the internal health and functioning of the organization. To understand the structure and operations of these various entities, it is helpful to remember how the responsibility for delivering social services is divided between the public, private, and nonprofit (or voluntary) sectors. In this chapter, we discuss the difference between public and private human services and nonprofit organizations, paying particular attention to how nonprofit organizations are structured, managed, and funded and their relationship to other socially oriented entities.

8.1 GOVERNMENT-MANAGED AND -FUNDED SOCIAL SERVICES

The public sector encompasses the work done by government agencies and offices at the federal (national), state, county, and municipal (city or town) levels. These entities may provide social services directly to individuals and families or fund and oversee programs run by nonprofit organizations. This funding may come in the form of grants and contracts that enable these organizations to deliver goods and services to support families and communities. Funding may also take the form of reimbursements for services covered by programs such as Medicaid and Medicare, which pay for health care services for qualifying individuals.

Most states in the US have an umbrella health and human services agency that oversees offices statewide. Example branches may include the following:

- Department of Children and Families: Manages the foster care system and is responsible for responding to cases of abuse and neglect
- Department of Transitional Assistance: Manages social benefit programs such as SNAP, WIC, and TANF (see Chapter 10 for detailed information on government programs)
- Department for Refugees and Immigrants: Provides workforce support and/or citizenship programs

Many states also have agencies that address the needs of older adults and people living with developmental disabilities. Every state has its own structure and organization designed to meet critical needs. Cities and towns also provide services that may be funded by state and federal agencies. For example, local housing authorities can provide rental assistance through Section 8 vouchers or affordable housing. The Section 8 program is a federal housing program funded by the U.S. Department of Housing and Urban Development. Some local housing authorities provide social services for residents, including youth or workforce development.

8.2 ROLE AND TAX STATUS OF NONPROFIT ORGANIZATIONS

The nonprofit sector encompasses businesses that are granted special tax status in exchange for providing a public benefit. Many of the oldest institutions in the United States are nonprofit organizations. Their role in society is so deeply embedded that it is easy to take them for granted. The nonprofit sector has evolved to conduct much of the work society considers to be important for our collective well-being but outside the bounds of what the public and private sectors are expected or allowed to do. This includes providing various types of support for individuals and families; nurturing socially, culturally, and environmentally robust and healthy communities; protecting animals and the environment; and much more. Although the nonprofit sector includes organizations with a wide range of missions, in this chapter we focus on those that provide community and human services.

Nonprofit Mission Statements

Nonprofit organizations often express their commitment to serving the public good through a succinct **mission statement**, which is a brief summary of the reason the organization exists and its primary goals. An effective mission statement can engender trust within the community served, attract donors, and help keep the organization's staff and board of directors focused on their purpose. Here are some examples:

- *Black Girls Code* (wearebgc.org): We build pathways for young women of color to embrace the current tech marketplace as builders and creators by introducing them to skills in computer programming and technology.
- *The National Alliance to End Homelessness* (endhomelessness.org): The National Alliance to End Homelessness is a nonpartisan organization committed to preventing and ending homelessness in the United States.
- *Indigenous Environmental Network* (ienearth.org): IEN is an alliance of Indigenous Peoples whose shared mission is to protect the sacredness of Earth Mother from contamination and exploitation by respecting and adhering to Indigenous knowledge and natural law.

Charitable Organizations

The official term for a nonprofit organization that provides community and human services is "charitable organization," meaning that it serves the public good through the pursuit of its mission. The term comes from the Internal Revenue Code, the compilation of federal tax laws in the United States. That might seem like an odd place for human services organizations to be defined, but it reflects the critical role that tax status plays in delineating their scope and functions. The first step in establishing a charitable organization is to legally register it as a business entity in its state. If the business can demonstrate that it was founded to provide a social benefit per section 501(c)(3) of the Internal Revenue Code (1986), it can apply to the Internal Revenue Service (IRS) to be recognized as a charitable organization.

Charitable organizations play such an important role in addressing individual, family, and community needs that are not met by government agencies or private businesses that the government grants them two tax-related benefits: tax-exempt status and eligibility to receive tax-deductible gifts. At the federal and state levels, the government incentivizes the creation of charitable organizations by granting them tax-exempt status, meaning that they do not have to pay taxes. In exchange for not paying taxes, charitable organizations are not allowed to redistribute surplus funds to anyone associated with the organization. The term "nonprofit" can be misleading because it suggests that the organization cannot make more money than it spends. In fact, a healthy nonprofit organization should always have a cushion in case of an unexpected risk to its income, such as an economic downturn that leads to a decrease in donations. However, unlike a private, for-profit business, if a nonprofit organization has money left over after paying for operating costs such as employee salaries and rent, it must invest the funds back into its work. Giving the excess funds to individuals or diverting them for other purposes can jeopardize the organization's tax-exempt status.

To further incentivize public support for charitable organizations, the government grants them eligibility to receive tax-deductible donations. Depending on their income and the size of their gifts, corporate and individual donors to these organizations may be able to claim their contributions as tax deductions. The rules governing tax-exempt status and eligibility to receive tax-deductible gifts at the federal level are found in section 501(c)(3) of the Internal Revenue Code. Additional rules governing nonprofit tax status are set at the state level.

Public Charities

The 501(c)(3) category includes more than 1 million organizations (National Center for Charitable Statistics, 2020). Although these organizations provide vastly different services to people across the socioeconomic spectrum, they share an obligation to provide a social benefit.

Depending on their purpose and structure, charitable organizations are typically designated as public charities or private foundations. As the name suggests, public charities serve the public and typically work directly with individuals, families, and communities. This category includes many organizations that provide social services such as public health clinics, shelters for housing-insecure individuals, after-school programs, food pantries, and houses of worship and faith-based organizations. They receive government funding and financial support from individuals, foundations, and businesses.

Private Foundations

Private foundations such as the Rockefeller Foundation and Ford Foundation play a significant role in funding nonprofit human services organizations and are also designated as 501(c)(3) entities. Private foundations are typically established by an individual, family, or corporation as the sole or primary funder for the purpose of making grants to other nonprofit organizations, often through a competitive application or screening process. The money provided to establish and maintain a private foundation is often held in an endowment, which is an investment portfolio managed to generate income to support the foundation's operations and grant-making. Private foundations are required to give away 5 percent of their assets annually and conform to other rules outlined in the Internal Revenue Code (Box 8.1).

BOX 8.1   Looking Beyond 501(c)(3): 501(c)(4) and Other Designations

The Internal Revenue Code identifies a wide range of organizations that are tax-exempt but not eligible to receive tax-deductible gifts, typically because their work provides a social benefit that may not be applicable to the general public. These include labor unions [described in section 501(c)(5)], trade associations [501(c)(6)], and even cemeteries [501(c)(13)]. Section 501(c)(4) outlines the attributes and rules governing social welfare organizations engaged in political lobbying (an activity that public charities can engage in, but only on a limited basis) and political campaigns (which public charities may not engage in at all).

The Internal Revenue Code draws a line between what 501(c)(3) and 501(c)(4) organizations can and cannot do, but some organizations appear to straddle both designations. Planned Parenthood, for example, is associated with providing reproductive health care services and education to the public as well as advocating for sexual health care and reproductive rights. How is that possible? This work is done by two different legal entities: Planned Parenthood Federation of America focuses on service delivery as a 501(c)(3) organization, whereas Planned Parenthood Action Fund engages in policy and advocacy work as a 501(c)(4) organization.

8.3 HOW NONPROFIT ORGANIZATIONS ARE FUNDED

Nonprofit organizations incur many of the same kinds of expenses as for-profit businesses, such as salaries and benefits, rent, utilities, maintenance, travel, equipment, liability insurance, and internet service. Their programs and services may generate additional expenses such as food, school supplies, buses, medical equipment, delivery vans, and more—a list as expansive as the wide range of services nonprofit organizations provide.

Their tax-exempt status and designated role in society position nonprofit organizations to secure funding from a variety of sources, including municipal, state, and federal government agencies; foundations; private businesses and corporations; and individuals. Some of this funding is obtained via mechanisms similar to those seen in the private sector, such as government contracts and the sale of goods and services, whereas some flows through philanthropic channels, including individual donations and foundation grants.

Although there are many funding sources for nonprofits, they are not all a good fit for every organization. Different funders are motivated to give for different reasons. To be financially sustainable, nonprofit organizations must seek out funders whose interests align with their missions. Most also pursue funding from a variety of sources to avoid being vulnerable to economic and political disruptions that could affect their revenue, such as a recession or a political election. Leaders of nonprofit organizations must understand why various funders give and what they are looking for in return. Within the nonprofit sector as a whole, fees for services and goods provided to the government and private entities are the largest source of revenue, followed by private contributions, government grants, investment income, and other sources (Figure 8.1).

Because of the stiff competition they face for limited resources, nonprofit organizations may be tempted to pursue funding opportunities that do not align with their mission or priorities. In the short term, bringing in money may relieve financial pressure, but it can come with obligations that pull the organization off course into **mission drift**. This phenomenon speaks to a challenge in obtaining funding: There is no guarantee that the entities which control the resources will choose to fund the priorities that nonprofit organizations identify in their communities.

Government Contracts, Grants, and Reimbursements

In addition to running social service programs, some government agencies also fund nonprofit organizations to run them. This funding may come in the form of contracts or grants for the provision of goods and services related to the government agencies' purposes.

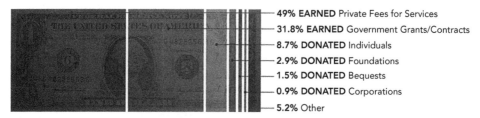

- **49% EARNED** Private Fees for Services
- **31.8% EARNED** Government Grants/Contracts
- **8.7% DONATED** Individuals
- **2.9% DONATED** Foundations
- **1.5% DONATED** Bequests
- **0.9% DONATED** Corporations
- **5.2%** Other

FIGURE 8.1 Non-profit Revenue Sources *Source*: Used with permission of National Council of Nonprofits

Another form of government funding is reimbursement for services. For example, Medicaid and Medicare are government-funded health insurance programs that pay health care facilities and providers for services provided to low-income and older individuals and some other eligible populations.

Government contracts, grants, and reimbursements are critical to many service providers' business models and long-term sustainability. The application process and administrative and reporting requirements for government funding can be cumbersome and time-consuming.

Philanthropy and Private Giving

The word **philanthropy** is derived from Greek roots meaning "love of humankind." The term broadly means supporting the common good but typically refers to giving by private foundations and individuals. Because the priorities, funding amount, and application processes vary tremendously from foundation to foundation, nonprofits must identify where their greatest chances of success lie so they can prioritize which grants to pursue. Grants often come with limitations on how they may be spent.

Individuals and families support nonprofit organizations in many ways, including monetary contributions that may range from a few dollars to millions, participation in events and fundraisers, and bequests in their wills. Personal contributions often come with no restrictions, so they give the organization more freedom to decide how to use the funds than foundation grants. Donations of time and services may also factor into an organization's business model and program strategy. When an organization is dependent on individuals donating money or their time, cultivating strong relationships is essential to maintain their support.

Corporate Giving

Private businesses have multiple incentives to fund nonprofit organizations, including improving relations with their communities, generating goodwill for their brands, and making employees feel good about where they work. This funding may be channeled through corporate foundations that award grants to nonprofits and internal giving programs often run by human resources, community relations, or marketing departments. Corporate giving is often focused on communities where companies have operations and may focus on issues related to their products or brand. Some businesses make in-kind donations of their products or services, and some sponsor fundraising events such as walkathons and galas, which provide visibility and marketing opportunities.

Funding Intermediaries

This category of funders includes public charities whose mission involves funding other public charities. Unlike private foundations, which are typically created and funded by an individual, family, or corporation, funding intermediaries often aggregate money from multiple sources and then redistribute it to nonprofit organizations that are aligned with their missions. The United Way is an example of a public charity that accepts contributions from many individuals and businesses and then redistributes the funds to organizations serving their communities.

BOX 8.2   **Reimagining the Nonprofit Sector and Philanthropy**

There is growing awareness of the power imbalance that often exists between low-income and historically oppressed communities of color and the elected officials, policymakers, and funders, including wealthy philanthropists, foundations, and corporations, who control much-needed resources and determine which social needs will be addressed and how. Even within nonprofit organizations, people of color are often underrepresented in executive leadership roles and on boards of directors (Faulk et al., 2021; Osili et al., 2018). This can have the paradoxical effect of further disempowering the very communities that the policies and funding are intended to support.

Mutual aid, discussed in this chapter, is an example of how communities can bypass these power dynamics by addressing their needs directly. Similarly, emerging trends in philanthropy, including participatory grant-making and trust-based philanthropy, are intended to restructure the relationship between nonprofit organizations and funders by redistributing power in decision-making processes. The worker self-directed nonprofit organization Justice Funders, (https://justicefunders.org/) based in Oakland, California, has developed a model to support a Just Transition for Philanthropy (https://justicefunders.org/thought-leadership/just-transition-for-philanthropy/) that prioritizes the collective well-being over the wealth and power of a few and puts the power of controlling wealth into the hands of communities.

Revenue Generation and Social Enterprise

Revenue generation refers to a business model in which nonprofit organizations sell goods or services to government agencies, private businesses, or individuals to fund their operations. Nonprofit organizations have long recognized the merits of this approach, which takes many forms, from hospitals charging for medical services to museums requiring admission fees. Another well-known example is the Girl Scouts' annual cookie sale.

Social enterprises are nonprofit and for-profit entities whose business model is designed to generate revenue and address a social or environmental need. The need may be met through the structure of the business—for example, by employing community members who might otherwise face barriers to employment—or through the products or services sold, such as affordable hygiene products marketed in communities in which girls and women might not otherwise have access to them (Box 8.2).

8.4 ACCOUNTABILITY AND GOVERNANCE

On its surface, the nonprofit sector appears to offer an admirable and effective solution to meeting a variety of social needs, and hundreds of thousands of nonprofit organizations work hard every day to serve their communities. However, as Professor Peter Frumkin (2002), who researches philanthropy and nonprofit management, and others have observed, the question of accountability in the nonprofit sector is complicated. Unlike private businesses, nonprofit organizations do not have owners or shareholders who are financially incentivized to provide a consistently high-quality product.

Some external oversight and accountability are provided by the IRS and state attorneys general offices, which ensure nonprofits' compliance with federal and state legal requirements, and **watchdog organizations**, which monitor their financial health and programs.

Internally, the **board of directors** is group of people who hold responsibility for the organization's legal, financial, and programmatic well-being. Board members are typically unpaid volunteers. They are also considered fiduciaries, meaning they are expected to prioritize the organization's needs ahead of their own. These conditions make it imperative for nonprofit organizations to have clarity about their organizational structure and governance practices. Board members are expected to adhere to three duties (Board Sources, 2017):

- *Duty of care* requires board members to protect the organization's tangible and intangible assets, from its funding and facilities to its reputation and goodwill.
- *Duty of loyalty* means they must honor the organization's mission and put its needs above their own and avoid all conflicts of interest.
- *Duty of obedience* requires board members to keep the organization in compliance with all applicable laws and regulations as well as with its own regulations and bylaws.

These three duties establish ethical expectations and practical responsibilities, including hiring and supervising the chief executive officer (CEO) or executive director (ED), supporting fundraising efforts, monitoring the organization's financial health, defining strategic priorities, reviewing and signing contracts, and finding their own successors.

The organization's **bylaws** are internal rules intended to guide the board of directors' practices and decision-making and provide a framework for holding board members accountable, especially when disagreements or problems arise. Bylaws may define the qualifications and expectations of board members; the structure of the board, including officer positions; the frequency and timing of board meetings; conflict-of-interest policies; succession processes; term lengths; the process for hiring executive directors; and the process for dissolving the organization.

A nonprofit board must include a chairperson or president, a treasurer, and a secretary. Additional positions, such as vice chair, may also be required by the bylaws. A variety of committees may also be established as needed to facilitate the board's work on critical issues; these may include a search committee for hiring a new executive director and a committee to support fundraising and event planning. Ideally, a board's leadership and composition should reflect the diversity of the population it serves, with mechanisms in place to ensure that community members are well represented.

8.5 DEVELOPMENT AND EVALUATION OF NONPROFIT PROGRAMS

The foundation of an organization's ability to evaluate its impact is laid almost as soon as it conceptualizes the social problems or challenges it intends to address. Clarity about needs to be met or gaps to be filled can lead to clarity about what success will look like. A **needs assessment**, whether conducted by the organization or an external party, can help provide this clarity.

From there, an organization can draw on its experience and expertise, familiarity with its community, stakeholders' input, and research to set specific goals and design programs and services to achieve them. Thorough planning helps avoid building a flaw into the design of the intervention. For example, an organization might fail to account for all the primary languages spoken within the community and be unable to reach as many beneficiaries as intended, or the methodology chosen may not be as effective in the local cultural context as the organization anticipated. External variables, including political, economic, social, and environmental factors, can influence whether a plan can be implemented as envisioned and achieve its intended results. For example, the COVID-19 pandemic demonstrated how the spread of an infectious disease could disrupt students' learning in ways an academic support program might not have been designed to address.

Although no one can anticipate every variable that can affect an organization's intended outcomes, several tools can be used to minimize the kinds of planning gaps that can undermine a program or project before it is even launched. Used in combination, these tools can increase an organization's confidence about what it should do to achieve its intended impact:

- **Stakeholder analysis** involves acquiring a thorough understanding of all the individuals, groups, organizations, businesses, and other entities that are affected by the issue the organization is addressing and may be impacted by its work.
- **Asset mapping** identifies existing resources and capacities in the community.
- Developing a **theory of change** based on research about the issue and a deep understanding of its community can help the organization focus on interventions that are likely to be effective.
- A **logic model** is a method used to identify and test assumptions about planned actions and expected outcomes.

Evaluation Methods

How do we know when a nonprofit organization is doing a good job? This seemingly simple question is complicated by the complexity of the social challenges many nonprofit organizations address and the influence external funding has on their decision-making and financial sustainability. Factors such as compelling communications, highly qualified staff, and healthy funding streams are critical to an organization's work and help attract donors, but they do not guarantee that the work is effectively delivering on the social benefit the organization is committed to providing to the individuals and community it serves. Even the most thorough planning process does not guarantee success.

To hold themselves accountable to their beneficiaries and donors, nonprofit organizations often engage in evaluation to assess their impact. By measuring actual results in relation to organizational goals and objectives, evaluation helps determine whether programs and services are working or whether course corrections are needed to ensure that resources are being used as effectively as possible to serve the community.

Evaluation can be conducted using a variety of methods, including interviews, surveys, focus groups, observation, and analysis of documents and records. Once an organization determines which programs or services it wants to evaluate and which questions it seeks to answer, it must select an appropriate method to obtain data that will answer those questions. For example, determining whether students in an after-school program feel welcome and respected requires a different approach than understanding whether the program is leading to improved academic performance. A variety of factors can influence that choice, including whether the priority is to determine if the program is being implemented as planned (its process) or what results are being achieved (its outcomes).

Evaluation can be designed to answer specific questions or to assess the longer term impact of multiple interventions or the organization's work as a whole. Evaluation design should account for factors such as the age and primary language of participants, the wording of instructions and questions, where it will be conducted and by whom, and how the results will be analyzed. The ethical research questions discussed in Chapter 6 apply to nonprofit evaluation practices: Organizations must ensure that the process is culturally appropriate, sensitive to concerns individuals may have about sharing personal information, respectful of participants' privacy, and anonymized. All data collected must be kept confidential and secure.

Although it would be ideal for organizations to make evaluation a routine practice, several barriers may prevent them from doing so. Staff workloads may make it difficult to administer evaluation tools and collect data. Cost may be a deterrent if the evaluation method requires outside consulting support or specialized software. Life circumstances may prevent some individuals' participation—for example, if clients are transient or fearful of providing personal information about themselves or family members due to their immigration status. Organizations contemplating evaluation must anticipate potential barriers and strive to develop an approach that is ethical, effective, and affordable.

8.6 STRUCTURE AND MANAGEMENT OF HUMAN SERVICES ORGANIZATIONS

Organizations have systems and structures for making decisions and setting internal policies (or rules) that guide how they operate. These systems and structures establish the chain of command, including how supervision will be performed and by whom, and define what role each person has in helping the organization meet its goals. The organizational structure identifies and assigns responsibilities to departments, teams, and, in some cases, key individuals, and it includes the reporting structure (which employees report to which team leader or department manager). An organizational chart is a visual often used to document the reporting structure (Figure 8.2).

Hierarchical Structure

Most human services organizations in the United States are structured as hierarchies. Although human services organizations vary widely in size and scope, there are some typical structures that apply. In nonprofit organizations, the group at the top of the organizational chart is the board of directors, whose governing responsibilities were discussed previously.

The CEO or ED reports to the board. This person is responsible for implementing the organization's mission and goals by managing its financial health, day-to-day operations, and internal and external relationships. The CEO/ED's leadership responsibilities

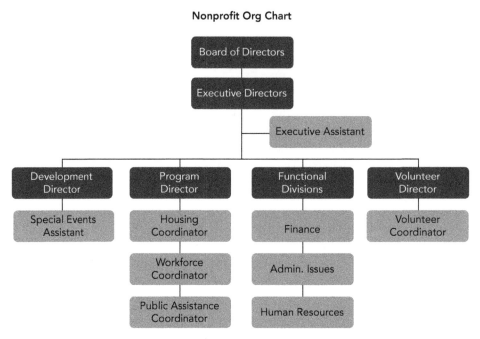

FIGURE 8.2 Non-profit Organizational Chart *Source*: Image via Donorbox nonprofit blog

make it unlikely that they will perform any of the direct service roles associated with the organization's operations. Rather, they supervise the heads of programs and teams responsible for providing community-facing work such as case management, counseling, provision of services, advocacy, and program coordination and evaluation. The ED also supervises leadership of other key units and activities such as human resources, accounting, fundraising (also called development), communications, and information technology. A CEO/ED's day may include a range of activities, from approving program budgets and equipment purchases to meeting with potential donors and community members. The ability to manage relationships effectively is critical to their success. This includes internal relationships with board members and staff and external relationships with funders, community members, partner organizations, coalitions, and other stakeholders.

Alternative Structures
Although hierarchies are the most common type of structure within human services organizations, other models are used as well. Some organizations striving to disrupt power imbalances have found that hierarchical organizational models do not align with their values. During the 1970s, many organizations addressing intimate partner violence and sexual assault utilized an organizational structure known as collectivist, flat, or lateral, in which responsibilities were often rotated, and no one person held more decision-making authority than another. In these models, there can still be teams; however, decision-making is generally done using a consensus-based method.

Some organizations use a cooperative model, which relies on some of the same decision-making strategies as collectives, but they are generally organized around a product, service, or resource. In these models, people may use their labor to contribute to the operation of an organization or to leverage greater purchasing power. For example, in a child care cooperative, a group of families may share responsibility for providing child care and purchasing supplies.

Supervision

The organizational models discussed in the previous section utilize different philosophies and policies around supervisor–supervisee relationships. Effective supervision is critical in all types of human services organizations. A structured system of supervision allows organizations to ensure that they provide consistent, ethical, and high-quality services to the individuals and communities they serve. Supervisory relationships can also ensure that organizational policies are understood and adhered to, while concurrently providing mentorship to younger or less experienced staff. Supervisory positions generally require a specified educational background and a minimum number of years of experience in the field or in a similar management role.

Human services students commonly engage in activities such as service-learning, internships, and field placements. In these situations, the role of the supervisor is critical in helping students understand organizational policies and practices and in the development of skills. Supervisors can also help students reflect on the ways that their attitudes and values might be influencing their work with clients or community members. When pursuing licensure, such as in clinical social work practice, supervision is a requirement to meet the standards set by the state. Due to the sensitive and intensive nature of the work, it is critical that human services professionals continually have an opportunity to self-reflect and identify areas of growth to provide the highest level of care and to avoid burnout. Although there are some roles in which you might be working one-on-one with clients or client systems, it is important to contextualize yourself within the larger mission of the organization.

8.7 MUTUAL AID "SOLIDARITY NOT CHARITY"

Although mutual aid models received significant attention during the COVID-19 pandemic, these models have been a mainstay throughout U.S. history, particularly for underserved Black, Indigenous, and people of color communities (Figure 8.3). In the 18th century, people who were formerly enslaved could not depend on White institutions for aid, so the need for collective support prompted the creation of **mutual aid organizations**. Among the first was the Free African Society, founded in 1787 in Philadelphia. Members in good standing could expect a number of benefits from the mutual aid fund. Particularly in the first years of the society, important aspects of support for members included payments for burials and providing financial aid for widows and other family members of the deceased, finding apprenticeships for children to learn a trade, and paying tuition for members' children if places in free schools were not available. Over time, society expanded to care for the social and economic well-being of its members by helping newcomers to the city feel welcome and by providing assistance during periods of financial difficulty brought on by unemployment, injury, or illness. During the yellow

FIGURE 8.3 Mutual Aid: "Just Enough" *Source:* Brenna Quinlan, 2019, digital artwork

fever epidemic of 1793, members nursed the sick, transported the ill to quarters outside the city where they could be quarantined and given medical aid, dug graves, and buried the dead.

The Black Panthers were popularly known during the 1960s as a group that sought to promote social, economic, and political power for Black people in the United States. However, they were also famous for creating systems of mutual aid, including medical clinics, school lunches, and services for the elderly (Spade, 2020). Mutual aid activities have continued in the United States, particularly after catastrophic events such as 9/11 and Hurricane Katrina. Mutual aid organizations have provided critical immediate relief for individuals during the COVID-19 pandemic and have inspired communities to consider what is possible through these models.

Some mutual aid models operate in the periphery of capitalism and often address important issues such as health, food, and shelter. Others coordinate support for different reasons. Mutual help groups, also called self-help groups or support groups, are nonprofessional peer-led models that provide support for social and emotional needs of their participants. Among the most well-known are Alcoholics Anonymous (AA), Narcotics Anonymous, Gamblers Anonymous, Sex and Love Addicts, Depression Anonymous, and Self-Management and Recovery Training (SMART) Recovery. Although their philosophies about substance use disorders or mental health care may differ, they are grounded in principles of peer support. Their models and practices do not work for everyone, but they have been shown to be effective for many. "Mutual help groups such as AA can help people make and maintain beneficial changes to their alcohol use while also helping to reduce health care costs by providing a free and responsive recovery support system" (Kelly & Yeterian, 2011, p. 352).

8.8 NETWORKS OF ORGANIZATIONS

Human services organizations do not function in a vacuum. They also partner with other organizations to work toward shared goals. When we examine the interactions between and among these organizations and their collective impact, you can also think of them as cells and organs within the body. Some are like cells grouped together working with similar goals within an organ, and others are like organs that work together as parts of systems that in turn must work together in order for the body to function. Whether they are formal or informal, hierarchical or cooperative, large or small, these organizations perform critical functions, and "the whole is greater than the sum of their parts." Just like with the human body, individual parts of the system, or groups of systems, may not function optimally at all times, and sometimes they may work together to achieve greater impact.

Organizations that operate on a local level often lack a statewide, regional, or national view or voice. To be more effective, they may join larger networks, sometimes called alliances or coalitions, that may be organized around one or more factors such as a social need, population, or geographic area. These networks provide a range of benefits for members, including training, cost-savings programs, and an advocacy platform. Effective communication and resource sharing benefit organization staff, policymakers, and end users. For example, the Alabama Coalition for Immigrant Justice is a grassroots, statewide network of individuals and organizations that works to advance and defend the rights of immigrants in Alabama. The coalition consists of six nonprofit organizations and hundreds of individual members. Another example is the Iowa Coalition Against Sexual Assault, which represents dozens of organizations across the state "to improve services for survivors of sexual harassment, abuse, and assault, and to prevent sexual violence before it occurs."

Many statewide entities also participate in national organizations such as the National Council of Nonprofits, allowing information to flow both up from the local level and down to organizations from the state and national level. Fox (2010) explains that "networks and coalitions involve interconnected systems of communication, grounding the emergence of a transnational public sphere" (p. 486).

SPOTLIGHT ON SERVICE-LEARNING

When you participate in a service-learning activity or placement, understanding how the organization is structured, governed, managed, and funded can help you understand what you see and experience.

1. Review the organizational chart. How are leadership and supervisory responsibilities distributed?
2. Identify members of the board of directors. What are their qualifications and relationship to the organization? Does the board's composition reflect the population served by the organization?
3. Explore Charity Navigator, an online evaluator of nonprofit organizations. See what you can learn about your organization's funding and financial health. This information will help you understand how the organization functions and provide perspective on the contribution you are making within the organization as a whole.

SUMMARY

- Most states have an umbrella health and human services agency that oversees several branch operations statewide. Although the agency structure and organization vary by state, these agencies work to meet critical and often immediate needs.
- The nonprofit sector has evolved to conduct much of the work society considers to be important for collective well-being. Nonprofits are defined as "charitable organizations" based on their tax-exempt status.
- Nonprofit organizations secure funding from a variety of sources, including local, state, and federal government agencies; foundations; businesses and corporations; and individual donors. Funding methods include government sources such as contracts for services, grants, and reimbursements, along with corporate giving, revenue generation, and private philanthropy.
- Nonprofits are governed by a board of directors, whose members must adhere to the three duties of care, loyalty, and obedience.
- Nonprofit organizations evaluate their programs and services using a variety of methods, including interviews, surveys, focus groups, observation, and analysis of documents and records.
- Most human services organizations have hierarchical structures, although other models exist.
- A structured system of supervision provides the means for human services organizations to ensure that they provide consistent, ethical, and high-quality services to the individuals and communities they serve.
- Mutual aid is a decentralized organizational model sometimes used to provide critical services during disasters; it may also involve collective support for members. Mutual help groups may be led by nonprofessional peers.
- Individual organizations are often part of local, state, regional, or national networks or coalitions. Networks may be organized around one or more factors, including a social need, population, or geographic area, and can provide benefits such as enhanced communication channels and cost-saving programs.

REVIEW QUESTIONS

Assessment Questions

1. Explain the tax status of nonprofit organizations and how they must be operated to maintain this status.
2. What is the most common structural organization for nonprofits?
3. Why do nonprofit organizations engage in evaluation? What are some methods for conducting evaluations?
4. What is mutual aid? How has it played a significant role in history?

Reflection Questions

1. Think about the various ways that nonprofits can be funded. What do you think are some of the benefits and drawbacks of each source of funding?

2. How can clarity about its mission statement help a nonprofit organization achieve impact in its community?
3. When have you experienced high-quality supervision in a past job? How did it impact your success? What were the key characteristics of the supervisor?
4. What is the potential of mutual aid for solving complex social and economic problems?

REFERENCES

Board Source. (2017). *Roles and responsibilities*. https://boardsource.org/fundamental-topics-of-nonprofit-board-service/roles-responsibilities

Faulk, L., Kim, M., Derrick-Mills, T., Boris, E. T., Tomasko, L., Hakizimana, N., Chen, T., Kim, M., & Nath, L. (2021). *Nonprofit trends and impacts 2021*. Urban Institute.

Fox, J. A. (2010). *Coalitions and networks* (Working paper series qt1x05031j). Center for Global, International and Regional Studies, UC Santa Cruz.

Frumkin, P. (2002). *On being nonprofit: A conceptual and policy primer*. Harvard University Press.

Internal Revenue Code U.S.C. § 501(c)(3) (1986).

Kelly, J. F., & Yeterian, J. D. (2011). The role of mutual-help groups in extending the framework of treatment. *Alcohol Research & Health*, *33*(4), 350–355.

National Center for Charitable Statistics. (2020, June). *The nonprofit sector in brief 2019*. https://nccs.urban.org/publication/nonprofit-sector-brief-2019#the-nonprofit-sector-in-brief-2019

Osili, U., Zarins, S., Bergdoll, J., Kou, X., Grossnickle, T., Schipp, D., Canada, A., Adrillo, T., Ernst, L., Knutson, J., Coleman, A., & Vernetta, W. (2018). *The impact of diversity: Understanding how nonprofit board diversity affects philanthropy, leadership, and board engagement*. Indiana University Press.

Spade, D. (2020). Solidarity not charity: Mutual aid for mobilization and survival. *Social Text*, *38*(1), 131–151.

CHAPTER 9

Community-Based Practice and Organizing

Learning Objectives

After completing this chapter, you will be able to:

9.1. Explain the similarities and differences between community involvement, community development, and community organizing.

9.2. Briefly describe the origins of community organizing and how its history influences contemporary efforts to bring about positive social change.

9.3. Explain the role of community organizers.

9.4. List the key principles and strategies used in community organizing.

9.5. Describe how just transition frameworks are used to improve quality of life in communities where they form the basis for social change.

Communities have the power to support individual well-being, as a tool for social change. Black Lives Matter. Stop Asian Hate. Me Too. Occupy Wall Street. All of these social protest movements have been covered extensively by the news media. What do these movements have in common? What can they teach us about activism and social change?

Individuals do not always have the power to create positive change. However, through collaboration, people with common goals can work together to bring about positive change. In human services, we acknowledge that social change can occur at all levels of society. In direct service settings, we approach change on the individual, family, or group level (micro level). When the goal is to change systems, we do this by developing programs, creating networks, and working to change public policy (meso and macro level). Activism and community organizing are methods used to empower individuals and groups to create lasting change for larger groups and communities. Human services professionals have a unique perspective about the impacts and shortcomings of policies and the inequities inherent in our institutions. Understanding the ways in which community organizing can bring about change will serve you throughout your career.

9.1 COMMUNITY INVOLVEMENT, DEVELOPMENT, AND ORGANIZING

Community can be defined in various ways. Place-based definitions consist of neighborhoods, towns, or cities. The definition of community can also encompass cultural groups and others with shared identities, such as BIPOC or LGBTQ+ groups. **Social action** relies on collective efforts and power to bring about positive change for communities.

The U.S. Department of Housing and Urban Development (HUD) developed a Healthy Community Index (HCI) with criteria for what is considered a livable community. The HCI provides an indication of the quality of life that residents are likely to experience. These measurements include the following:

- Access to fresh, quality food
- Access to health care
- Access to parks and open space
- Excessive housing cost burden (housing costs are 35 percent or more of household income)
- High school graduation rate
- Proportion of neighborhood infants born with low birth weight
- Proportion of neighborhood located close to industrial facilities reporting toxic air emissions
- Reading proficiency

You can see how the HCI considers a wide range of factors that determine the health and wellness of a community. Unsurprisingly, residents of low-resource communities experience hardships in many of these areas. The HCI measures provide a sense of how well institutions and systems are functioning (or not functioning) within a community and whether existing policies are serving the needs of residents. Community involvement, community development, and community organizing are ways in which improvements in policy, institutions, and systems can be achieved.

Community Involvement

Community involvement can be a meaningful way to develop and deepen community cohesion and improve local conditions. Being engaged in one's community can enhance overall well-being and deepen social connection and social capital. Volunteering with a parent–teacher organization and participating in community clean-ups or fundraisers are examples of community involvement that fall under the broad category of civic engagement. Robert Putnam's renowned book, *Bowling Alone*, explains that deep social networks and community involvement enhance the quality of life for residents, even if they themselves are not directly involved (Putnam, 2000). Such activities can improve the quality of life for members of a community, but they are not generally designed with the aim of changing policy, institutions, or systems or disrupting power.

Community Development

Cities, towns, and villages contain "systems of systems" that include education, housing, business, recreation, law enforcement, and human services organizations. Sometimes these systems work well together, but there is always room for improvement. **Community development**, sometimes called community economic development (CED), promotes higher functioning communities through a process that "involves participants in constructive activities and processes to produce improvements, opportunities, structures, goods, and services that increase the quality of life, build individual and collective capacities, and enhance social solidarity" (Staples, 2004, p. 7). Human services professionals are a part of a larger constellation of social change efforts, and human services organizations are likely to be involved in community development efforts.

Community development activities consist of revitalizing the economic, physical, and social infrastructures and networks of a specific community or set of neighborhoods. Activities include gathering input and direction from affected residents, thus empowering both individuals and institutions within the geographically defined area. Community development benefits residents and ensures that discriminatory practices are avoided in the work (Soifer et al., 2014, p. 7).

One important role of the CED model is to provide opportunities for low-income communities to develop expanded access to affordable housing and employment (Box 9.1). CED grants fund Community Development Corporations that support low-income neighborhoods through the development of resources such as new business incubators and manufacturing or agricultural initiatives. Some economic development agencies are central hubs of the community, serving as a community center, fostering collaboration among many social and educational services.

Asset-based community development (ABCD) represents a meso-level practice that has been adapted since its first iteration in the early 1990s (McKnight, 2017). ABCD supports economic and social development within communities and uses community knowledge and skills to support community goals and objectives. Applying an ABDC mindset resonates with the strengths-based perspective discussed in previous chapters. The Northeast Assets Leadership Project describes seven attributes of ABCD (Walker, 2006):

- Use an asset lens to examine community strengths.
- Be inclusive of all citizens.

BOX 9.1	Promise Zone Initiative

Where we live is predictive of our access and opportunities for education, employment, and economic self-sufficiency (Chetty et al., 2014). The Promise Zone (PZ) Initiative considers the role of community as the point of economic intervention, rather than at the individual level (The White House, 2014). Developed with HUD in 2014, the PZ Initiative strives to improve the quality of life within "distressed" communities (Kitchens & Wallace, 2022). It focuses on jobs, education, housing, and community violence. The PZ Initiative also partners with the AmeriCorps VISTA program to capitalize on local community engagement.

The Harlem Children's Zone is an example of a "cradle-to-college" initiative within a PZ neighborhood. Per this model, high-quality early childhood care programs are paired with high-quality preschool and kindergarten through grade 12 programs. This educational focus is linked to access to health care, through school-based clinics and parent and community engagement.

- Map the assets to provide details of community strengths and use the process to map assets as a way to connect within and between community members.
- Take immediate action to improve the community.
- Center decision-making within the community to reflect and meet community goals.
- Facilitate bottom-up leadership to support, rather than lead, community initiatives.
- Cultivate a sense of community ownership.

Community Organizing

Throughout history, humans have actively resisted oppressive forces. Sometimes via non-violent resistance and sometimes by force, people have organized themselves to oppose the status quo. When communities seek to disrupt the status quo, to disrupt business as usual, they employ "people power." **Community organizing** involves efforts to pressure leaders, groups, or individuals for more structural forms of change through community organizing direct action.

When an issue consists of many locations, organizations, and platforms, seeking to shift multiple institutions, social norms, and attitudes, it is understood as a broader social movement. Black Lives Matter (BLM) started as a social media hashtag and is now a global movement consisting of many social movement organizations that use community organizing strategies as they strive to achieve social and institutional change to end anti-Blackness and other forms of racism.

Many of the techniques used by BLM are similar to other forms of organizing, and there are some overlaps with community development (Table 9.1). Fisher and DeFilippis (2015) define community organizing broadly as the "process of building power through involving a constituency in identifying problems they share and the solutions to those problems" (p. 364). Staples (2004) defines community organizing as the "collective action by community members drawing on the strength of numbers, participatory processes, and indigenous leadership to decrease power disparities and achieve shared goals for social change" (pp. 1–2). Whether organizing is place-based, issue-based, or both, the techniques and strategies used are often the same. Staples (2004) explains that "social action brings people together to convince, pressure, or coerce external decision-makers to meet collective goals either to act in a specified manner or to modify or stop certain activities" (p. 9).

TABLE 9.1   Overlaps Between Community Development and Community Organizing

Community Development	Intersections and Overlap	Community Organizing
Change-makers work collaboratively; conflict does not need to be central	Focuses on structural change	Conflict is common and done strategically
Often led by formal entities or organizations	Led by people from the community	Utilizes a grassroots approach
	Engages community members in the process	

9.2 ORIGINS OF COMMUNITY ORGANIZING

The origins of community organizing are most often associated with Saul Alinsky, community and political activist. In the 1930s, Alinsky joined with other like-minded people in the meatpacking district of Chicago, which was a hub of community organizing and social action. The meatpacking yards in Chicago were a place of unsafe, unsanitary, and exploitative work conditions. Many people today are familiar with these conditions from reading Upton Sinclair's 1906 book, *The Jungle*.

Alinsky's Principles and Practices

Alinsky learned organizing practices from the labor unions of the time (Schutz & Miller, 2015). Building on these lessons and working with local resident Joseph Meegan, in 1939, he helped found the Back of the Yards Neighborhood Council (BYNC), a collaboration of ethnic schools, churches, and various social clubs. The BYNC motto was "We the people will work out our own destiny." The organization used confrontational methods such as protests in and outside factories to fight for fair treatment for workers and economic improvements. Still in operation, the BYNC is a community organization whose mission is "to enhance the general welfare of all residents, organizations, and businesses in our service area."

Alinsky was a prolific organizer, and in 1940 he collaborated with other local leaders to create the Industrial Areas Foundation (IAF), a national community organizing network consisting of multifaith organizations, unions, and other civic groups (Graf, 2020). The IAF trained community organizers based on the following principles (Graf, 2020):

- Importance of power
- Self-interests (your own, your allies', and your opponents')
- Relational power: one-to-one relationship building

IAF supported the creation of the Community Service Organization, an important California Latinx organization that trained labor and civil rights activist Cesar Chavez.

Alinsky continued to refine his approach by supporting organizing efforts throughout the country, including working with Minister Franklin Florence in Rochester, New York, where issues of racial inequity and injustice were profound (Figure 9.1). Malcolm X gave assurance to the Black community in Rochester that Alinsky could be trusted

FIGURE 9.1 Franklin Florence (second from right) continued to be an important civil rights leader, as seen here when he and Raymond Scott (left) were arrested during a 2008 protest at the County Office Building. *Source*: Photo by Jeremy Moule/provided by CITY Magazine (Rochester, NY).

(Beck & Purcell, 2013). Alinsky supported FIGHT (Freedom, Independence, God, Honor, Today), a grassroots organization that demanded more employment and training opportunities at the Eastman Kodak Company for Black residents (Tiffany, 2021).

Kodak had reneged on an agreement to give jobs to local people. Alinsky and members of FIGHT managed to buy some of the company's stock and gain control of additional shares by proxy from sympathetic shareholders. This gave them the right to attend the 1967 shareholders' meeting. Alinsky gave press and television interviews, stirring up interest and tension about the issue. On the day of the shareholders' meeting, several hundred people from Rochester protested outside, and Alinsky and Black leaders from FIGHT marched into the meeting. This was a dramatic act—Black people walking into a situation dominated by White power was almost unheard of in 1960s America (Beck & Purcell, 2013).

This campaign ultimately resulted in a change in hiring practices at Kodak and many other area corporations (Wadhwani, 1997). Alinsky continued to influence community organizing and chronicled his approach in his seminal book *Rules for Radicals* in 1971.

Influence on Modern-Day Movements

Community organizers and grassroots movements from the past influence modern movements, and many contemporary organizers self-identify as working in the Alinsky style or tradition. The strategies developed by Alinsky and his peers are the core of most contemporary campaigns, regardless of their political leaning. For example, the Tea Party movement that emerged after the election of Barack Obama used these tried-and-true organizing strategies. Advocating for a smaller government and rejecting what would become the Affordable Health Care Act, a network of local Tea Party groups emerged throughout the nation using many of the tactics developed by Alinsky, including person-to-person community-based outreach and door-to-door canvassing, paired with disruptive tactics in an attempt to stop the creation of a national health insurance program (Fisher & DeFilippis, 2015). Although Alinsky was well known for his work, the organizations and movements that he supported were often led by members of the impacted community. These types of activities and organizations are often referred to as "grassroots" because they are "bottom up" in structure.

Some other examples include the following:

- Many Asian American activists, such as Grace Lee Boggs and Yuri Kochiyama, directly learned from Black organizers such as James Boggs (Grace's husband) and Malcolm X to understand the importance of forming collective antiracist alliances (Aguilar-San Juan, 2015). Kochiyama, whose family was imprisoned in an internment camp, was known to be grateful for reparations for descendants of Japanese Americans; however, she fought for the majority of her life to also gain reparations for descendants of slavery (Kochiyama, 1994).
- Fans of K-pop musical group BTS in 2020 famously used their online fandom (the BTS ARMY) to disrupt numerous racist events in the name of social justice and spread the message of antiracism through many areas of Asia and the United States (Lee & Kao, 2021).
- Leaders of the Stop Asian Hate movement, which gained nationwide traction from 2020 to 2021 in the United States, learned from how social media, attention to intersectional identity, and decentralized leadership functioned effectively in the BLM organization (e.g., Ho, 2020).

9.3 ROLE OF COMMUNITY ORGANIZERS

Community organizers come from all types of backgrounds. Some hold degrees in social work, community development, or law, and others are trained by networks of professional community organizations (Fisher & DeFilippis, 2015). Early in his career, President Barack Obama was a community organizer.

> Community organizing provides a way to merge various strategies for neighborhood empowerment. Organizing begins with the premise that (1) the problems facing inner-city communities do not result from a lack of effective solutions, but from a lack of power to implement these solutions; (2) that the only way for communities to build long-term power is by organizing people and money around a common vision; and (3) that a viable organization can only be achieved if a broadly based indigenous leadership—and not one or two charismatic leaders—can knit together the diverse interests of their local institutions. (Obama, 2012, p. 29)

The role of a community organizer is to facilitate a process that aligns the goals of the **campaign**, an organized plan designed to achieve a goal, with the best strategy. Community organizers listen and help articulate the concerns of the group, and they work alongside community members to provide technical support and help facilitate a larger sustained plan for change. These plans will often encompass several campaigns designed by people impacted by the issue (Box 9.2).

People who participate in organizing activities or campaigns are sometimes called **activists**. Their activities can range from hosting listening sessions to scheduling meetings with elected officials or designing and implementing actions such as rallies or marches. They may engage in creative communication/protest tactics such as a guerilla projection, which consists of projecting a still or moving image onto a building or other public place without permission, with the goal of promoting awareness of a particular issue (Figure 9.2).

FIGURE 9.2 Guerilla projection in Brooklyn, NY *Source*: The Illuminator Collective

9.4 PRINCIPLES AND STRATEGIES OF COMMUNITY ORGANIZING

Heather Booth, community organizer and activist, established the Midwest Academy in Chicago in 1973. The academy has emerged as a leader in teaching strategy, tactics, and movement building to many organizations, including the American Civil Liberties Union, the Audubon Society, and NARAL Pro-Choice Texas. The academy provides frameworks for how to design and implement an effective campaign. It encourages groups to have broad goals and many subgoals. Determining which goal to lead with is critical to both the short- and long-term success of a campaign.

The Midwest Academy advocates three core principles for direct action:

- Win real, immediate, concrete improvements in people's lives.
- Give people a sense of their own power.
- Alter the relationships of power.

Using both an internal and an external focus, the Midwest Academy suggests that community organizing groups can change power relations by doing the following:

- Building strong lasting organizations
- Changing laws and regulations
- Electing people who share your perspective and priorities

Recruitment and Communication

Alinsky-style organizing emphasizes person-to-person communication to develop relationships and engage people in campaigns. Organizers may map their campaigns to better understand who is impacted by the issue and who might be interested in participating. In workplace organizing, this can be very clear. When engaging in issue- or place-based activities, identifying potential members can be more challenging.

People's willingness to actively support causes varies across a wide spectrum. Milbrath and Goel (1977) developed a typology of political participation to articulate levels of engagement seen in our political systems (Dobratz, 2015):

- *Apathetics*: Those who are withdrawn from the political process
- *Spectators*: Those showing minimal involvement, who are engaged at a very basic level
- *Gladiators*: Those functioning as "active combatants" and leaders

In community organizing, you can see similar levels of engagement. This list might also include "foot soldiers," people who routinely show up and inform other people about the campaign. Understanding people's level of commitment to a cause or outcome is key to engaging them during the recruitment phase and for promoting leadership.

In organizing, leaders (gladiators) are identified from the impacted community. They are connected to a wide network within the community. They can motivate others, communicate effectively, and have an ability to listen and magnify the concerns of the group. Identifying leadership within the organization and taking time to develop and encourage engagement are all part of the organizer's job. When a foot soldier with leadership potential is identified, an organizer might provide support and guidance to help elevate that person into a leadership role.

The National Education Association identified important ways to listen and communicate during one-on-one recruitment meetings. Listen for the following:

- Issues: Topics, problems, concerns, and public policy that people care about.
- Interests: A person's stake in an issue.
- Values: The moral principles people live by.
- Capacity: What an individual can contribute to an issue or group (e.g., money, time, special skills, networks).
- Commitment: What an individual is actually willing to do. A person's commitment is directly related to the depth of their interest. (p. 3)

Issue Framing

> Framing is what we choose to say and how we choose to say it. But it's also what we leave unsaid.
>
> —Kendall-Taylor and Gibbons (2018, n.p.)

How we understand issues influences what we believe we should do about them. When someone is directly impacted by an unjust system or action, their understanding is different from that of someone who has learned about it via news reports or social media. Much of our understanding is derived from *how* we came to understand an issue. Issue framing considers how we express who is involved and impacted. For example, when advocates were fighting for paid family medical leave and wage replacement during job absence, at the state level, they intentionally framed this issue broadly to demonstrate that many people will have the need for wage replacement to care for a family member, even individuals without children. When paid family leave is framed as a maternity leave issue, it limits the number of people who see the value. When the issue is framed as necessary support for multigenerational caregiving, this expands the focus from families with small children to all families.

Implicit values can be embedded into the language of framing. Are we appealing to someone's emotions or to their reason? Researchers studying campaigns for same-sex marriage found that framing that focused on love (Figure 9.3) versus rights or equity resonated with a broader section of the population (see Kendall-Taylor & Gibbons [2018] or Harrison & Michelson [2017]). Developing effective communication strategies and adjusting as needed are parts of any campaign.

Targets, Allies, and Opponents

Organizers may engage in a power-mapping exercise to determine for a given issue who are the decision-makers who have real power to make a change. Targets can and often do consist of many people. Targets can consist of people who hold elected office or individuals who are part of a governing board, such as a board of trustees. Organizers typically

FIGURE 9.3   Rally celebrating the legalization of same-sex marriage in all 50 states in 2015. *Source: The Times-Picayune/The Advocate.*

develop specific strategies for each target, which can range from active allies to those who are completely opposed (Figure 9.4):

- Active allies: People who support the cause and are fighting alongside members/ leaders
- Passive allies: People who support the cause but are not (yet) doing anything about it
- Neutrals: The unengaged and uninformed
- Passive opposition: People who do not support the cause but are not actively working against it
- Active opposition: People who do not support the cause and are actively organizing against it

Sometimes, groups with similar goals or values are working on the issue from a different focus or perspective; these groups may become allies. Active allies are critical for amplifying and expanding your base of support. In the campaign for paid family leave

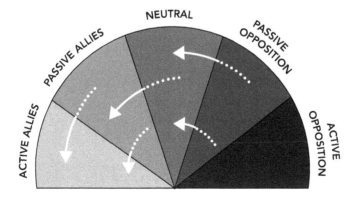

FIGURE 9.4   Spectrum of Allies *Source:* George Lakey, Training for Change

in Massachusetts, there were many active allies, including labor unions. At the same time, there were also many groups in opposition, such as the small business lobby (Gardinier, 2008). In developing a campaign, understanding the opposition is as important as leveraging allies.

Strategic Escalation and the Decision Dilemma

> When authorities ignore the demands of the people, people can pressure them to listen and act. But to win, people must keep up the pressure. A target rarely gives in after one action.
>
> —Kyokusiima (Beautiful Trouble tool kit, n.p.)

Often, the first time the public becomes aware of a campaign is when there is an action, such as a rally. Public actions are rarely the first or only activity that organizers engage in; rather, these are products of lots of time and hard work. Most campaigns design a strategy that begins with lower pressure activities, such as emails, meetings, or calls to decision-makers. Activities then progress to include more public-facing actions, such as marches or protests, to pressure decision-makers.

In the design and execution of a campaign, it is important to put decision-makers into a situation in which they have to make a choice; this is known as a **decision dilemma**. Decision-makers need to know that there will be accountability based on their action(s). Decision-makers should be clear about the "ask" and understand when and why they need to act. They also need to understand the potential range of responses from the group based on their action or inaction.

Student Organizing

For many decades, student organizing has been one of the most vital forms of activism in existence. In recent years, student organizers have pressured their respective administrations to lessen the environmental footprint of their campus and to more effectively prevent and respond to on-campus sexual assault and racist structures and policies. The student-led divestment campaign has focused on getting universities to stop investing endowment funds into fossil fuel companies. Such campaigns have taken years to develop traction and produce results; for example, in late 2021, Harvard University finally announced that it would divest and no longer allow any of its $42 billion endowment to be invested in fossil fuel enterprises. This did not happen without intense student pressure, and it took nearly 10 years to achieve this outcome.

On-campus community organizers may have a larger goal but begin their efforts with smaller, winnable campaigns that allow participants to see some success and recruit additional members while setting themselves up for their larger ambitions. Organizers engage in a thoughtful process of identifying both what to focus on and how to apply pressure (Figure 9.5).

TRY IT YOURSELF

What issues currently exist on your campus that you would like to see changed? What groups or allies would you seek out to support a community organizing effort?

BOX 9.2   Help Wanted: Hiring a Community Organizer, Job Posting

The Carolina Federation is a statewide organization that brings local people together across race and the rural–urban divide to build political and electoral power in their own communities and across North Carolina. We are hiring two Lead Organizers to lead our efforts to grow grassroots political power in county-level chapters across North Carolina. At a time when the right-wing still holds power in North Carolina and far too many campaigns overlook the importance of long-term investment in local communities, we are developing a bold approach to multi-racial organizing and voter engagement for our state. Our approach to building power is defined by our relentless commitment to bringing new people into political action, our deep investment in local leadership and our intentional integration of cultural work with community and electoral organizing. By unleashing the full potential of our diverse communities, we can create real change in the lives of our people, win elections that were previously unwinnable and transform the political terrain. By rooting ourselves in our movement traditions, our grassroots democratic practice and our solidarity with each other, we can dismantle the concentrated corporate power that seeks to control our government and our economy.

About the Lead Organizer Position

In this moment of both challenge and opportunity, we are looking to bring on two (2) experienced Lead Organizers to guide our grassroots political power building in the Triad and the Southeast.

We are seeking Lead Organizers who would:

1) be thrilled to be part of growing and innovative independent political organization
2) fit our culture of courageous leadership and playful camaraderie, and
3) share a deep love for people and a ferocious commitment to power and transformation.

These two positions will be the beating heart of our statewide base-building efforts, responsible for leading the innovation, implementation and expansion of our county-level work, while supporting and developing our talented county-level organizers and their exceptional member leaders. Broadly, each Lead Organizer will be responsible for the following:

- Direct supervision of county-level organizers with weekly check-ins, regular coaching and deep attention to their development as movement leaders.

- Facilitation, coordination and development of county-level member leadership teams.
- Support for member-led issue and electoral campaigns at the county and statewide levels.
- Significant involvement in the formation of one to two new county-level chapters.
- The Lead Organizers will report to the Organizing Director.

Qualities We're Looking for in Our Lead Organizers

Our organization values the recruitment of staff with strong political alignment and key leadership qualities that match both the role and the kind of work we do. This is because we believe that skills and competencies can be taught, while values, alignment and leadership qualities are more deeply ingrained. Because the work we do is political, fast-paced, deeply relational, and about power, we look for many of the following qualities:

Politically Clear: You know why building power through elections, issue campaigns, and transformative organizing is essential. You are convinced that racial, economic, gender, and environmental justice are what we need, and you lift up the leadership and dignity of working-class people and people of color.

A Leader Who Unleashes More Leadership: You take responsibility for motivating others, coordinating effective collective action and building powerful teams—even in the face of obstacles. But most of all you unleash leadership in others, igniting responsibility and ownership in those you lead.

Interdependent: You bring your best, rely on the strengths of others and know that we are responsible for each other's well-being.

Courageous and Determined: You draw from deep values and beliefs, so you continue to take action towards goals, even in the face of change, fear, loss, conflict, and uncertainty.

Ambitious, Innovative, Relentless: You believe that you and others are capable of greatness. You believe not only that we can win but that we have a duty to win. When things get difficult you get creative and keep trying and learning until we succeed.

FIGURE 9.5   Emma Sulkowicz carries her mattress with her everywhere in protest to the university's handling of her sexual assault. Her action became a symbol of organizers and activists across the country. *Source*: Andrew Burton/Staff.

9.5 JUST TRANSITION PRINCIPLES

The notion of a **just transition** is compelling for those committed to social change. Just transition is the core principle that a healthy economy and a clean environment can and should coexist and that the process should not come at the cost of workers' or community residents' health, environment, jobs, or economic assets (Just Transition Alliance, 2020).

Using this approach, advocates fight for economic models that are regenerative (circular) instead of extractive (Figure 9.6). Regenerative economic approaches structure service, commerce, and resources in ways that benefit the communities where they are housed. Extractive economies are based on activities that benefit individuals and businesses outside of the community. The regenerative approach allows community residents and institutions to maintain some control over their economic autonomy, quality of life, and environmental realities. Working toward a just transition requires the application of community development practices to create institutions and networks that meet the needs of residents and community organizing to change social and economic policies.

Communities working within the just transition model often partner with labor unions, advocacy coalitions, environmental groups, mutual aid organizations, and small

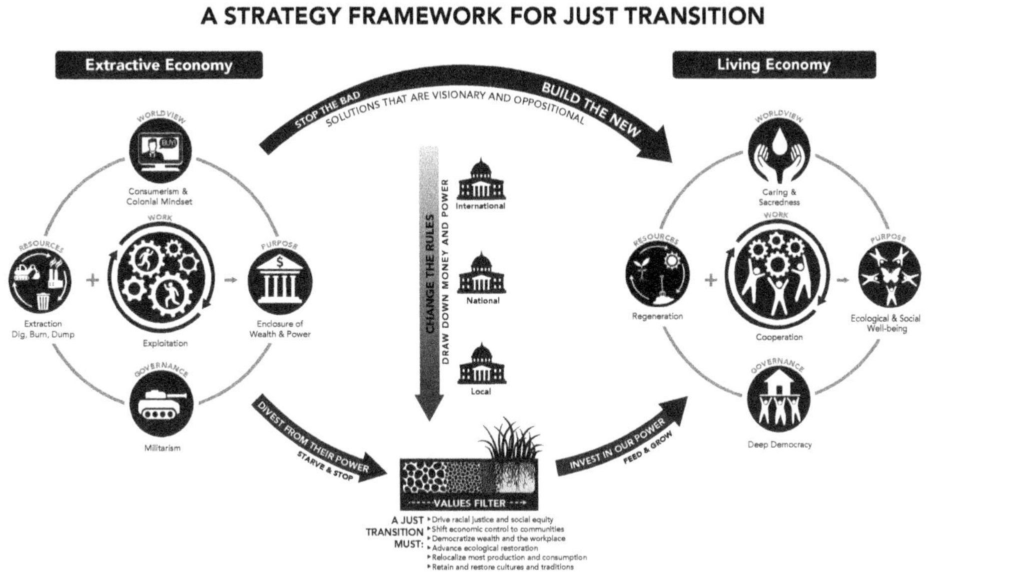

A STRATEGY FRAMEWORK FOR JUST TRANSITION

FIGURE 9.6 Two economic models: extractive versus regenerative. *Source*: Developed by Movement Generation with Climate Justice Alliance. Icons designed by Micah Bazant; framework graphic designed by Design Action Collective.

businesses. Organizational activities may include job training or retraining for community members, home ownership programs, facilitation of a community **land trust**, promoting environmentally sound energy practices, and/or fostering community or arts enrichment programs (Just Transition Alliance, 2020). Because this model strives for profound structural change, tools of organizing are often applied to shift larger policies that destabilize or harm communities, such as housing and environmental laws.

An example of a just transition model can be found on the West Side of Buffalo, New York. A key facilitator there is PUSH Buffalo, which stands for People United for Sustainable Housing. Using a just transition framework, PUSH Buffalo "mobilize residents to create strong neighborhoods with quality, affordable housing; to expand local hiring opportunities; and to advance economic and environmental justice in Buffalo" (PUSH, 2019). Their accomplishments include the following:

- Building green, affordable housing
- Creating a sustainable workforce training center for local residents in geothermal, solar, and sustainable landscaping
- Creating a co-op academy to foster the creation of just businesses
- Providing youth development opportunities

PUSH recognizes that affordable, sustainable homes, a healthy local economy, and job prospects have a huge potential for making real, lasting change and improving the lives of community residents. In addition to these initiatives, they also participate in larger advocacy efforts through campaigns centered around tenants' rights and the creation of a net-zero carbon economy.

SPOTLIGHT ON SERVICE-LEARNING

Think about these questions. They can also be the basis for small-group discussion.

1. How does your organization use framing to articulate its work?
2. What, if any, community organizing strategies have been used to develop the community where your organization is located?
3. Do staff in your organization participate in lobbying or other advocacy activities? If yes, how have these activities contributed to positive change in the community?

SUMMARY

- Communities consist of shared space, identities, or goals held by a group. Through collaboration, individuals can work together to achieve common goals and objectives.
- ABCD represents a meso-level practice that has been adapted since it originated in the early 1990s. ABCD can be broadly used to support economic and social development; it relies on community knowledge and skills to support community goals and objectives.
- Sometimes by nonviolent resistance and sometimes by force, people have organized to oppose the status quo and bring about positive change. Community organizing engages individuals and groups in campaigns that work toward structural forms of change.
- Community organizers facilitate processes that align the goals of the campaign with the best strategy. They listen, help articulate the concerns of the group, and work alongside community members to provide technical support and help facilitate a larger sustained plan for change.
- The origins of community organizing are most often associated with Saul Alinsky, who worked during the 1930s to improve working and living conditions in the meatpacking district of Chicago.
- Alinsky's work was based on key principles: importance of power, self-interests (your own, your allies', and your opponents'), and relational power through face-to-face relationship building.
- The three core principles associated with the Midwest Academy, a leader in teaching strategy, tactics, and movement-building, are (a) win real, immediate, concrete improvements in people's lives; (b) give people a sense of their own power; and (c) alter the relationships of power.
- Issue framing considers how ideas in a campaign are best presented to meet stated goals.
- Putting decision-makers into a situation in which they are forced to make a choice is known as creating a decision dilemma. Decision-makers need to know that there will be accountability based on their action (or lack of it).
- The just transition framework is based on the idea that a healthy economy and a clean environment can and should coexist and not come at the cost of workers' or community residents' health, environment, jobs, or economic assets.
- Organizations using this approach advocate for regenerative (circular) economic models that serve the interests of the community instead of extractive models that exploit or take advantage of a community for others' gain.

REVIEW QUESTIONS

Assessment Questions

1. What are some methods of promoting community development? Define asset-based community development and explain its value.
2. Why is the role of a community organizer important? How does organizing overlap with community development?
3. What are the spectrum of allies? Why is it important to understand from a community organizing perspective?
4. Name and describe three community engagement strategies.

Reflection Questions

1. What is an issue that you are passionate about or that is particularly prominent on your campus or in your community? How would you move from identification of a problem to coalition building to delivering on your goals?
2. Who do you know that might be a good community organizer? What are some of their strengths and characteristics that would make them effective in this role?
3. Provide an example of how you could reframe an issue or social problem to resonate with a larger audience.
4. Do you think there are any social issues that can't be addressed through community organizing methods? If yes, what are these issues and why? If no, what issues do you think might be most challenging to address?

REFERENCES

Aguilar-San Juan, K. (2015). "We are extraordinarily lucky to be living in these times": A conversation with Grace Lee Boggs. *Frontiers*, 36, 92–123. https://www.jstor.org/stable/10.5250/fronjwomestud.36.2.0092

Alinsky, S. (1971). *Rules for Radicals*. Random House.

Beck, D., & Purcell, R. (2013). *International community organising: Taking power, making change*. Policy Press.

Chetty, R., Hendren, N., Kline, P., & Saez, E. (2014). Where is the land of opportunity? The geography of intergenerational mobility in the United States. *Quarterly Journal of Economics*, 129, 1553–1623.

Dobratz, B. (2015). *Power, politics, and society: An introduction to political sociology*. Routledge.

Fisher, R., & DeFilippis, J. (2015). Community organizing in the United States. *Community Development Journal*, 50, 363–379.

Gardinier, L. (2008). "We thought we were going to get it done": Examining the paid family leave campaign in Massachusetts. *Journal of Workplace Rights*, 13, 401–419.

Graf, A. (2020). Lessons learned: Stories from a lifetime of organizing. ACTA Publications.

Harrison, B. F., & Michelson, M. R. (2017). What's love got to do with it? Emotion, rationality, and framing LGBT rights. *New Political Science*, 39, 177–197.

Ho, J. (2020). Anti-Asian racism, Black Lives Matter, and COVID-19. *Japan Forum*, 33, 148–159. doi:10.1080/09555803.2020.1821749

Just Transition Alliance. (2020). *What is Just Transition?* http://jtalliance.org/what-is-just-transition

Kendall-Taylor, N., & Gibbons, S. (2018). Framing for Social Change. Stanford Social Innovation Review. https://doi.org/10.48558/PYWW-XF45

Kitchens, C., & Wallace, C. T. (2022). The impact of place-based poverty relief: Evidence from the Federal Promise Zone Program. *Regional Science and Urban Economics*, 95, 103735.

Kochiyama, Y. (1994). The impact of Malcolm X on Asian-American politics and activism. In J. Jennings (Ed.), *Blacks, Latinos, and Asians in urban America: Status and prospects for politics and activism* (pp. 129–141). Praeger.

Kyokusima, (n.d.) Beautiful Trouble Toolkit, https://beautifultrouble.org/toolbox/principle/

Lee, W., & Kao, G. (2021). Why #BlackLivesMatter(s) to K-pop, BTS, and BTS ARMYs. *JASPM Journal, 11*, 70–87. doi:10.5429/2079-3871(2021)v11i1.7en

McKnight, J. (2017). Asset-based community development: the essentials. *ABCD Institute*, 1–4.

Milbrath, L. W., & Goel, M. L. (1977). Political participation: How and why do people get involved in politics? Rand McNally College Publishing Company.

Obama, B. (2012). Why organize? Problems and promise in the inner city. In M. Minkler (Ed.), *Community organizing and community building for health and welfare* (pp. 27–32). Rutgers University Press.

People United for Sustainable Housing. (2019). *PUSH Buffalo annual report.* https://www.pushbuffalo.org/wp-content/uploads/2020/05/PUSH-AnnualReport2019.pdf

Putnam, R. (2000). *Bowling alone: The collapse and revival of American community.* Simon & Schuster.

San Francisco nonprofit helps Latino families navigate road to self-sufficiency, economic security mission economic development agency and community partners employ holistic approach to deliver human services. (2014, October 20). States News Service.

Schutz, A., & Miller, M. (Eds.). (2015). *People power: The community organizing tradition of Saul Alinsky.* Vanderbilt University Press.

Sinclair, U. (1906). *The Jungle.* Doubleday.

Soifer, S., McNeely, J. B., Costa, C., & Pickering-Bernheim, N. (2014). *Community economic development in social work.* Columbia University Press.

Staples, L. (2004). *Roots to power: A manual for grassroots organizing* (2nd ed.). Praeger.

Tiffany, K. (2021, July/August). The Rise and Fall Of an American Tech Giant: Kodak changed the way Americans saw themselves and their country. *The Atlantic*, June 16. https://www.theatlantic.com/magazine/archive/2021/07/kodak-rochester-new-york/619009/

The White House. (2014, January 8). *Fact Sheet: President Obama's Promise Zones Initiative.* https://obamawhitehouse.archives.gov/the-press-office/2014/01/08/fact-sheet-president-obama-s-promise-zones-initiative

Wadhwani, R. D. G. (1997). Kodak, FIGHT and the definition of civil rights in Rochester, New York 1966–1967. *The Historian, 60*, 59–75.

Walker, J. (2006). Building from strength: Asset-based community development. *Communities & Banking, 17*, 24–27.

Weil, M., Reisch, M. S., & Ohmer, M. L. (Eds.). (2012). *The handbook of community practice.* SAGE.

CHAPTER 10

Understanding Social Policy

Learning Objectives

After completing this chapter, you will be able to:

10.1. Define social policy.

10.2. Describe the Social Security program and how it benefits older adults and some other populations.

10.3. Differentiate between entitlement and means-tested programs.

10.4. Explain how economic welfare programs, such as Temporary Assistance for Needy Families, assist low-income families.

10.5. Explain how programs associated with the War on Poverty addressed the causes and outcomes of poverty.

10.6. Compare and contrast alternative economic policies to address poverty.

10.7. Differentiate between the Medicare and Medicaid programs and compare these health care models with the Patient Protection and Affordable Care Act.

10.8. Explain the role of mental health policy within the context of broader health care policy.

10.9. Describe how educational policy has addressed issues of access and equity.

10.10. Explain how child welfare policies attempt to balance support for families and child safety.

Policies are rules, a plan, or method of action that governments and organizations create and implement to guide their operations. For example, tax policies dictate who must pay taxes, how much, and under what circumstances. In human services, policy influences how we practice and what resources are available to individuals, families, and communities. Some policies are enacted and implemented at a local level or state level, whereas other policies represent federal legislation or judicial actions. For example, policy changes in 2022 to the 1973 *Roe v. Wade* Supreme Court decision, which constitutionally protected a woman's right to choose to carry a pregnancy, meant that many states reduced or eliminated abortion access. Human services professionals need to understand social policy from both a historical perspective and the current role social policy plays in contemporary life to best support individuals, families, and communities. In this chapter, we discuss a range of social policies and explore how these policies directly and indirectly impact the health and welfare of children, families, and communities.

10.1   WHAT IS SOCIAL POLICY?

One way that governments respond to social problems is through policy. **Social policy**, also called *social welfare policy*, is a broad term that refers to the ways in which governments respond to the basic health and welfare needs of a society. Social policies can be enacted by federal, state, or local governments. They can be proactive, to support the general health and welfare of society, or reactive to address specific social problems or violations of human rights.

Social policies aim to address the distribution of social and economic resources and inequalities due to socioeconomic status, race, ethnicity, gender, sexual orientation, disability, age, or religion. These policies usually focus on issues that directly or indirectly impact children and families and include economic, health, education, and child welfare policy. Some social policies are designed to distribute benefits, such as the means to help individuals and families meet basic needs such as food and shelter. Sometimes these public benefit programs are referred to as "welfare." Although the origin of the word "welfare" means well-being, the word has come to have a negative association and has been stigmatized and politicized.

As discussed in Chapter 2, many of the original U.S. policies were established during the time of British colonization. During the early years as an independent nation, social policies were not at the forefront of public concerns, and social needs were often addressed at the local level. Social welfare programs at the time were inconsistent and varied based on location. With industrialization and the growth of cities and towns, these modest local programs played an important but insufficient role in creating a cohesive **safety net**, a system of government programs designed to support individuals and families when they experienced social or economic hardship. During the 20th century, state and federal governments implemented new policies and programs that became part of this safety net.

10.2   SOCIAL SECURITY

After tremendous economic growth in the early 1900s, the 1929 stock market crash began the economic tailspin in the United States known as the Great Depression. Millions of people were unemployed, banks failed, and investments were lost. The magnitude of the social and economic devastation required a comprehensive response. Piecemeal or local approaches were not sufficient to address the magnitude of the problem. The **New Deal** was a series of programs established by the administration of President Franklin D. Roosevelt between 1933 and 1939 designed to provide jobs and economic relief for the American people and implement reforms in many industries. New Deal programs included the Works Progress Administration, which created construction jobs for the unemployed, and Social Security.

10.3 ENTITLEMENT AND MEANS-TESTED PROGRAMS

One of the most important New Deal initiatives was the establishment of the **Social Security** program via the Social Security Act of 1935. Roosevelt's Secretary of Labor was Frances Perkins, a member of the settlement house movement and the first woman to serve as a cabinet secretary. She played a significant role in designing the Social Security program and advocated for a system of universal health care, a concept we are still debating today. Perkins was instrumental in establishing the National Industrial Recovery Act, which created both the Public Works Administration and the National Recovery Administration, helping to create industrial regulation codes, shorten working hours, raise wages, and restrict child labor. As the chair of the Committee on Economic Security, she was considered the key architect of the Social Security Act, one of the most significant policies created in U.S. history (Francis Perkins Center, 2021).

The Social Security Act helped create a safety net; however, U.S. social programs are not as comprehensive as those of many other developed nations. Other countries' social programs include universal health care, free or low-cost higher education, paid family leave, and universal child care. U.S. social programs are limited and less comprehensive than those of some other nations, which is why the U.S. system of social welfare is sometimes referred to as the "reluctant social welfare state."

The Social Security Act set up the structure to issue "old age pensions," funded by a worker payroll tax. Although upon retirement, workers receive a guaranteed income, it is important to note that Social Security payments rarely meet the financial needs of older adults, who must often depend on other social welfare programs to help with medical costs and other expenses. The Social Security program also provides benefits for people with disabilities and dependents of deceased workers. Social Security is considered an **entitlement program**, which is a program available to all individuals who meet eligibility requirements.

Social Security Benefits

There are no income requirements for Social Security. Eligibility criteria include age (age 62 years or older) and work credits calculated by the number of years of work (Social Security Administration, n.d.). Benefits are progressive, which means that a greater percentage of earnings are provided for workers at the lower end of the economic spectrum. For example, a lower income worker may receive 50 percent of their former earnings, whereas a higher income worker may receive 25 percent. While the percentage of previous earnings is higher for lower income workers, monthly payments are higher for higher income workers (Figure 10.1).

Social Security is best known as a retirement program, but it also provides disability insurance and benefits for children/dependents of deceased workers (Center on Budget and Policy Priorities, 2019). In the event that a working parent dies, survivor benefits are issued to qualifying family members to ease the financial burden of the lost wages. Should a worker become injured or unable to work due to illness, they may be eligible for Social Security Disability Insurance. Workers make contributions to this program through their taxes, and benefits are based on those contributions. Individuals who live with substantial barriers to employment, including disability, may also receive benefits through the Social Security Income program.

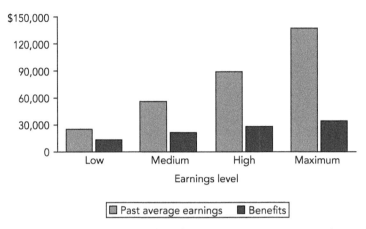

FIGURE 10.1   Progressive Social Security benefits chart. *Source*: Center on Budget and Policy Priorities http://www.cbpp.org.

10.4 ECONOMIC WELFARE PROGRAMS

A small provision within the Social Security Act allowed for the creation of the Aid to Dependent Children (ADC) program. This program was rooted in the mothers' pension model and provided benefits to widowed mothers and families in which the father was unable to work. The structure of the program intentionally centered on the father as breadwinner. Although it was a federal initiative, states were granted authority to determine eligibility criteria and amount of the benefit. ADC was a **means-tested** entitlement program, so individuals were required to meet income limits to be eligible for benefits.

ADC varied from state to state. Policymakers in the South wanted to ensure this benefit did not disrupt the exploitation of Black labor in the agricultural industry (Soss et al., 2011). In many states, Black women were often prohibited from receiving this benefit, and if benefits were available, rules were established to ensure that women would not share these resources with men. This regulation prohibited households with men from eligibility. It was common practice for local authorities to conduct home "inspections" in the middle of the night to determine if a man was living in the house, thereby rendering a family ineligible (Reich, 1962; Soss et al., 2011).

In the 1960s, ADC became **Aid to Families with Dependent Children (AFDC)**. AFDC was an entitlement grant program that provided cash welfare payments to eligible children based upon state determined criteria. This program continued to be a source of political and social tension, and many politicians campaigned for its reform or dissolution. Most famously among them was Ronald Reagan, who campaigned on an anti-welfare platform first for governor in California and later for U.S. president. Images of "lazy Black welfare queens" exploiting tax-paying Americans were used as a political strategy to question the value and purpose of means-tested benefits such as AFDC. Although welfare fraud did exist, it was actually a very small problem relative to the needs of vast numbers of poor families receiving welfare (Kohler-Hausmann, 2007).

Temporary Assistance for Needy Families

AFDC remained in place until the Clinton administration, when the 1996 Personal Responsibility Work Opportunity and Reconciliation Act was passed to create the **Temporary Assistance for Needy Families (TANF)** program. This new legislation was known as "welfare reform." The TANF program issued block grants to states. Block grants are federal funds given to states that can be used broadly. New TANF eligibility standards included a work requirement, time limits, and family caps (limiting the economic benefit regardless of family size). The results of welfare reform meant that even if a family was poor, if it did not meet the new eligibility standards, it could not receive the benefit. The role of economic aid as a safety net was limited for many families.

In 2016, the TANF program was evaluated. How did 20 years of this program help or hinder poverty rates for children and families? Moffitt and Garlow (2018) concluded that the welfare rolls were reduced, and more women entered the workforce. However, these outcomes can be partially explained by limits in eligibility to access welfare benefits and economic trends that were associated with increased employment. Did TANF decrease poverty rates? If the goal of welfare reform was to meet the needs of children and families living in poverty, especially deep poverty, the evidence suggests that this program has failed. Figure 10.2 shows that for every 100 families living in poverty, only 23 were receiving TANF. Prior to welfare reform, 68 out of 100 families had access to AFDC (Meyer & Floyd, 2020).

GI Bill

In 1944, the Servicemen's Readjustment Act was passed, commonly known as the GI Bill. This program provided eligible veterans with substantial benefits after their military service, including unemployment benefits, access to training and education, and home loan benefits (U.S. Department of Veterans Affairs, 2013). Between 1944 and 1952, the Veterans Administration backed nearly 2.4 million mortgages for World War II veterans (U.S. Department of Veterans Affairs, 2013). These mortgages allowed many veterans to

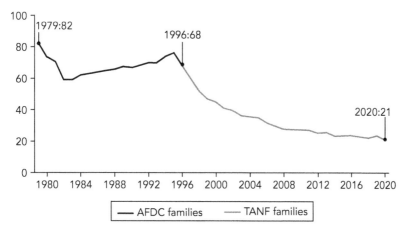

FIGURE 10.2 TANF's reach declined over time. *Source*: Center on Budget and Policy Priorities http://www.cbpp.org.

become first-time homebuyers and thus helped fuel the development of homes in sub-urban communities. African American veterans were often denied access to these mortgages, or they did not apply for fear they would be denied.

As the postwar economy and housing market grew and new suburban developments were built, discriminatory practices such as **redlining** limited Black Americans' access to home ownership by limiting their access to mortgages (Rothstein, 2017). Redlining lim-ited who was eligible for a mortgage and thus ensured that the sale of housing was mostly to White individuals and families. This practice reinforced existing segregation and dis-criminatory practices in the housing industry. Homeownership remains one of the most useful tools for intergenerational transmission of wealth. Therefore, lower rates of home-ownership among African American veterans negatively impacted that generation and subsequent generations (Rothstein, 2017).

10.5 WAR ON POVERTY

Sometimes referred to as the Great Society, the **War on Poverty** was the second major suite of 20th-century social welfare programs. Originating under President Lyndon Johnson, War on Poverty initiatives included key public health programs such as Medicare and Medicaid (discussed in Section 10.7), which were part of the Social Security Amendments of 1965.

Economic Opportunity Act of 1964

The Economic Opportunity Act of 1964 (EOA) provided job training and employment opportunities. The EOA expanded educational access and employment opportunities through programs such as the Job Corps, the Work Study program, and Volunteers in Service to America. These programs offered education, training, and work opportunities to low-income youth and adults (McLay, 2019). Another feature of the EOA was Com-munity Action Agencies. These organizations were private nonprofits that received federal funds to implement anti-poverty programs that promoted self-sufficiency. These programs were to ensure "maximum feasible participation" of the poor, and more than 1,000 of these organizations are in operation throughout the country today.

Civil Rights Movement

The War on Poverty developed out of the advocacy and action of many social justice lead-ers, including Martin Luther King, Jr., and John Lewis (Figure 10.3). The Civil Rights Act of 1964 prohibited discrimination on the basis of race, color, religion, sex, or national origin. Discrimination was outlawed in employment policies and public benefits. The act also addressed inequalities in voting rights and mandated the desegregation of schools (U.S. Department of Labor, n.d.). In 2013 and 2021, two important Supreme Court cases found some aspects of the Voting Rights Act of 1965 unconstitutional, rolling back decades of oversight to ensure voting access to historically disenfranchised voters of color.

Nutrition Support Programs

Immediately following the passage of the EOA, President Johnson created the Food Stamps program, now called the **Supplemental Nutrition Assistance Program (SNAP)**. SNAP is a food assistance program for low-income families, including seniors and

FIGURE 10.3   Civil rights leaders from left to right: John Lewis, Whitney Young, A. Philip Randolph, Dr. Martin Luther King Jr., James Farmer, and Roy Wilkins. *Source*: Everett Collection Historical/Alamy Stock Photo.

individuals with disabilities (Center on Budget and Policy Priorities, n.d.). An earlier iteration of this program began in 1939 when recipients would buy physical stamps to purchase food. A dollar's worth of stamps equated to $1.50 worth of food, and there were restrictions on what could be purchased. The Food Stamp Act of 1964 made the program permanent and included regulations for implementation of the program, including eligibility requirements, restrictions for items such as alcohol and prepared hot foods, and prohibited discrimination on the basis of race, religion, national origin, or political beliefs (Shahin, 2017).

The federal **Special Supplemental Nutrition Program for Women, Infants, and Children (WIC)** provides grants to states to fund supplemental foods, nutrition education, and health care referrals for low-income women, infants, and young children who are determined to be at nutritional risk. The program serves low-income women who are pregnant, postpartum (up to 6 months after birth), or breastfeeding (up to the child's first birthday) and children up to age 5 years (Box 10.1).

Head Start
Head Start is a program designed to prevent a cycle of poverty by providing support for young children and their families. In 1965, Head Start began as a short-term summer enrichment program for low-income children at risk of negative academic and developmental outcomes. Head Start preschool programs offer free high-quality early educational opportunities for children (Joshi et al., 2016). Although its primary goal is to provide a foundation for school readiness, the program has expanded to offer holistic services that include health and wellness programs, such as health screenings and food programs. Head Start programs also focus on providing access to support services for families, such as programs that provide housing support and continuing adult education (U.S. Department of Health and Services, 2015). Head Start was also instrumental in its early support for other methods of early educational intervention, such as assisting in funding the public television show *Sesame Street* (Office of Head Start, 2019).

BOX 10.1 **COVID and Food Security**

The social and economic impact of the COVID-19 pandemic highlighted the important role of food assistance in the United States. During the pandemic, a Census Bureau survey found that 22 million adults reported not having enough to eat over a 7-day period (Center on Budget and Policy Priorities, 2021). In 2020, federal spending on SNAP increased almost 50 percent and cost approximately $90 billion (Evich, 2021). The rise in costs came from both an increased need for food assistance due to high rates of unemployment and increased benefit levels. Spending on food assistance programs was one aspect of the American Rescue Plan Act of 2021, which allocated $12 billion to address food insecurity by extending SNAP benefits, providing a pandemic electronic benefit transfer program to offset food loss from school closures, enhanced the WIC program, and provided additional federal resources to states for the administration of food programs (Rosenbaum et al., 2021).

10.6 ALTERNATIVE ECONOMIC POLICIES TO ADDRESS POVERTY

There is a debate about whether the policies and programs designed as a part of the War on Poverty are effective. Today, there are still too many children and adults living in poverty or deep poverty. And yet, we also can see the positive impact of various safety net programs that have become part of our national identity. The following sections discuss tax policies and an alternate benefit model aimed at poverty relief.

Earned Income Tax Credit

In response to growing political concern about AFDC in the 1960s and 1970s, the earned income tax credit (EITC) was established. A Senate Committee report (Senate Committee on Finance, 1975) stated that the EITC should "assist in encouraging people to obtain employment, reducing the unemployment rate, and reducing the welfare rolls" (p. 33). The EITC translated into larger tax refunds for the working poor, and the terms have been expanded multiple times. Although the tax credit helps many low-income workers, it may not address the needs of the non-working poor and some single working parents with children (Bitler et al., 2017).

Child Tax Credit

The Child Tax Credit passed in 1997 was intended to reduce tax liability via a tax credit. Depending on earnings, families may be eligible for a tax refund. Under President Joe Biden, the American Rescue Plan of 2021 expanded the Child Tax Credit as part of pandemic relief efforts through December 2021. The average family received $2,000 to $3,600 in the form of monthly payments (versus a lump sum refund during tax season). The amount was based on income, family size, and age of children. One of the strengths of this model is that this income did not count against income eligibility for programs such as SNAP, TANF, or WIC. In December 2021, Congress failed to renew the benefit. According to the Urban Institute, expanding the Child Tax Credit to 2025 would reduce child poverty by 5.8 percent, from 14.2 percent to 8.4 percent, using 2018 as a benchmark for a typical year. That means that 4.3 million fewer children would be in poverty in a typical year, representing more than a 40 percent decrease in child poverty (Acs & Werner, 2021).

Universal Basic Income

Some policy advocates propose different ways to address poverty relief, such as a **universal basic income** (UBI), which would provide a basic income for all adults. Although UBI is not a policy at the federal or state level, it is an anti-poverty intervention that advocates believe is worth considering. UBI models provide individuals with a regular cash transfer to be spent at the recipient's discretion. Although UBI was supported by the 2020 presidential candidate Andrew Yang, it is not a new concept. More than 50 years ago, Martin Luther King, Jr., advocated for a UBI program (King, 2010).

One example of UBI is the Stockton Economic Empowerment Demonstration (SEED) project in California. SEED provided 125 randomly selected residents with $500 per month for 24 months (2019–2021). Participants were issued a debit card with the monthly allotment to be used in any way the participants saw fit. Observing spending patterns from the debit cards, researchers determined that most purchases were for household goods and food. Families who participated in this project articulated a reduction of stress with the availability of these resources (West et al., 2021). Some cities are experimenting with basic income models to determine their viability and efficacy to reduce family poverty such as Phoenix, Los Angeles, Gainesville, Atlanta, and St. Paul.

10.7 HEALTH CARE POLICY

The federal government has played a large role in developing and implementing anti-poverty programs and has also been a key player in supporting health care as a basic entitlement for certain groups, such as senior citizens (Medicare) and low-income children and families (Medicaid).

Medicare and Medicaid

Medicare is a federally administered health insurance program and an example of an entitlement program. Taxpayers pay into the Medicare trust fund, which provides health insurance primarily for people aged 65 years or older. Medicare benefits are available regardless of income, but recipients must pay a monthly premium (for those receiving Social Security benefits, premiums are deducted from the monthly Social Security check).

Medicaid is a joint federal–state health insurance program for certain low-income individuals and families and qualifying elderly adults and individuals with disabilities. Medicaid programs are administered at the state level and differ according to state guidelines. Medicaid serves to address the barriers of affordability of private and employer-based health insurance but has not historically been able to meet the needs of all people living in poverty. For example, there is no federal funding for poor non-elderly adults who do not meet other eligibility criteria such as being pregnant, disabled, or parents/guardians of children (Rosenbaum, 2009). Children make up approximately two-fifths of those enrolled in Medicaid, whereas one-fifth are low-income seniors or people with disabilities. The costs of Medicaid for seniors and people with disabilities accounts for about half of Medicaid costs in 2018 (Center on Budget and Policy Priorities, 2020).

Patient Protection and Affordable Care Act

Political and ideological differences in the United States surrounding funding for health care have resulted in opposing viewpoints. Today, the expanded role of government in health care funding is viewed as a liberal or progressive cause, and the role of individual responsibility as a conservative cause. In the past, the lines between political beliefs were not always as stark.

The **Patient Protection and Affordable Care Act (ACA)** passed in 2010 under the Obama administration. Although this legislation and associated programs are often referred to as Obamacare, the provisions of the policy have a long history, and the ideas behind expanded health care coverage represent both liberal and conservative presidents and administrations (Freed & Das, 2015). Figure 10.4 compares elements of Nixon's health care plans and the ACA.

The ACA impacted health care coverage in four important ways:

- It led to implementation of a federal health insurance marketplace (healthcare. gov) to offer health insurance coverage from private insurers to individuals and families who do not have access to health insurance through an employer.
- It created subsidies for individuals and families between 100 and 400 percent of the federal poverty level to help them buy health care insurance from private insurers.
- It created small business insurance marketplaces to support health insurance plans for employers with 50 or fewer employees.
- It sought to expand Medicaid by allowing people earning up to 133 percent of the federal poverty level to qualify for Medicaid benefits.

Pres. Nixon's 1971 Plan:	**Pres. Obama's Affordable Care Act, 2010:**
• All employers required to provide basic health insurance, including a range of specific coverage requirements	• Employers with more than 50 emplyees must offer affordable insurance with a minimum set of benefits to most employees, or pay extra if their employees qualify for a tax credit to buy insurance on a marketplace instead.
• Employees required to share the cost of insurance, up to a cap	
• Insurance companies can only vary benefit packages to an extent	• Smaller employers can buy through a special program, and smallest employers can get a tax credit.
• Special insurance programs at reasonable rates for self-employed/others	
• Replace most of Medicaid for poor families with a completely federal plan open to any family below a certain income level: cost-sharing rises with income.	• "Affordable" coverage is that which costs less than 9.5 percent of household income. Subsidies and tax credits available to many.
	• Medicaid expanded by offering states funding to cover individuals earning up to 133 percent of poverty level (fully at first then tapering back to 90 percent over time).
Nixon's 1974 Plan:	
• All employers must insure all full-time employees, with employee cost-sharing up to a cap, and federal subsidies to aid employers.	• Minimum package of insurance benefits for all newly eligible individuals.
• Replace Medicaid with a plan open to anyone not eligible for employee health insurance or Medicare, and those who can't afford their coverage.	• Pays primary care providers equal rates for Medicaid & Medicare patients

FIGURE 10.4   Nixon versus the ACA. *Source*: Freed, G. L., & Das, A. (2015). Nixon or Obama: Who is the real radical liberal on health care? *Pediatrics, 136*(2), 211–214.

Another aspect of the ACA was its focus on prevention of health problems by developing, expanding, and funding new programs focused on public health; increasing access to preventive health care; and creating incentives for prevention and wellness services (Chait & Glied, 2018).

Contested Elements of the ACA

Since the ACA was passed in 2010, its components have been contested and debated. Two contested aspects of the ACA were the individual mandate and Medicaid expansion. The individual mandate required legal residents to have health insurance, and those without health insurance were required to pay a penalty (Eibner & Saltzman, 2015). As of 2019, the federal penalty was removed, but a few states assess their own penalty for being uninsured.

Medicaid expansion was another widely debated issue. The ACA originally sought to expand eligibility for Medicaid by increasing the income cap to up to 133 percent of the federal poverty level. In 2021, the Supreme Court ruled that states could choose to expand Medicaid and that expansion would not be mandated. Today, eligibility for Medicaid varies based on a state's acceptance or rejection of Medicaid expansion.

Effects of the ACA

Ten years after the ACA was enacted, policy analysts examined the benefits and limitations of the legislation (Blumenthal et al., 2020; Rapfogel et al., 2020). A policy report from the *New England Journal of Medicine* highlighted several important outcomes:

- The overall number of people with access to health care coverage increased. Insurance access through state-level health insurance exchanges, increased access to Medicaid, and extended access to dependent coverage for young adults contributed to these increases. Specifically, more lower income individuals had access to care, especially in states that expanded their Medicaid coverage.
- Although there are considerable costs associated with health care, the total costs of the program were less than expected, which was associated with lower growth in health care costs.
- The known health effects and health-related impacts suggest some benefits associated with the ACA, but most health experts believe additional research is needed to better understand the relation between the policy and health outcomes.

10.8 MENTAL HEALTH SERVICES

The ACA focused on access to broad health coverage, including mental health services. However, the role of the federal government in mental health care did not start with the ACA. Several major policies have addressed mental health care.

After World War II, several steps were taken to expand the federal government's role in mental health care. The 1946 National Mental Health Act was established to fund research on the causes and correlates of mental illness and support enhanced interventions and treatments to foster mental health (Brand, 1965). The National Institute of Mental Health (NIMH) was established in 1949. This federal agency contributes to mental health care and policy through research on the prevention and treatment of mental illnesses (NIMH, 2015).

A "bold new approach" to mental health care was established in 1963 when President John F. Kennedy signed the Community Mental Health Act (originally called the Mental Retardation Facilities and Community Health Centers Construction Act). This law was a reaction to existing practices of institutionalization and refocused mental health care within the community, highlighting that there were both economic and social benefits to community-based care. The institutionalization of people with mental illness was both expensive and less effective than community-based solutions, known as "behavioral health care" (Centers for Medicare & Medicaid Services, n.d.). Behavioral health care is an expansive way to look at mental health care to understand the complex interactions and impacts of personal, family, and community factors. This approach considers ecological factors within the micro, meso, and macro levels.

The Mental Health Parity Act of 1996 and the Paul Wellstone and Pete Domenici Mental Health Parity and Addiction Equity Act of 2008 focused on ensuring that the coverage provided by health insurance companies for mental health and substance use disorder is similar to coverage for physical health. In combination with the ACA, mental health parity impacts insurance providers and policyholders in both small and large group health plans. The intent of mental health parity laws is to ensure equitable treatment regardless of the type of health issue. In practice, however, there are barriers to equity (Shana, 2020). Research highlighted barriers to services that include a lack of access to care and high costs for mental health services (HeadStarter Network, 2019).

Mental health policy was further impacted by the founding of the National Alliance for the Mentally Ill (NAMI) in 1979 (National Alliance on Mental Illness, 2021). NAMI advocates for people with mental illness and focuses on social and health policies that expand access to high-quality effective treatments and services for individuals with mental illness and their families and caregivers. NAMI has four primary policy positions: improving health, responding to crises, supporting inclusion and nondiscrimination, and stopping harmful practices such as conversion therapy used on members of the LGBTQ community.

10.9 EDUCATION POLICY

Today, U.S. public education is considered both a pathway to success and a form of anti-poverty policy. Ample research has demonstrated the relationship between high-quality early educational intervention and developmental and economic benefits (e.g., increased high school graduation rates and lower rates of social welfare use) (Karoly et al., 2006). But the history of public education was not built on policies or practices of equity and access.

The first public school in the United States was established in 1635 in Boston, Massachusetts. However, access to education was limited for most children until the 1830s when Horace Mann advocated for free, public, and universally accessible education. These noble ideals were not immediately implemented. Access to a free public education remained limited due to location, race, ethnicity, gender, and disability. Children from rural areas, children of color, girls, and children with disabilities had less access to public schools (Kober & Rentner, 2020).

Discrimination and Access to Education

Unequal access to education has been a part of our nation's history, and educational policy has both helped and hindered the goals of educational equity. For example, one of the first federal welfare agencies was enacted after the Civil War to provide aid to formerly enslaved people. Known as the Freedman's Bureau, this agency provided medical and food assistance. The Freedman's Bureau also built schools and established teacher-training programs ("Freedmen's Bureau," 2020). Although these services were underfunded and only implemented for 7 years, these efforts contributed to the development of historically Black colleges.

A set of post–Civil War policies and practices known as Jim Crow laws were established to diminish opportunities and access to resources for Black citizens. These laws restricted access to voting, employment, and housing. Jim Crow laws also led to the development and enforcement of "separate but equal" policies. In 1896, the U.S. Supreme Court reinforced these practices of segregation in *Plessy v. Ferguson*.

In 1954, the Supreme Court reversed its decision and ruled that decades of discrimination were unconstitutional under the 14th Amendment. The 14th Amendment specified that the state could not deny equal protection under the law. *Brown v. Board of Education* ended the practice of racial segregation in public schools and ruled that "separate but equal" policies were unconstitutional.

Elementary and Secondary Education Act

In 1965, the Elementary and Secondary Education Act was passed as part of the War on Poverty. The original policy focused on the development of educational standards and accountability (Paul, 2016). Subsequent amendments have included Title I, which created funding sources to enhance educational outcomes for districts with higher percentages of low-income students.

Title IX

Congress passed Title IX of the Education Amendments in 1972. This legislation prohibits discrimination based on sex (pregnancy, sexual orientation, or gender identity) in any educational institution that receives federal financial assistance. Title IX applies to students in public kindergarten through grade 12 programs and any college, university, or postsecondary program that receives federal funding. It recognizes the role of educational systems to be accountable to prevent sex-based discrimination and harassment. Title IX helped address inequalities such as discriminatory admissions practices and limited opportunities in athletics (U.S Department of Justice, 2012). Since Title IX, there have been substantial changes in women's educational outcomes. According to a report from the White House Council on Women and Girls (2011), the percentage of women with a college degree increased 59 percent between 1970 and 2009.

Protecting the Rights of People with Disabilities

Discrimination against people with disabilities was not addressed by federal law until the 1970s. Section 504 of the Rehabilitation Act of 1973 was the first civil rights law for persons with disabilities to be enacted in the United States. It prohibits discrimination against people with disabilities in programs that receive federal financial assistance.

The **Individuals with Disabilities in Education Act** (IDEA) was first passed in 1975 as the Education for All Handicapped Children Act; it was reauthorized as IDEA in 1990. This policy required states that received federal education funds to provide a free and appropriate public education (FAPE) to all children, including children with disabilities (De Los Santos & Kupczynski, 2019). Ensuring FAPE required schools to develop and implement Individualized Education Programs (IEPs) that specify the educational plan for the child. Subsequent amendments have expanded access to educational services for children with disabilities from birth (early intervention services) to age 21 years (transition from high school to adulthood), raised the standards for special education teachers, and enhanced standards on curriculum and accountability for educational outcomes (Individuals with Disabilities Education Act, 2021).

The Americans with Disabilities Act (ADA) passed in 1990. The ADA, IDEA, and Section 504 combine to protect children and adults with disabilities from exclusion and discriminatory treatment in education, employment, and the community.

No Child Left Behind

In 2001, the bipartisan-supported No Child Left Behind Act (NCLB) was passed by Congress to address educational inequality. It was later signed into law by George W. Bush in 2002. NCLB was an update to the Elementary and Secondary Education Act, originally passed in 1965 under President Johnson. The intent of NCLB was to support educational growth and excellence for all students regardless of race, ethnicity, gender, or ability (Klein, 2015). In a famous speech to the National Association for the Advancement of Colored People, President Bush (2000) stated that NCLB would address the "soft bigotry of low expectations" and ensure that all children received a high-quality education.

What were the results of NCLB? Many studies were conducted, and results show that although there were some student gains in certain academic subjects, the overall intent of the law to reduce educational inequality was not sufficiently met (Dee & Jacob, 2010). Some criticism centered on the law's focus on accountability through testing. "High-stakes" tests were associated with grade advancement, as well as benchmarks for graduation. Other research examined the role of the policy on aspects of educational growth and development associated with social and emotional well-being (Whitney & Candelaria, 2017). Although addressing the gaps in educational outcomes is worthwhile, some educators questioned the value of using standardized tests as the metrics of success (Darling-Hammond et al., 2007). NCLB funds were tied to test scores, and this meant that schools with the means and resources to prepare for state tests were financially rewarded, while lower income schools did not benefit from additional federal educational spending.

Every Student Succeeds Act

In 2015, NCLB was replaced with the Every Student Succeeds Act (ESSA) (Meibaum, 2016). The ESSA limits the role of the federal government and was a direct result of criticism of NCLB implementation and outcomes. ESSA removed many of the specific accountability measures of NCLB, such as Adequate Yearly Progress. The ESSA provided more flexibility for states to decide on metrics of assessment and evaluation for student outcomes and teacher effectiveness. The act also provides support for schools with achievement gaps using input from the school and local community (National Association of Secondary School Principals, 2015). Rather than use lower test scores as a funding penalty, ESSA looks to examine ways in which schools can enhance their services through increased numbers of school counselors and student access to advanced courses (Walker, n.d.). The ESSA does continue testing as a means of evaluation, but there is more input into the testing processes and fewer "high-stakes" outcomes are implemented (Klein, 2016).

As with many recent educational reforms, the mission, goals, and outcomes of the policy are not always aligned. But like the original intent of NCLB, the ESSA was advocated as a policy that would provide flexibility, shared accountability, and a focus on addressing both the quality of education and equity in access (Klein, 2016).

Educating Children Experiencing Homelessness

Access to education can be limited for children experiencing homelessness or housing insecurity. First passed in 1987, the McKinney–Vento Act focuses on services to ensure the educational continuity of children experiencing housing insecurity and homelessness. Federal funds are distributed by state governments to provide support services. These services include transportation; basic school supplies; tutors and other forms of academic support; and specialized training for teachers, administrators, and other school staff (Institute for Children, Poverty & Homelessness,2019).

10.10 CHILD WELFARE POLICY

Child welfare refers to the health and well-being of children. The **child welfare system** at the state level has various names, such as Child Protective Services, the Department of Children and Families, or the Department of Social Services. Although child welfare has become synonymous with the foster care system, child welfare is a broad term that encompasses a range of policies that support optimal outcomes for children. Other policies that support child welfare include health and education policy. Policies relating to economics, housing, and employment also affect the well-being of children. All these policies directly or indirectly impact children's growth and development.

The United States has struggled since its inception to identify and protect the rights of children. Whereas child welfare policies had been previously enacted at the state level, our modern understanding of child welfare can be traced back to the Social Security Act of 1935, which was the first piece of federal legislation to organize policies to directly support the welfare of children beyond more piecemeal state approaches (Murray & Gesiriech, 2004). Child welfare policies also seek to support children who do not have caregivers or guardians, such as some of the 175,000 children estimated to have lost a parent or grandparent caregiver due to COVID-19 (Hillis et al., 2021).

Child Abuse Prevention and Treatment Act

A defining moment in the modern child welfare movement happened with the passage of the Child Abuse Prevention and Treatment Act (CAPTA) of 1974. CAPTA supports a national system for the prevention and treatment of child abuse and neglect. The act provided financial assistance to states to develop child abuse prevention programs, conduct research on child welfare, and assess critical issues and best practices (Feit et al., 2014). Since 1974, CAPTA has been revised and amended to address many key issues, such as the inclusion of community-based family resources and supports and issues of domestic violence, substance use, and human trafficking. A 2018 CAPTA amendment focused on issues of individuals who make good-faith efforts to report child abuse and neglect (Child Welfare Information Gateway, 2019a).

CAPTA also required each state to develop protocols regarding mandated reporting. Mandated reporters are individuals who are required to report suspected child maltreatment due to their position or role in the community, such as medical professionals, teachers, and social workers, but any adult who suspects child maltreatment can and should report (Child Welfare Information Gateway, 2019b). It is the responsibility of child welfare agencies to investigate cases of suspected child maltreatment.

Indian Child Welfare Act

The passing of CAPTA in 1974 did not specifically address the needs of all children and families. This was especially true within the Native American community, which had experienced a long history of forced assimilation and prejudice. Native American children were more likely to be removed from parental care, and once removed, these children were most likely placed outside of their communities.

In 1978, the Indian Child Welfare Act (ICWA) was passed, seeking to address the historic and contemporary discrimination and disenfranchisement of Native American children and families (U.S. Department of Health and Human Services, 2015a, p. 23). ICWA focused on maintaining children within their families and communities and offered a set of standards for children who were removed from their biological parents or families. Specifically, ICWA mandated that child welfare workers provide resources and support to families, identify child placements that prioritize the child's ability to stay within their community, and work with the family and tribe throughout the process (National Indian Child Welfare Association, 2020).

Adoption Assistance and Child Welfare Act

The Adoption Assistance and Child Welfare Act of 1980 was passed to address the rising number of children in the foster care system and the increased time spent under state care (Murray & Gesiriech, 2004). One of the primary goals of the act was to reduce the barriers to adoption through enhanced financial assistance. This was especially true for children with disabilities, who often require special services. Prioritizing the stable placements of children in foster care was the primary goal of permanency planning, including provisions to maintain sibling relationships. Another important component of the act was to ensure that state child welfare systems made "reasonable efforts" to maintain families by implementing prevention efforts and supporting family reunification services. The Family Preservation and Family Support Services Program followed in 1993 to provide support for families at risk for child maltreatment and child removal (Murray & Gesiriech, 2004).

Multiethnic Placement Act

The Multiethnic Placement Act (MEPA) of 1994 addressed adoption and foster care placements based on factors such as race and ethnicity. MEPA was passed to try to address the disproportionality in the foster care system. Black, Indigenous, and people of color (BIPOC) children were overrepresented in the foster care system and were less likely to be adopted than White children. MEPA established new recruitment protocols and practices to increase the racial and ethnic diversity of foster parents and adoptive parents (Snowden, 2007).

Adoption and Safe Families Act

The Adoption and Safe Families Act (ASFA) of 1997 also sought to support the best interests of the child. The act highlighted the primacy of child safety and identified accountability standards for states to ensure improved child outcomes. ASFA provided incentive programs to increase the number of adoptions and reduce the time children spent in foster care.

Discrimination in Child Welfare

Child welfare policy has been intertwined with factors such as race and socioeconomic status. Poverty is a risk factor for maltreatment of children, especially when linked to other risk factors and especially when prevention, intervention, and treatments are unavailable or inaccessible (Martin & Citrin, 2014). The child welfare system has also been more likely to involve BIPOC children and families, with disproportionately more children of color involved in the system and more children of color staying longer in out-of-home care (Dettlaff & Boyd, 2020). Although many policies have been enacted to address these disproportionalities, additional policies and practices must consider the implications and impacts of implicit and structural bias (see Chapter 7) in the child welfare system.

SPOTLIGHT ON SERVICE-LEARNING

Think about these questions. They can also be the basis for small-group discussion.

1. What policies most directly impact your service-learning placement?
2. Think about the mission and goals of the organization and the clients/populations it serves. How do anti-poverty, education, health, and/or child welfare policies influence the organization's capacity and role in providing services within the community?

SUMMARY

- Social policy is a broad term that refers to the ways in which governments respond to basic health and welfare needs of a society.
- The Social Security Act was a major piece of legislation known as the New Deal. One major element was the Social Security program, which funded a federal retirement pension program based on worker payroll taxes.
- Aid to Dependent Children was a means-tested entitled program originally developed as a part of the Social Security Act to provide income to widowed mothers and their children.
- Welfare reform in 1996 was known as the Temporary Assistance for Needy Families (TANF) program. TANF shifted away from an entitlement model and added

new eligibility standards, including time limits and work requirements, limiting its capacity to serve as an economic safety net.

- The GI Bill provided eligible veterans with benefits such as access to training and education and home loans. Although many of these benefits helped foster economic security for veterans, the program was not equitable and often discriminated against African American veterans.

- The War on Poverty is the term used to describe a suite of anti-poverty programs developed and implemented during the Johnson administration. Programs included economic programs, educational programs, and nutritional support programs.

- Nutrition support programs such as SNAP and WIC are food assistance programs that target low-income families at nutritional risk.

- Head Start is an early educational intervention that offers preschool-aged children holistic services that provide a foundation for school readiness. Programs include high-quality preschool curriculum, food programs, and health screenings.

- Alternative policies to address poverty include the Earned Income Tax Credit, Child Tax Credit, and Universal Basic Income. These policies offer different strategies to provide additional income to low-income families through tax credits or income support. These programs are similar in that they allow families to make choices for how best to use the funds to meet their family's needs.

- Health care policy refers to any policy that focuses on physical or mental health and wellness. Examples include Medicare, Medicaid, the Patient Protection and Affordable Care Act, and mental health parity policies.

- Education policy includes a range of policies that support public education. Educational policies address diverse needs such as educational accountability and standards, prohibit discrimination, provide educational accommodations for students with disabilities, and provide services for children experiencing homelessness. Examples of educational policy include the Elementary and Secondary Education Act, Title IX, Individuals with Disabilities in Education Act, No Child Left Behind, Every Student Succeeds Act, and the McKinney–Vento Act.

- Child welfare policy includes a range of policies intended to bolster the welfare of children and families. The main policies associated with child welfare are foster care and adoption policies. Child welfare policies have historically marginalized communities of color, and there remains a need to address disproportionality within the system.

REVIEW QUESTIONS

Assessment Questions
1. What is Social Security? Why do we have it?
2. Explain the difference between Medicare and Medicaid.
3. Name at least four education-related acts and describe their significance.
4. How does child welfare legislation try to balance the well-being of the child and the best interest of the family?

Reflection Questions
1. Which policies from this chapter do you think are most effective at reducing poverty?
2. What other anti-poverty policies or practices would you recommend?
3. Describe the timeline of mental health care policies in the United States. What issues within the system still need to be addressed? What should have been considered or included but wasn't?
4. How has racism affected the accessibility of social benefits? What changes could be made to make social policies more equitable?

REFERENCES

Acs, G., & Werner, K. (2021, July 29). *How a permanent expansion of the Child Tax Credit could affect poverty.* Urban Institute. https://www.urban.org/research/publication/how-permanent-expansion-child-tax-credit-could-affect-poverty

Bitler, M., Hoynes, H., & Kuka, E. (2017). Do in-work tax credits serve as a safety net? *Journal of Human Resources, 52*(2), 319–350.

Blumenthal, D., Collins, S., & Fowler, E. (2020). The Affordable Care Act at 10 years—Its coverage and access provisions. *New England Journal of Medicine, 382,* 963–969. https://www.nejm.org/doi/full/10.1056/NEJMhpr1916091

Brand, J. (1965). The National Mental Health Act of 1946: A retrospect. *Bulletin of the History of Medicine, 39*(3), 231–245. http://www.jstor.org/stable/44447563

Bush, G. W. (2000, July 10). George W. Bush's speech to the NAACP. *The Washington Post.* https://www.washingtonpost.com/wp-srv/onpolitics/elections/bushtext071000.htm

Center on Budget and Policy Priorities. (2019). *Top ten facts about social security.* https://www.cbpp.org/sites/default/files/atoms/files/8-8-16socsec.pdf

Center on Budget and Policy Priorities. (2020). *Policy basics: Introduction to Medicaid.* Retrieved October 1, 2021, from https://www.cbpp.org/research/health/introduction-to-medicaid

Centers for Medicare & Medicaid Services. (n.d.). *The Mental Health Parity and Addiction Equity Act (MHPAEA).* Retrieved July 19, 2021, from https://www.cms.gov/CCIIO/Programs-and-Initiatives/Other-Insurance-Protections/mhpaea_factsheet

Chait, N., & Glied, S. (2018). Promoting prevention under the Affordable Care Act. *Annual Review of Public Health, 39*(1), 507–524. https://doi.org/10.1146/annurev-publhealth-040617-013534

Child Welfare Information Gateway. (2019a). *About CAPTA: A legislative history.* U.S. Department of Health and Human Services, Children's Bureau.

Child Welfare Information Gateway. (2019b). *Mandatory reporters of child abuse and neglect.* U.S. Department of Health and Human Services, Children's Bureau.

Darling-Hammond, L., Noguera, P., Cobb, V. L., & Meier, D. (2007). Evaluating" no child left behind". *NATION-NEW YORK-, 284*(20), 11.

Dee, T., & Jacob, B. A. (2010, Fall). The impact of No Child Left Behind on students, teachers, and schools. *Brookings Papers on Economic Activity,* 149–207.

De Los Santos, S. B., & Kupczynski, L. (2019). Painting a picture: A timeline of students with disabilities in United States history. *National Forum of Special Education Journal, 30*(1).

Dettlaff, A. J., & Boyd, R. (2020). Racial disproportionality and disparities in the child welfare system: Why do they exist, and what can be done to address them? *Annals of the American Academy of Political and Social Science, 692*(1), 253–274.

Eibner, C., & Saltzman, E. (2015). *How does the ACA individual mandate affect enrollment and premiums in the individual insurance market?*

RAND Corporation. https://www.rand.org/pubs/research_briefs/RB9812z4.html

Evich, H. B. (2021, January 27). Food stamp spending jumped nearly 50 percent in 2020. *Politico*. Retrieved September 18, 2021, from https://www.politico.com/news/2021/01/27/food-stamp-spending-2020-463241

Feit, M., Joseph, J., & Petersen, A. (Eds.). (2014). *New directions in child abuse and neglect research*. National Academies Press.

Frances Perkins Center. (2021). *Honoring and preserving the woman behind the new deal*. Retrieved October 23, 2021, from https://francesperkinscenter.org

Freed, G. L., & Das, A. (2015). Nixon or Obama: Who is the real radical liberal on health care? *Pediatrics, 136*(2), 211–215. https://doi.org/10.1542/peds.2015-1122

Freedmen's Bureau. (2020, July 22). *Encyclopedia Britannica*. https://www.britannica.com/topic/Freedmens-Bureau

HeadStarter Network. (2019, January 10). *The origin story of Head Start*. Retrieved October 9, 2021, from https://www.headstarternetwork.org/blog/2019/1/10/the-origin-story-of-head-start

Hillis, S. D., Blenkinsop, A., Villaveces, A., Annor, F. B., Liburd, L., Massetti, G. M., Demissie, Z., Mercy, J., Nelson, C., 3rd, Cluver, L., Flaxman, S., Sherr, L., Donnelly, C., Ratmann, O., & Unwin, H. J. T. (2021). COVID-19-associated orphanhood and caregiver death in the United States. *Pediatrics*, e2021053760.

Individuals with Disabilities Education Act. (2021). *About IDEA*. Retrieved October 10, 2021, from https://sites.ed.gov/idea/about-idea

Institute for Children, Poverty & Homelessness. (2019). *The McKinney–Vento Homeless Assistance Act*. https://www.icphusa.org/mkv

Johnson, L. (1964, August 20). Remarks upon signing the Economic Opportunity Act. http://www.presidency.ucsb.edu/ws/index.php

Joshi, P., Geronimo, K., & Acevedo-Garcia, D. (2016). Head Start since the War on Poverty: Taking on new challenges to address persistent school readiness gaps. *Journal of Applied Research on Children, 7*(1), Article 11. http://digitalcommons.library.tmc.edu/childrenatrisk/vol7/iss1/11

Karoly, L. A., Kilburn, M. R., & Cannon, J. S. (2006). *Early childhood interventions: Proven results, future promise*. RAND Corporation.

King, M. L., Jr. (2010). *Where do we go from here: Chaos or community?* (Vol. 2). Beacon.

Klein, A. (2015, April 10). No Child Left Behind: An overview. *Education Week*. https://www.edweek.org/policy-politics/no-child-left-behind-an-overview/2015/04

Klein, A. (2016, March 31). The Every Student Succeeds Act: An ESSA overview. *Education Week*. https://www.edweek.org/policy-politics/the-every-student-succeeds-act-an-essa-overview/2016/03

Kober, N., & Rentner, D. S. (2020). *History and evolution of public education in the US*. Center on Education Policy.

Kohler-Hausmann, J. (2007). "'The crime of survival': Fraud prosecutions, community surveillance, and the original 'welfare queen'". *Journal of Social History*, 329–354.

Martin, M., & Citrin, A. (2014). *Prevent, protect, and provide: How child welfare can better support low-income families* [SPARC brief]. https://cssp.org/wp-content/uploads/2018/11/Prevent-Protect-Provide-Brief.pdf

McLay, M. (2019). A high-wire crusade: Republicans and the War on Poverty, 1966. *Journal of Policy History, 31*(3), 382–405.

Meibaum, D. L. (2016). An Overview of the Every Student Succeeds Act. *Southeast Comprehensive Center*.

Meyer, L., & Floyd, I. (2020, November 30). *Cash assistance should reach millions more families to lessen hardship*. Center on Budget and Policy Priorities.

Moffitt, R. A., & Garlow, S. (2018). *Did welfare reform increase employment and reduce poverty?* https://inequality.stanford.edu/sites/default/files/Pathways_Winter2018_Employment-Poverty.pdf

Murray, K. O., & Gesiriech, S. (2004). *A brief legislative history of the child welfare system* [Research paper]. The Pew Commission on Children in Foster Care.

National Alliance on Mental Illness. (2021). *Policy priorities.* https://www.nami.org/Advocacy/Policy-Priorities

National Association of Secondary School Principals. (2015). *Every Student Succeeds Act (ESSA) overview.* https://www.nassp.org/a/every-student-succeeds-act-essa-overview

National Indian Child Welfare Association. (2020, December 23). *About ICWA.* Retrieved October 18, 2021, from https://www.nicwa.org/about-icwa

National Institute of Mental Health. (2015, July 9). *Mission.* National Institutes of Health (NIH). https://www.nih.gov/about-nih/what-we-do/nih-almanac/national-institute-mental-health-nimh

Office of Head Start. (2019). *Head Start services.* Retrieved October 12, 2021, from https://www.acf.hhs.gov/ohs/about/head-start

Paul, C. A. (2016). *Elementary and Secondary Education Act of 1965.* Social Welfare History Project. http://socialwelfare.library.vcu.edu/programs/education/elementary-and-secondary-education-act-of-1965

Rapfogel, N., Gee, E., & Calsyn, M. (2020, March 23). *10 ways the ACA has improved health care in the past decade.* Center for American Progress. https://www.americanprogress.org/issues/healthcare/news/2020/03/23/482012/10-ways-aca-improved-health-care-past-decade

Reich, C. A. (1962). Midnight welfare searches and the Social Security Act. *Yale Law Journal, 72,* 1347. https://digitalcommons.law.yale.edu/cgi/viewcontent.cgi?article=9026&context=ylj

Rosenbaum, D., Neuberger, Z., Keith-Jennings, B., & Nchako, C. (2021). Food Assistance in American Rescue Plan Act Will Reduce Hardship, Provide Economic Stimulus. *Center on Budget and Policy Priorities, Washington, DC.*

Rosenbaum, S. (2009). Medicaid and national health care reform. *New England Journal of Medicine, 361*(21), 2009–2012. https://doi.org/10.1056/NEJMp0909449

Rothstein, R. (2017). *The color of law: A forgotten history of how our government segregated America.* Liveright.

Senate Committee on Finance. (1975). Tax Reduction Act of 1975, Report to accompany H.R. 2166, 94th Cong., 1st sess., March 17, 1975, S. Report 94-36, p. 11.

Shahin, J. (2017). *Commemorating the history of SNAP: Looking back at the Food Stamp Act of 1964.* U.S Department of Agriculture. https://www.usda.gov/media/blog/2014/10/15/commemorating-history-snap-looking-back-food-stamp-act-1964

Shana, A. (2020, June 17). Mental health parity in the US: Have we made any real progress? *Psychiatric Times.* Retrieved October 10, 2021, from https://www.psychiatrictimes.com/view/mental-health-parity-in-the-us-have-we-made-any-real-progress

Snowden, R. (2007, September 21). *Briefing The Multiethnic Placement Act: Minority children in state foster care and adoption.* Retrieved October 10, 2021, from https://www.cwla.org/briefing-the-multiethnic-placement-act-minority-children-in-state-foster-care-and-adoption

Social Security Administration. (n.d.). *Understanding Supplemental Security Income Social Security entitlement.* Retrieved October 12, 2021, from https://www.ssa.gov/ssi/text-entitle-ussi.htm

Soss, J., Fording, R. C., & Schram, S. F. (2011). *Disciplining the poor: Neoliberal paternalism and the persistent power of race.* University of Chicago Press.

U.S. Department of Health & Human Services. (2015). *Major federal legislation concerned with child protection, child welfare and adoption.* https://nfpcar.org/CAPTA/History/majorfedlegis.pdf

U.S. Department of Justice. (2012). *Equal access to education: Forty years of Title IX.* https://www.justice.gov/sites/default/files/crt/legacy/2012/06/20/titleixreport.pdf

U.S. Department of Labor. (n.d.). *Legal highlight: The Civil Rights Act of 1964.* Retrieved October 9, 2021, from https://www.dol.gov/agencies/oasam/civil-rights-center/statutes/civil-rights-act-of-1964

U.S. Department of Veterans Affairs. (2013). *Education and training: History and timeline.* https://www.benefits.va.gov/gibill/yellow_ribbon/yrp_list_2013.asp

Walker, T. (n.d.). *With passage of Every Student Succeeds Act, life after NCLB begins.* Retrieved October 10, 2021, from https://www.nea.org/advocating-for-change/new-from-nea/passage-every-student-succeeds-act-life-after-nclb-begins

West, S., Baker, A. C., Samra, S., & Coltrera, E. (2021). *Preliminary analysis: SEED's first year.* Stockton Economic Empowerment Demonstration.

White House Council on Women and Girls. (2011, March). *Women in America: Indicators of social and economic well-being.*

Whitney, C. R., & Candelaria, C. A. (2017). The effects of No Child Left Behind on children's socioemotional outcomes. *AERA Open,* 3(3), 2332858417726324. https://doi.org/10.1177/2332858417726324

Williams, E., Waxman, S., & Legendre, J. (2020, March 9). *State earned income tax credits and minimum wages work best together.* Center on Budget and Policy Priorities. https://www.cbpp.org/research/state-budget-and-tax/state-earned-income-tax-credits-and-minimum-wages-work-best-together

CHAPTER 11

Global Human Services

Learning Objectives

After completing this chapter, you will be able to:

11.1. Consider how global patterns impact working with newcomers.

11.2. Define *human trafficking* and explain how human services organizations assist individuals who have experienced trafficking.

11.3. Outline the scope of international human services, including definitions for different types of international populations and the various types of international aid organizations that exist.

11.4. Describe essential principles that should guide ethical international human services activities.

11.5. Explain the purpose of Fair Trade Learning Standards in promoting collaborative international programming efforts.

The COVID-19 pandemic served as a reminder that we live in an interconnected and interdependent world. The pandemic taught us on a daily basis that social, political, economic, and public health issues have impacts beyond the construct of international borders. Although global connections are not new, in recent decades, globalization has accelerated such relationships. **Globalization** describes the interdependence and interconnectedness of international systems, which include economies, governments, businesses, and media. Many corporations have become multinational, transportation (particularly air travel) has become more accessible, and the internet has made information and sharing of ideas faster and easier.

Human services organizations and the people they serve are affected by global macro forces, including the economy and politics of their home nation as well as those of the globalized world. Understanding the effects of these systems on communities and individuals can help practitioners comprehend the importance of policy and how global influences affect individual wellness and behavior. In this chapter, we consider the following questions: Which groups of people are impacted by geopolitics? How do human services professionals engage in the issues that emerge from these forces? How do we practice as global professionals? How do we learn and practice ethically in global settings?

11.1 WORKING WITH NEWCOMERS AND UNDERSTANDING GLOBAL PATTERNS

All of the attitudes, values, skills, and knowledge that have been discussed throughout this book are relevant to working with people of any background. In addition, developing an understanding of how geopolitics impacts programs, services, communities, and the lives of individuals is critical to making a difference as a human services professional. The circumstances that lead to a person relocating to a different country are varied and can present unique needs from a case management and organizational perspective. For example, clients may need support accessing legal services related to their immigration status and/or require support navigating education, housing, and employment systems.

Terminology Related to Immigration Status

Individuals and families who come to the United States do so under various circumstances and with differing legal statuses. The umbrella term *newcomer* is used to describe a person who is foreign-born and new to a host country. Individuals who have resided in certain countries for longer than a few years, such as the US, may have the legal status of naturalized citizen or permanent resident. People who enter a host country without a documented legal status may be called *undocumented*.

The anti-immigrant term "illegal alien" is not used in human services settings, and the field articulates reasons why this term is problematic:

- It is misleading and offensive because it connotes criminality; presence in the United States without proper documents is a civil offense, not a criminal one.
- It is legally inaccurate because it is akin to calling a criminal defendant "guilty" before a verdict is rendered.
- It is imprecise because it implies finality even though immigration status is fluid and, depending on individual circumstances, can be adjusted.
- It is technically inaccurate because it labels the individual as opposed to the actions the person has taken.
- It scapegoats individual immigrants for problems that are largely systemic.
- It divides and dehumanizes communities and is used to discriminate against people of color. (Bartnik, 2016, p. 72)

Impact of Climate Change

Climate change has global implications. Often, the nations with the least capacity to influence the climate are among the most impacted by climate change (Intergovernmental Panel on Climate Change, 2001) because increased globalization and production by countries in the Global North have historically polluted significantly more than have non-Western and Southern nations (Hickel, 2020). For example, during the 2020 hurricane season, Central America and southern Mexico were pummeled by back-to-back storms, resulting in many fatalities and extensive property and infrastructure damage. Many of the countries most affected that season, including Nicaragua and Honduras, were already experiencing economic, political, and social difficulties.

Natural disasters compound existing local problems and can contribute to the movement of people. The office of the United Nations High Commissioner for Refugees (UNHCR, n.d.) defines climate refugees as "persons displaced in the context of disasters and climate change." Migration trends from Central America into the U.S. southern border have received significant attention over the years, and although political unrest, economic instability, and violence are major drivers of people to the U.S. border, such factors have been further complicated by extreme weather and natural disasters.

Nonprofit and human services organizations provide immediate services, including shelter, food, support with the immigration process, and family reunification services. Some people may require legal or counseling services, which are often provided by human services organizations. In addition, organizations may provide integration services, which help clients adapt to local circumstances—for example, resettlement agencies that provide core services such as obtaining Social Security cards or enrolling children in school.

Trauma Experienced by Immigrants and Refugees

According to UNHCR, at least 82.4 million people throughout the world have been forced to flee their homes; among them are nearly 26.4 million refugees (Figure 11.1). The UNHCR defines a refugee as a person who has crossed an international border "owing to well-founded fear of being persecuted for reasons of race, religion, nationality, membership of a particular social group or political opinion" (1951 Convention Relating to the Status of Refugees).

FIGURE 11.1   Ai Weiwei covers Berlin landmark in 14,000 refugee life jackets *Source*: John Macdougall

Syria

The circumstances that lead a person to flee their home are dire and often life-threatening. For example, the Syrian civil war began in 2011 and has raged for over a decade, resulting in the murders of hundreds of thousands of people and the displacement of millions more. Many cities and towns were so severely damaged in the conflict that fundamental institutions such as hospitals and schools were destroyed. Critical infrastructure, including water and sanitation, was no longer operable in many areas of the country. Some escapees were internally displaced, meaning they left their communities but did not cross an international border; they are still living in Syria. Others migrated to countries such as Turkey, Lebanon, Jordan, or Germany, necessitating a greater need to coordinate services using a collaborative international scope. Nongovernmental organizations (NGOs) and humanitarian organizations provided basic services for people who relocated within Syria as well as those who crossed an international border, but the increased need and the wide dispersal of individuals have often outpaced available resources.

Ukraine

The unprovoked attacks by Russian military in Ukraine in 2022 have led to devastating effects to health, mental health, and public institutions and infrastructure, already strained by the ongoing coronavirus pandemic (Leon et al., 2022). The anticipation and implementation of international aid and NGOs contributing to the physical (e.g., shelter, clothing, food) and mental (e.g., therapeutic services, trauma care) well-being of displaced Ukrainians present major challenges that rely on the political and personal networks and alliances of local leaders. Leon et al. (2022) recommend that the provision of human services programming must be coupled with the stated goal to end the Russian military advances and resulting human death and suffering. The additional fallout created by the Russian-directed war revealed weaknesses in a European overreliance on fossil fuels (Żuk & Żuk, 2022), a major setback in progress on preventing climate change in the region, disruption of global food supplies (Lang & McKee, 2022), as well as the revelation that emergency services were often racially coded and exclusive toward non-White refugees fleeing Ukraine (Cénat et al., 2022). With all these complexities, consider how best international actors can aid ethically in the provision of much-needed resources. What guidelines should we follow, and what conditions and traumas of survivors must we prioritize when working under such extraordinary circumstances? The next section summarizes the types of trauma we can expect during and following an armed conflict, with examples of what human services practitioners can do.

Sources of Trauma for Refugee Populations

Historically, the United States has led the world in refugee resettlement (UNHCR, 2021a), although during the Trump administration, resettlement numbers fell drastically. Many nonprofit and social services agencies in the United States provide resettlement services to refugees. Depending on the circumstances that led to immigrating to the United States, complex mental health needs may arise from being separated from family and support systems. Many in the human services field are rightly concerned about the well-being of children and youth crossing international borders, an area that has been receiving increased attention. Miller et al. (2019, pp. 5–6) identify potential sources of trauma for immigrant and refugee youth:

- Anxiety about the possibility of parental deportation or safety of family members in the country of origin
- Family separation, either planned separation due to immigration logistics or separation as a result of immigration policy or detention
- Bullying or victimization at school
- Physical or sexual abuse
- Dangerous conditions during migration
- Intrafamilial conflict or violence
- Unsafe neighborhoods or gun violence (in country of origin and after relocation)
- Racism and microaggressions (both in country of origin and after relocation)

Acculturative Stress

Due to the complex and difficult circumstances that lead to the need to leave one's home, it is not surprising that refugees experience higher levels of post-traumatic stress disorder, anger, anxiety, and depression. **Acculturative stress** is a phenomenon in which individuals who have forcibly or intentionally left their country of origin experience difficulty coping and adapting to the host country's norms and environment, as well as disruptions to their psychological, social, and physical well-being (Berry, 2006). In addition to psychological effects, acculturative stress can also manifest in physical symptoms such as stomach pain or headaches, unhealthy coping strategies including substance use (e.g., Johnson et al., 2009; Park et al., 2014), or other social issues such as intergenerational family conflict (e.g., Caplan, 2007; Padilla & Borrero, 2006). These mental health challenges will often persist well past the initial reception and placement period (Blackmore et al., 2020) and can be made worse due to experiences of racial and ethnic discrimination (e.g., Torres et al., 2012).

Trauma-Informed Approach

There are many trauma-inducing events that lead people to leave their home country; therefore, a trauma-informed approach is critical in service provision. Trauma-informed care is often described as asking "What happened to you?" instead of "What is wrong with you?" According to Levenson (2017), "Trauma-informed care incorporates core principles of safety, trust, collaboration, choice, and empowerment and delivers services in a manner that avoids inadvertently repeating unhealthy interpersonal dynamics in the helping relationship" (p. 1). It also involves sensitivity on the part of the practitioner—for example, not asking clients unnecessarily to repeat their migration history, so as to avoid retraumatization.

11.2 HUMAN TRAFFICKING

Globalization and market forces contribute to exploitative migration in the form of **human trafficking**, which the UN defines as the recruitment, transportation, transfer, harboring, or receipt of people through force, fraud, or deception, with the aim of exploiting them for profit (Figure 11.2). The UN (n.d.) reports that traffickers often target the

FIGURE 11.2 Farm worker picking strawberries. *Source*: F Armstrong Photography.

most vulnerable populations: people who are undocumented, poor, or living in dysfunctional families.

The following are the three main types of human trafficking:

- Sex trafficking: Forcibly moving a person from one location to another for the purpose of sexual exploitation
- Forced labor: Forcing an individual into work or service using methods such as fraud and/or coercion
- Debt bondage: Tricking an individual into working for minimal or no pay to pay off a real or fictitious debt; also known as bonded labor or debt slavery

It is estimated that there are 40.3 million victims of human trafficking worldwide (Cameron et al., 2023). Human services professionals are critical in the fight to identify and stop trafficking and in providing services to trafficked individuals. According to the National Research Council (2013), human services provision can happen at the individual level by professionals that include case managers, social workers, or child protection workers and at the agency/systems level, including child welfare, youth shelters, or child protective services.

Human services organizations provide a range of services to trafficked individuals, including temporary and longer term shelter, intensive case management, victim outreach, support groups, counseling and therapeutic services, mentoring, and legal assistance (National Research Council, 2013). Individuals who have experienced trafficking may be eligible for protections and services afforded them by the Trafficking Victims Protection Act, including the following:

- Housing assistance
- Food assistance
- Income assistance
- Employment assistance
- English language training
- Health care
- Mental health services
- Foster care

Persons who have been trafficked may be eligible for public benefits including Temporary Assistance for Needy Families, the Supplemental Nutrition Assistance Program, and the Women, Infants, and Children Nutrition Program. In the United States, the National Human Trafficking Although some view human trafficking as an international occurrence or a situation in which people from other countries are trafficked to the United States, it happens to U.S. residents as well. The UN reminds us that people of all ages and backgrounds can become victims of human trafficking.

11.3 DEFINING INTERNATIONAL HUMAN SERVICES

Human services students often participate in global service programs. These experiences deeply affect the participant's understanding of global issues and the complexities of international development. They refine a person's cultural agility, defined by Caligiuri (2012) as "mega-competency that enables professionals to perform successfully in cross-cultural situations" (pp. 4–5), while also deepening an understanding of the practitioner's own culture and personal values.

Defining International Populations

Human services professionals engage in many international workspaces and may consult with international teams or work with international clients. Social worker George Warren (1943) has been credited with conceptualizing international social work as a distinct field in which professionals contribute to organized programming abroad. These programs include relief and rehousing as part of disaster recovery, refugee resettlement, other inter-country casework, as well as human services conferences that promote education, exchange, and learning about different cultural perspectives.

What is now accepted as a more complete and inclusive definition of international human services is that the field includes not only working with individuals abroad but also engaging with international or foreign-born individuals in one's own home context or country of origin. The diversity of such clients includes **cross-national** individuals, who relocate from one country to another, such as climate refugees and asylum seekers; and **transnational** clients, who maintain close personal, family, or business ties in multiple locations between their country of origin and country of residence. Transnational individuals have an identity that is more hybrid and fluid and not always fixed with one cultural frame of reference (Cameron et al., 2007; Nuttman-Shwartz & Berger, 2012; Sanders & Pederson, 1984).

A client's nationality may even be up for debate, as in the case of **stateless** individuals, who are not recognized as "citizens or nationals under the operation of any laws of any country" (UNHCR, 2021b). These can include some refugees, some descendants of conscripted soldiers, and people living in contested borderlands such as Palestinian and Kurdish peoples. As such, human services professionals must integrate an interdisciplinary lens by incorporating information from law and policy into practice.

International Aid Organizations

International nongovernmental organizations (INGOs) tend to be large in scope and serve many countries. INGOs have grown substantially during the past 50 years. Turner (2010) indicated that the number of INGOs grew from 832 in 1950 to 27,472 in 2006.

Between the 1940s and 1960s, many countries were gaining independence from colonial powers. For example, numerous independent nation-states emerged during this time in sub-Saharan Africa. Recall that in Chapter 1 we discussed the failure of governments and business to address unmet needs; this was also the case in some Latin American countries. In locations with emerging governments, civil society and nonprofit organizations developed alongside each other in supplemental, complementary, and sometimes adversarial roles (Young, 2006).

International development refers to organized efforts to bring resources, skills, and knowledge to economically disadvantaged countries. Financial aid from wealthy counties to lower resourced countries is sometimes referred to as "aid." These supports may take the form of grants or loans supporting infrastructure (e.g., sanitation projects), humanitarian aid for recovery from natural disasters, or aid to support health needs (e.g., vaccines and medications). Many of these efforts are organized by organizations such as the World Health Organization or the UN. These projects are implemented by local entities such as governments, NGOs, and businesses.

International nongovernmental organizations can support local efforts through the provision of social services and health care. For example, Oxfam, an INGO founded in London, England, but now based in Kenya, has offices in many major cities and programming around the world. Oxfam supports many social and economic causes, including education, health, and fair trade. Médecins Sans Frontières (MSF), or Doctors Without Borders, is an INGO that provides direct medical care to communities that lack sufficient services. During the Ebola virus crisis of 2013–2016, MSF was critical in providing treatment throughout West Africa.

Other INGOs such as Human Rights Watch monitor and report on human rights abuses throughout the world and serve advocacy and watchdog functions. Through the lens of international human rights and humanitarian law, they address a range of issues, including the rights of children, women, the LGBTQ+ community, and other groups minoritized by race, ethnicity, or religion. Some U.S.-founded INGOs manage their operations abroad in collaboration with local groups and communities; such organizations tend to provide the same type of services overseas that are provided in the United States. Finally, there are also government-funded human services programs, each with its own unique, complex history of responding to local challenges.

Faith-Based Organizations

The role of faith-based organizations is highly visible in global human services practice. Recall our Chapter 2 discussion of Salvation Army operations in more than 130 countries, with its global expansion beginning in the late 19th century. In some instances, faith-based institutions were deeply enmeshed with political and economic systems. In other instances, faith traditions were imposed during colonialism, and communities were forced or coerced into adopting new beliefs and rejecting previously held values.

Faith-based INGOs are among the most expansive service providers in global settings. Many play a critical role in providing basic necessities such as food and shelter. It is important to recognize that these organizations operate in a complex political, cultural, and economic environment—one complicated by a history that may involve imperialism, proselytization, or other forms of oppression. At the same time, religious institutions may be at the center of people's lives and can be one of the most critical forms of support within communities. Human services practitioners are likely to experience religious diversity and be exposed to perspectives and beliefs that are different from their own, especially when working globally or with newcomers.

Many newcomers seeking services in the United States will rely on faith-based organizations. Organizations such as Catholic Charities have been critical in providing services for people crossing the U.S.–Mexican border, helping clients access the most basic services such as food, shelter, and health care. The Hebrew Immigrant Aid Society, Jewish Family Services, and other faith-based agencies provide resettlement services for refugees, including intensive case management, English language classes, and access to legal services. Islamic Relief Worldwide is an international organization whose main goals are to help Muslim individuals suffering from hunger and malnourishment and to provide emergency supplies to vulnerable Muslim communities enduring a crisis such as COVID-19.

11.4 PRINCIPLES OF ETHICAL INTERNATIONAL SERVICE

To function ethically in an international work environment, there are some key considerations to adopt to avoid costly cross-cultural mistakes. The International Federation of Social Workers' "Statement of Ethical Principles" on working in international contexts (2018) outlines nine principles for ethical professional behavior abroad, including the recognition of inherent human worth and dignity, promoting human rights, promoting social justice, and treating people as whole persons. Practitioners need to show respect for a different culture's norms and values and prioritize local human rights. They must respect the spirit of the community in which they are working.

Avoiding Ethnocentrism

Ethnocentrism, the belief that one's own ethnicity is superior or more normative than that of another country or ethnicity, can be dangerous (Thomas, 1996). The imposition of a person's own ethnic, national, or cultural norms or values in an environment that does not operate on such norms at best leads to cultural miscommunication and an opportunity for correction and self-reflection. At worst, these attitudes and behaviors are ethnocentric, lead to potential disruption of justice, rob local people of their ability to self-determine their outcomes, and can be seen as a form of colonization. A belief in American exceptionalism and that U.S. human services practices and resources are superior to others will put U.S. students at a disadvantage in developing cross-cultural relationships. These attitudes make a person less open to learning and valuing the norms and accepted practices of different cultures. In fact, other types of bias related to country of origin, race, income level, gender, culture, religion, and sexuality may pose a challenge when working with individuals from a different social identity group. Best practices suggest that it is wise to suspend judgment and behave more like a *seeker* by demonstrating cultural humility and learning to appreciate and, when appropriate, to integrate customs, norms, and values from the local culture.

No White Saviors, an example of an organization that decenters an ethnocentrism perspective, is a primarily female and African-led online advocacy movement that began in Uganda and that works to promote antiracist social justice awareness of **white saviorism** and put an end to it. Its work helps ensure equitable distribution of economic, political, and material resources, particularly to Black, Indigenous, and people of color (BIPOC) communities. White saviorism, also known as the white savior industrial complex, has been identified by Cole (2012) as well-intentioned practices of White individuals working with communities of color that have the result of benefiting White individuals, capitalism, and colonization, in that White individuals are portrayed as "noble" and "heroic" leaders who alone can help struggling BIPOC communities seen as incapable of helping themselves. White saviorism reframes intercultural engagement as providing the White "savior" with clout and other social rewards and prestige, rather than emphasizing local empowerment and creativity. Such efforts position rich, White, democratic countries and NGOs as having "superior" knowledge and resources and a desire to potentially impose, indoctrinate, and perpetuate their own cultural norms in foreign cultures.

The concept of white saviorism is the opposite of an ethical partnership. An important question to ask in considering international service is how an individual can best help in the context of local needs and local culture. Human services practitioners must understand how a history of colonization, capitalism, and enslavement has impoverished and robbed many countries that are now often prime destinations for human services programs and projects (Box 11.1). Following the period in the 1970s and 1980s wherein international human services professionals began to interrogate the comparative aspect of international aid (Healy & Link, 2012), practitioners continue to question the ethics of what countries help and what countries are helped. The field continues to evolve, asking how and where resources were developed or stolen in both historical and contemporary time periods, thereby requiring us to grapple with the ethics of international engagement in a way that understands the historical context of aid programs. For example, Kagal and Latchford (2020) identify how a Black feminist approach to international human services demands self-reflection over whose voices and lives are being centered; why human services practitioners select certain countries to provide or develop resources; and interrogating the reproduction of how positionality, power, and responsibility are negotiated.

Motivation

Mohan (2008) suggests the motivation to engage in international human services should be to promote experiences and new knowledge that "foster equality and justice as vehicles of international understanding, collaboration, and collective human development" (as cited in Nuttman-Shwartz & Berger, 2011). This type of motivation for service actively

---

BOX 11.1   **Orphanage Tourism**

Ethical, legal, and logistical challenges can arise in relation to international programs. One of the particularly fraught examples is the practice of orphanage tourism (Figure 11.3). UNICEF (2021) explains that these programs "can fuel human trafficking, trap [local] children in inappropriate environments and harm their development. Shockingly, many children in orphanages are not orphans. Instead, they have been separated from their families to attract fee-paying volunteers." Although this is an extreme example of how outside involvement can be damaging within local communities, even modest levels of outsider involvement can result in unintended consequences.

FIGURE 11.3   ChildSafe campaign against orphanage tourism. *Source*: https://thinkchildsafe.org/children-are-not-tourist-attractions.

contributes to social justice and contributes more inclusive information to the professional knowledge base. It also de-emphasizes strictly self-motivated interest in international human services work. Thus, proper motivation that is collaborative in nature can help minimize saviorism and ethnocentrism when working with international clients.

Researching the Location

A potential practitioner should consider the country of their placement. Questions to ask include the following: Are there existing relationships with local actors and organizations in this country? What is the motivation for wanting to work in this location and context? In what capacity would you serve in this location?

For students interested in fieldwork sites abroad, four models exist for how to appropriately select a location (Nuttman-Shwartz & Berger, 2012):

- Independent/one-time model, in which a student whose interests lie in a specific country engages in a placement there
- Neighbor-country model, in which a student is placed in a nearby nation (e.g., Canada or Mexico for U.S. students) where there is more similarity and common ground for collaboration

- On-site group model, such as field supervision or study abroad, which sometimes includes local liaisons or host families
- Exchange/reciprocal model, in which academic and field resources from both host country and country of origin are shared

Students must become knowledgeable about international politics, human rights conditions, and resource availability in the country in which they are interested. Before making assumptions about the quality of life and characteristics of the country of choice, Xu (2006) recommends researching country- and region-specific agencies that serve local populations and analyzing potential gaps in access to care to understand potential roles in that environment. It is often more empowering for practitioners to partner with or contribute to existing, locally developed programming instead of providing temporary or unsustainable aid from a country or organization with greater resources.

By engaging in proper research about a location of interest, students may discover some critical boundaries, which could dictate a change of plans. For example, imagine a gay individual with an interest in working in a country with discriminatory laws against homosexual people and practices. For ideological and/or safety reasons, this person might choose to investigate opportunities in a different country. However, it is also possible that this individual might also believe that working abroad could be of value as a way to raise visibility over issues of sexual orientation and gender identity, and to provide safe counsel for local LGBTQ+ individuals struggling to self-advocate.

Risk Evaluation

Evaluating the personal and professional risks associated with an international placement invites reflection about one's own tolerance of contradiction and ability to manage flexibility and ambiguity, which are key characteristics of effective cross-cultural partnerships and service (e.g., Caligiuri & Tarique, 2012; Wittenberg & Norcross, 2001).

Engagement from outside organizations, groups, and individuals is not without risks. Legitimate questions about what an outsider can or should do within other cultures need to be considered. This insider–outsider tension exists in our home communities as well, but it is even more profound when engaging in global human services work. Social, economic, and political challenges within local communities are complex. Individuals working in a community in which they do not know the language, culture, customs, and history must think about being perceived as an outsider intending to "help" provide local aid.

Using our own frames of reference to understand challenges and to design solutions involves certain risks. These risks range from the engagement being ineffective to actually being harmful and unethical. When an outside system or organization engages with a community or country other than its own, there are tremendous risks for misalignment, flawed, and even dangerous programs. Easterly (2006) defines outside bureaucrats who administer aid resources as "Planners," people and organizations that think they already know all the answers. Planners use top-down goal setting in the absence of local voices and have little or no understanding of local conditions. Conversely, Easterly (2006) encourages practitioners to think and act as "Searchers," who admit that they do not know the answers in advance. A Searcher believes that only insiders have enough knowledge to find solutions and that most solutions must be homegrown.

11.5 FAIR TRADE LEARNING STANDARDS

There are many examples of impactful international service and education partnerships. With thoughtful program design and the right mindset, educational and volunteer program models can be done well and run effectively. Through a collaborative process, Hartman et al. (2014) developed a list of Fair Trade Learning Standards intended to guide the structure of these programs. The following guidelines emerged from lessons and practices among international educators, researchers, NGO representatives, and community members:

- *Dual purposes*: Programs are organized with community and student outcomes in mind. Community-driven outcomes and student learning about ethical global engagement must be held in balance with one another.
- *Environmental sustainability and footprint*: Program administrators should engage in dialogue with community partners about environmental impacts of the program and the balance of those impacts with program benefits.
- *Deliberate diversity, intercultural contact, and reflection*: Program administrators and community partners should work to enhance diversity of participants at all points of entry and should nurture structured reflective intercultural learning and acceptance within all programs. This involves deliberate intercultural contact and structured reflective processes by trusted mentors.
- *Global community building*: The program should point toward better future possibilities for students and community members. For community members, the program should encourage multidirectional exchange to support learning opportunities. For students, the program should facilitate a return process with reflective opportunities.
- *Community preparation*: Community organizations and partners should receive clear pre-program expectations, partnership parameters, and sensitization, including the fullest possible awareness of possible ramifications.
- *Local sourcing*: Program participants' needs should be met through Indigenous sources. Maximum local ownership and economic benefit are central to the ethos of community partnership. An example would be contacting local eateries, host families, or local cooks to support economic development while offering an opportunity to learn about locally available foods.
- *Direct service, advocacy, education, project management, and organization building*: Students should be trained in the appropriate role of the outsider in community development programs with a focus on local sustainability and capacity development. Ideally, community members should have a direct role in training.
- *Reciprocity*: Outcomes for communities should be as important as student outcomes.
- Purpose: Program leaders systematically encourage student reflection and growth regarding responsible and ethical behavior in a global context.
- *Student preparation*: Students should be prepared by pre- or in-field trainings that equip learners with the basic conceptual and experiential tools to optimize field learning. Students may be expected to acquire a working knowledge of the host country's history, current events, and culture.
- *Connect context to coursework and learning*: Program leaders engage documented best practices in international education, service-learning, and experiential education through reflection to connect experiential course components with course, civic engagement, and intercultural learning goals.

CASE STUDY 11.1 **Matthew Lee, Building an Effective Cross-National Partnership**

Professor Matthew Lee spent years developing contacts, learning the language, and living and working in Croatia to understand the interplay of its historical, geographic, religious, and economic systems and identity (Figure 11.4). His goal was to create a curriculum that would best meet the needs of local partners in Croatia, align with his own interests in antiracist and anti-nationalist pedagogy, and provide an opportunity for U.S.-based students to participate more fully and ethically through a study-abroad course. It took many years to cultivate relationships with people in key positions who had resources and similar interests in cross-cultural learning and themes of ethnic conflict and identity.

Factors key to the project's success were a concentration on fostering mutual trust and a level of communication with partners whose talents and capabilities befitted the style of an outside-the-classroom educational experience and allowed for mutual, reciprocal learning. Interactions with local leaders, educators, and NGOs were more productive because of Lee's efforts to learn and speak the language, understand local events and culture, and be flexible in developing mutual goals. Any attempts at international partnership must be based on curiosity about and respect for local context and values. They also require taking risks and developing a willingness to create key relationships that allow for better understanding and cooperation.

Think About . . .

1. Imagine you had an interest in working in a foreign context. How would you go about developing contacts and a cultural understanding of the global forces and politics in the location of your choice?
2. What resources would you need to engage in international efforts abroad ethically?

FIGURE 11.4 Professor Matthew Lee lectures on antisocial behavior as part of an ongoing partnership with the University of Osijek in Croatia. *Source*: Photo provided by author.

SPOTLIGHT ON SERVICE-LEARNING

Think about these questions. They can also be the basis for small-group discussion.

1. How has globalization influenced the community where you are serving?
2. What larger geopolitical forces have compelled people to relocate to this area?
3. What programs are in place to support newcomers?

SUMMARY

- Globalization refers to the interdependence and interconnectedness of international systems, including economies, governments, products, businesses, and media.
- Human services organizations and the people they serve are impacted by macro forces including the economy and politics.
- People immigrating to the United States may have unique needs from a case management perspective. Complex mental health needs can arise from being separated from family and support systems, which requires trauma-informed care.
- Human trafficking is the recruitment, transportation, transfer, harboring, or receipt of people through force, fraud, or deception, with the aim of exploiting them for profit. The three main types of human trafficking are sex trafficking, forced labor, and debt bondage.
- An inclusive definition of international human services is to include both working with individuals abroad and also engaging with international or foreign-born individuals in one's own home context or country of origin.
- Over the past four decades, the number of INGOs that provide aid in various forms has grown. Faith-based organizations have played a large role in international aid efforts.
- It is important that individuals engaged in international service be conscious of avoiding attitudes and behaviors based in ethnocentrism or white saviorism.
- Preparation for working abroad should include doing research about the country of placement and becoming knowledgeable about international politics, human rights conditions, and resource availability.
- Engagement from outside organizations, groups, and individuals can create challenges in a community in which outsiders do not know the language, culture, customs, and history. The best solutions arise when local participation and local frames of reference are involved in addressing challenges.

REVIEW QUESTIONS

Assessment Questions

1. How can global forces impact a client? Name at least four potential sources of trauma that may be experienced by immigrant and refugee youth.
2. Define *white saviorism* and *ethnocentrism*. What can be done to prevent this type of thinking?
3. What are the three main types of human trafficking? What types of services and protections are available to individuals who have experienced trafficking?
4. What are some risks tied to outside organizations and individuals providing services in countries other than their own?

Reflection Questions

1. What should you take into consideration to avoid cross-cultural mistakes? What actions could you take to increase your cultural competency?

2. Think of an experience you have had or heard about that involves cross-cultural or international human services. Were sufficient actions taken to avoid cross-cultural mistakes or harmful mind frames such as ethnocentrism? What were these actions? What other actions could have been taken?

3. If you were working with a recent immigrant, how would you ask questions about their interest in or need for local services? How would you evaluate the appropriateness of these services for improving their well-being?

REFERENCES

Bartnik, A. (2016). *Illegal, undocumented or unauthorized: A few reflections on unauthorized population in the United States.* https://ruj.uj.edu.pl/xmlui/bitstream/handle/item/40933/bartnik_illegal_undocumented_or_unauthorized_2016.pdf?sequence=1

Berry, J. W. (2006). Acculturative stress. In P. T. P. Wong & L. C. S. Wong (Eds.), *Handbook of multicultural perspectives on stress and coping* (pp. 287–298). Springer.

Blackmore, R., Boyle, J. A., Fazel, M., Ranasinha, S., Gray, K. M., Fitzgerald, G., Misso, M., & Gibson-Helm, M. (2020). The prevalence of mental illness in refugees and asylum seekers: A systematic review and meta-analysis. *PLoS Medicine, 17*(9), e1003337.

Caligiuri, P. (2012). *Cultural agility: Building a pipeline of successful global professionals.* Wiley.

Caligiuri, P., & Tarique, I. (2012). Dynamic cross-cultural competencies and global leadership effectiveness. *Journal of World Business, 47,* 612–622. https://doi.org/10.1016/j.jwb.2012.01.014

Cameron, E. C., Cunningham, F. J., Hemingway, S. L., Tschida, S. L., & Falicov, C. J. (2007). Working with transnational immigrants: Expanding meanings of family, community, and culture. *Family Process, 46,* 157–171. https://doi.org/10.1111/j.1545-5300.2007.00201.x

Cameron, E. C., Cunningham, F. J., Hemingway, S. L., Tschida, S. L., & Jacquin, K. M. (2023). Indicators of gender inequality and violence against women predict number of reported human trafficking legal cases across countries. *Journal of Human Trafficking, 9,* 79–93.

Caplan, S. (2007). Latinos, acculturation, and acculturative stress: A dimensional concept analysis. *Policy, Politics, & Nursing Practice, 8,* 93–106. https://doi.org/10.1177/1527154407301751

Cénat, J. M., Darius, W. P., Noorishad, P.-G., McIntee, S.-E., Dromer, E., Mukunzi, J. N., Solola, O., & Williams, M. T. (2022, April 27). War in Ukraine and racism: The physical and mental health of refugees of color matters. *International Journal of Public Health, 67.* https://doi.org/10.3389/ijph.2022.1604990

Cole, T. (2012, March 21). The White-savior industrial complex. *The Atlantic.* https://www.theatlantic.com/international/archive/2012/03/the-white-savior-industrial-complex/254843

Convention relating to the Status of Refugees (189 U.N.T.S. 150, entered into force April 22, 1954). United Nations. 1951.

Easterly, W. (2006). The White man's burden. *Lancet, 367*(9528), 2060.

Hartman, E., Paris, C. M., & Blache-Cohen, B. (2014). Fair Trade Learning: Ethical standards for community-engaged international volunteer tourism. *Tourism and Hospitality Research, 14*(1–2), 108–116. https://doi.org/10.1177/1467358414529443

Healy, L. M., & Link, R. J. (2012). *Handbook of international social work: Human rights, development, and the global profession.* Oxford University Press.

Hickel, J. (2020). Quantifying national responsibility for climate breakdown: An equality-based attribution approach for carbon dioxide emissions in excess of the planetary boundary. *Lancet Planetary Health, 9,* e99–e404. https://doi.org/10.1016/S2542-5196(20)30196-0

Intergovernmental Panel on Climate Change. (2001). *Climate change 2001: The scientific basis.* Cambridge University Press. https://www.ifsw.org/global-social-work-statement-of-ethical-principles/

International Federation of Social Workers. (2018, July 2). *Global social work statement of ethical principles.* https://www.ifsw.org/global-social-work-statement-of-ethical-principles

Johnson, T. P., VanGeest, J. B., & Cho, Y. I. (2009). Migration and substance use: Evidence from the U.S. National Health Interview Survey. *Substance Use & Misuse, 37,* 941–972. https://doi.org/10.1081/JA-120004160

Kagal, N., & Latchford, L. (2020). Towards an intersectional praxis in international development: What can the sector learn from Black feminists in the global North? *Gender & Development, 1,* 11–30. https://doi.org/10.1080/13552074.2020.1717179

Lang, T., & McKee, M. (2022). The reinvasion of Ukraine threatens global food supplies. *BMJ, 376,* o676. https://doi.org/10.1136/bmj.o676

Leon, D. A., Jdanov, D., Gerry, C. J., Grigoriev, P., Jasilionis, D., McKee, M., Meslé, F., Penina, O., Twigg, J., Vallin, J., & Vagerö, D. (2022). The Russian invasion of Ukraine and its public health consequences. *Lancet, 15,* 1–2.

Levenson, J. (2017). Trauma-informed social work practice. *Social Work, 62,* 105–113.

Miller, K. K., Brown, C. R., Shramko, M., & Svetaz, M. V. (2019). Applying trauma-informed practices to the care of refugee and immigrant youth: 10 clinical pearls. *Children, 6,* 94.

Mohan, B. (2008). Rethinking international social work. *International Social Work, 51,* 11–24. https://journals.sagepub.com/doi/pdf/10.1177/0020872807083911

National Research Council. (2013). *Confronting commercial sexual exploitation and sex trafficking of minors in the United States.* National Academies Press.

Nuttman-Shwartz, O., & Berger, R. (2012). Field education in international social work: Where we are and where we should go. *International Social Work, 55,* 225–243. doi:10.1177/0020872811414597

Padilla, A., & Borrero, N. (2006). The effects of acculturative stress on the Hispanic family. In P. T. P. Wong & L. C. J. Wong (Eds.), *Handbook of multicultural perspectives on stress and coping* (pp. 299–317). Springer. https://doi.org/10.1007/0-387-26238-5_13

Park, S.-Y., Anastas, J., Shibusawa, T., & Nguyen, D. (2014). The impact of acculturation and acculturative stress on alcohol use across Asian immigrant subgroups.

Substance Use & Misuse, 49, 922–931. https://doi.org/10.3109/10826084.2013.855232

Sanders, D. S., & Pederson, P. (1984). *Education for international social welfare.* University of Hawaii, School of Social Work.

Thomas, K. M. (1996). Psychological privilege and ethnocentrism as barriers to cross-cultural adjustment and effective intercultural interactions. *Leadership Quarterly, 7,* 215–228.

Torres, L., Driscoll, M. W., & Voell, M. (2012). Discrimination, acculturation, acculturative stress, and Latino psychological distress: A moderated mediational model. *Cultural Diversity and Ethnic Minority Psychology, 18,* 17–25. doi:10.1037/a0026710

Turner, E. A. (2010). Why has the number of international non-governmental organizations exploded since 1960? *Cliodynamics, 1*(1), 81–91.

UNICEF. (2021). *Volunteering in orphanages.* https://www.unicef.org/rosa/what-we-do/child-protection/volunteering-orphanages

United Nations. (n.d.). *Human trafficking FAQs.* https://www.unodc.org/unodc/en/human-trafficking/faqs.html

United Nations High Commissioner for Refugees. (n.d.). *About us.* https://www.unhcr.org/en-us/about-us.html

United Nations High Commissioner for Refugees. (2021a). *Resettlement in the United States.* https://www.unhcr.org/en-us/resettlement-in-the-united-states.html

United Nations High Commissioner for Refugees. (2021b). *Statelessness in the United States.* https://www.unhcr.org/en-us/statelessness.html

Wittenberg, K. J., & Norcross, J. C. (2001). Practitioner perfectionism: Relationship to ambiguity tolerance and work satisfaction. *Journal of Clinical Psychology, 57,* 1543–1550. https://doi.org/10.1002/jclp.1116

Xu, Q. (2006). Defining international social work: A social service agency perspective. *International Social Work, 49,* 679–692. https://doi.org/10.1177/0020872806069075

Young, D. R. (2006). Complementary, supplementary, or adversarial? In E. T. Boris & C. E. Steuerle (Eds.), *Nonprofit and government: Collaboration and conflict* (pp. 37–80). Urban Institute Press.

Żuk, P., & Żuk, P. (2022). National energy security or acceleration of transition? Energy policy after the war in Ukraine. *Joule, 6,* 709–712.

CHAPTER 12

Stress and Self-Care

Learning Objectives

After completing this chapter, you will be able to:

12.1. Define *stress* and compare various types of stress, based on their duration and nature.

12.2. Describe how multiple stressors can impact the experience of trauma in childhood.

12.3. Provide a brief overview of the body's stress response.

12.4. Define burnout and describe several key factors that contribute to burnout among human services practitioners.

12.5. List factors that can contribute to stress among Black, Indigenous, and people of color (BIPOC)/minority practitioners.

12.6. Define *self-care* and *radical self-care*, and provide examples of self-care strategies and activities.

12.7. Examine the different ways that human service professionals can set professional boundaries to improve self-care.

12.8. List ways that institutions can promote self-care and wellness in their staff, contractors, and volunteers.

Human services professionals work in high-stress settings. They must manage stress experienced by their clients, as well as their own personal and professional stress. This chapter provides a broad overview of stress, considers the role of multiple or severe stressors, and discusses how human services professionals can navigate stress for their clients and themselves. We consider ways in which stress can be mediated to reduce negative outcomes. We also examine how stress can lead to burnout and how human services professionals can address the challenges of working in a trauma-heavy field, including learning and implementing effective self-care strategies.

12.1 WHAT IS STRESS?

Stress is defined as the body's reaction to a change, challenge, or demand. We experience stress as physical and/or emotional tension (Cleveland Clinic, 2021). **Stressors** are stimuli or events that cause a state of tension and strain. Stressors can range from minor inconveniences such as running late for a meeting to major life events such as a job loss or death of a loved one. Each person handles stress differently, but research has shown that the more stressors a person is faced with, the more difficult it is to cope and adapt (Felitti et al., 1998; Larkin et al., 2012). **External stressors** are those caused by environmental demands, whereas **internal stressors** consist of our internal expectations, motivations, and demands.

Types of Stress
Stress can be categorized by how long it lasts:

- **Acute stress** is short term in duration and related to a particular event or context. An example of acute stress is tension and worry about an upcoming exam.
- **Chronic stress** is ongoing and pervasive and can impair the body's ability to respond to new situations (Chrousos, 2009). Experiencing sustained physical or emotional abuse and living in deep poverty are examples of chronic stress.

Stress can also be categorized by its nature (Center on the Developing Child at Harvard University, n.d.):

- **Positive stress**, also called eustress, is short term and can be motivating and exciting and contribute to the development of confidence and coping skills. This type of stress is associated with temporary worry or nervousness related to positive events such as the first day of school or work, moving to a new community, receiving a promotion, getting married, and having a baby. Positive stress is associated with brief increases in heart rate and temporary elevation of stress hormones.
- **Negative stress**, also called distress, is what typically comes to mind when we think of stress. Negative stress can be acute or chronic, causes worry and anxiety, and can lead to mental and physical problems.
- **Tolerable stress** describes negative stress that can be managed if the person experiencing it has resources and support that promote coping and adaptation, despite adversity. For example, an individual dealing with the aftermath of a car accident may be struggling with physical recovery and emotional effects, but the stressful event is defined, and the person can adapt and recover with social support, health care and time.
- **Toxic stress** occurs when a stressful event is prolonged and associated with trauma, such as child maltreatment, sustained exposure to family or community violence, or the accumulation of unmitigated risk factors. Without adequate intervention or treatment, toxic stress can impact cognitive, social, and physical functioning. It is associated with negative outcomes that include anxiety, depression, memory and learning problems, substance abuse, cancer, and heart disease.

Timing of Stress
The timing of a stressful life event may have an impact on development. Research has explored the impact of factors such as domestic violence, caregiver drug use, and severe poverty within the first few months of life. Findings suggest that factors such as early

caregiver neglect are associated with later sensory integration issues and problems with self-regulation (Hambrick et al., 2019). Research on the impact of early-in-life stress suggests a sensitive period of development during which brain and body development are uniquely impacted by the balance of risk and protective factors:

> That is to say, the quality of a child's early environment and the availability of appropriate experiences at the right stages of development are crucial in determining the strength or weakness of the brain's architecture, which, in turn, determines how well he or she will be able to think and to regulate emotions. (National Scientific Council on the Developing Child, 2008, p. 1)

Therefore, the timing of stress and trauma affects outcomes associated with that stress. A stressful event later in life may be associated with fewer long-term negative consequences, especially if there are supportive individuals and resources available. Imagine an 8-year-old child fleeing a war zone, having lost their father to gunfire in the process. Because the early encounter occurred during a more sensitive period of development, how this child will develop over time and deal with future traumatic events is likely to be different from how an adult experiencing the same event would do so.

12.2 EFFECTS OF MULTIPLE STRESSORS AND TRAUMA DURING CHILDHOOD

The Adverse Childhood Experiences (ACE) study documented how multiple stressors and childhood trauma can impact social, physical, and economic wellness (Figure 12.1). The original study (Larkin et al., 2012) examined more than 17,000 adults' ACEs through their primary care doctors' reports. Participants reported on the incidence of 10 risk

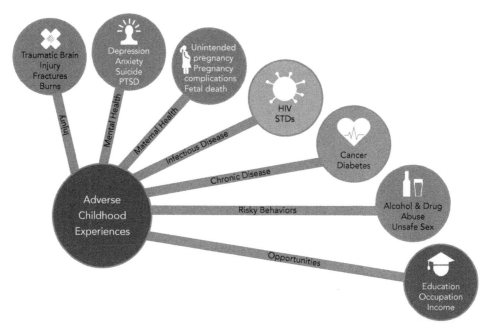

FIGURE 12.1   Early adversity has lasting impacts. *Source*: CDC.gov.

factors from childhood, including child abuse and neglect, a parent with mental illness, an incarcerated parent, domestic violence, divorce, and family substance abuse. Almost two-thirds (64 percent) of the sample reported at least one ACE risk factor, and 12.4 percent reported four or more risk factors. Overall, adults who reported more ACEs also had higher rates of negative behavioral, physical, and mental health outcomes such as smoking, alcoholism, obesity, heart disease, and depression (Centers for Disease Control and Prevention, 2020).

Physiological Effects of Stress

Although some stress is necessary for healthy development, in general, frequent stress or chronic stress can lead to negative physical and mental outcomes. To understand the impact of stress, we need to understand how stress affects the body. Both the brain and endocrine (hormone) systems activate in response to stress. During a stressful event, the brain produces chemicals and stress hormones that support a physical adaptive response (Kazakou et al., 2023; Shonkoff et al., 2005).

The sympathetic adrenomedullary system and the hypothalamic–pituitary–adrenal system contribute to the production of hormones such as adrenaline (also called epinephrine) and cortisol. When these hormones are secreted frequently or over long periods of time, they are associated with negative health outcomes such as high blood pressure, osteoporosis, and mental health issues such as anxiety and depression (Russell & Lightman, 2019). In addition, increased frequency and duration of stress hormones have also been associated with impairments to parts of the brain, such as the hippocampus, which is responsible for learning and memory (Shonkoff et al., 2005). Sustained stress can negatively affect overall wellness and physical, social, and cognitive outcomes (American Psychological Association, n.d.).

12.3 THE STRESS RESPONSE

The body's response to stress is commonly called the **fight-or-flight response**. This is a physical reaction to stress that prepares the body to either take action (fight) or retreat from the stressor (flight). When stress is perceived, adrenaline is pumped into the bloodstream, resulting in increased heart rate and blood pressure and more rapid breathing. More oxygen goes to the brain, increasing alertness. The brain triggers a series of hormonal events that culminate in the adrenal glands releasing cortisol into the bloodstream, which keeps the body "speeded up" and on high alert. Glucose and fats are released into the bloodstream to supply more energy, and metabolic changes can result in increased sweating. When the perceived threat/stressor is removed, cortisol levels fall, and the body rebounds and stabilizes (Russell & Lightman, 2019).

In some situations, especially when the stress is severe and long-lasting, the stress response stays activated, and stress hormones remain elevated. The physical implications of chronic stress may be compounded or exacerbated by other health-related risk factors. Chronic stress, combined with behaviors such as smoking, unhealthy diet, and alcohol or drug misuse, adds to the **allostatic load** (McEwen, 2008), which is "the wear and tear on the body and brain that result from being 'stressed out'" (McEwen, 2005, p. 315). The concept of allostatic load has led to understanding how changes in the amygdala, the part of the brain responsible for processing fear and other significant emotional events, can create neural pathways that cause even descendants of survivors of genocide and internment, as well as children of refugees (e.g., Brockie et al., 2013; Duru et al., 2012), to be predisposed to cope with stress less effectively than others. Practitioners need to be mindful of past generational history of trauma in working with clients with a genetic or cultural predisposition to respond to stress in a highly tense pattern of behavior or emotion.

Fight, Flight, Freeze, or Fawn

In addition to fighting or fleeing a stressor, reactions to stress can also include freezing and fawning (Gaba, 2020), two terms newer to the field that encapsulate the long-term human reaction to traumatic experiences. Freezing involves being incapable of moving or making a choice, such as not being able to move from the middle of the street when seeing an oncoming vehicle. At times, freezing behavior might appear to have a medical or neurological cause, with symptoms that could include pale skin, stiffness, or a change in heart rate (Frothingham, 2021). Fawning behavior seeks to appease the threat to avoid conflict or abuse (Gaba, 2020) and is common in people who experienced childhood verbal, physical, or sexual abuse and may become a pattern that continues into adulthood. For example, a child may attempt to appease a bully by giving up their lunch money to avoid a fight, hide their gender identity around a transphobic parent, or stay with a long-term partner who physically abused them to appease their abuser's sense of control. Because these stress responses can continue from childhood into adulthood, an effective human services practitioner might spend time assessing their client's coping and resilience strategies from youth to the present day. A developmental assessment may help discover new pathways to managing stress.

Resilience

For most people, stressful events can be addressed through personal and interpersonal support. For example, a child may reach out to a parent or teacher to help mitigate stress related to difficulty in a class or failing an exam. One's mindset about stress can reframe a stressful situation into a learning experience, which can be beneficial to development (McGonigal, 2016). Psychologists define **resilience** as the process of adapting well ("bouncing back") when faced with adversity, trauma, or significant sources of stress. Resilience refers to both the process of managing stressful events and the outcome, such as adapting to a situation and feeling competent or self-confident in the face of its impact (Pooley & Cohen, 2010). A resilient response to stress does not negate the stressful situation, but it highlights the mechanism through which people cope with stress, adapt, and persevere. Mechanisms of resilience are dependent not only on the individual response to stress but also on the balance of ecological risk and protective factors. For example, an individual with a strong social support network may be better able to adapt to stressful situations or events than an individual who lacks social connections.

12.4 WHAT IS BURNOUT?

Burnout is feeling physically and emotionally drained and exhausted due to workplace conditions and responsibilities (Corey, 2017). Human services professionals have demanding jobs and may be more subject to burnout than people in occupations that do not involve regular exposure to the difficulties of others.

People in any profession can experience burnout from overwork, not getting enough sleep, and not eating properly. For human services practitioners, burnout can result from taking on too many cases and not having a work–life balance. Both psychological and physical symptoms can occur from burnout (Mayo Clinic Staff, 2021), including the following:

- Feeling constantly tired and drained
- Feeling anxious or on edge
- Feeling trapped or defeated
- Lack of motivation and decreased satisfaction with work
- Ongoing pessimistic or cynical outlook
- Lack of appetite or overeating
- Difficulty completing daily tasks
- Headaches
- Stomachaches

Psychologists recommend engaging in a period of self-monitoring as a way for a person to understand if they are experiencing burnout. Attention is paid to thoughts, behavior, and emotional states, and noticing if overwork has become the norm and personal needs are not being met. Checking in with oneself involves asking questions such as "Am I doing too much?" "Am I being rewarded for my contributions and perspectives?" and "Am I hurting in some way because of a stressor in the workplace?" Healthy evaluation of self-monitoring may cause a practitioner to make changes in how they manage their work and life responsibilities.

Compassion Fatigue and Secondary Trauma

Human services professionals are particularly susceptible to a phenomenon called **compassion fatigue** (Bride et al., 2007), in which practitioners share in the emotional burden or trauma described by clients. This often leads to "taking the work home" and, as a result, feeling sad, drained, and upset, sometimes to the point of lashing out at family or friends. Compassion fatigue can lead to professionals using poor judgment in case planning or management or failing to provide useful, empathic support for clients. A practitioner's experience of empathically understanding the pain expressed by a client, combined with the stress of working with clients who have experienced traumatic past events, can cause what Figley (1995) refers to as **secondary trauma**. Common symptoms include sleeplessness, difficulty concentrating, and hyperarousal. Self-monitoring can help to successfully identify when a practitioner is experiencing compassion fatigue or secondary trauma (Bride et al., 2007), signaling a need to engage in self-care and consider ways to reduce workload, at least temporarily.

12.5 CHALLENGES FACED BY BIPOC AND OTHER MINORITY PRACTITIONERS

Many BIPOC and other minority-identified practitioners sometimes expect and experience microaggressive comments or situations with clients or other staff members. Such practitioners may also face the challenge of encounters with clients or systems that are demeaning to their own identity, as not all clients and contexts are free of dismissive or derogatory ideas or policies. Some nonminority managers do not exhibit equal respect for BIPOC employees and, as a result, may overburden them without compensation or make them feel even more vulnerable when their contributions are not valued or integrated into workplace decisions and functioning. In these types of situations, a minority practitioner's level of stress may be more heightened than that of other professionals who do not have to manage distress associated with oppressive systems and policies.

People of color working in human services sometimes experience a kind of workplace burnout called **racial battle fatigue**, a term coined by social scientist William Smith (2004). This type of burnout is related to the weakened position many BIPOC individuals experience in a work setting, which obligates them to take on extra tasks associated with promoting diversity and retention—work that is often undervalued and underpaid. Smith cites the "battle" aspect of this experience as a BIPOC individual navigating a predominantly White workspace and having the additional challenge of needing to know how and when to speak up (or not) for issues of racial equity and diversity and feeling pushed to take a leadership role regarding these issues. The "fatigue" aspect results in burnout, frustration, isolation, and even anger from not seeing substantial and programmatic change. Such experiences can be intensified by working with clients with stubbornly racist and prejudicial views.

To some extent, some minority practitioners feel a self-imposed sense of responsibility that motivates them to represent and collaborate with and for their community. This stepping up often occurs due to acknowledging the lack of culturally familiar services and practitioners available to clients. The result is that such a professional may increase their caseload or agree to do more pro bono work, which can contribute to burnout. What is the healthiest work-life balance for a BIPOC practitioner? Understanding the process of engaging in self-care offers many answers.

12.6 WHAT IS SELF-CARE?

Self-care is defined as activities used to preserve and improve one's own physical, mental, and emotional health. Self-care can include activities such as exercise, eating a healthy diet, getting adequate sleep, spending time alone or with family, unplugging from social media and work responsibilities, and responding to one's spiritual and religious needs (Corey, 2017). Self-care is essential for human services professionals and others in helping professions as part of a strategy for achieving work–life balance and maintaining wellness.

Self-Care Is Personal

Some individuals spend money on lavish vacations and expensive outings and consider these forms of self-care. Something as simple as a hot bath or a quiet walk in a local park, however, can also be an effective means of self-care. Depending on the person, a date night with a partner or cuddling with a pet on the sofa and binge-watching a favorite show or reading a book by a favorite author can be self-care. Research has shown that deep breathing exercises and using meditation and relaxation apps are effective self-care methods that promote stress reduction and better sleep. Each person needs to find activities and strategies that work for them.

CASE STUDY 12.1 | Sandika

Sandika (she/her) is a 47-year-old cisgender female Afro-Mexican American human services practitioner and the training director for a transgender health clinic in a major metropolitan city. Sandika has been stressed out lately because of her "overwhelming" caseload and passion for treating younger, Latinx, and immigrant LGBTQ+ clients. She overextends herself by taking more clients than she has time for and worries if she does not take clients that they will not find someone who "looks like them" and can offer queer-affirming bilingual services. During the COVID-19 pandemic, Sandika's agency granted her one-and-a-half days of work where she could see clients via Zoom and work from home; however, many of those days have been inundated with

doctor's appointments for herself or her husband Josue, whose recurrent back pain problems have forced him to also work from home, creating a more cramped and noisier environment.

Think About . . .

1. What would be the most helpful self-care strategies for this client?
2. What are individual practices the client can pursue?
3. What are some structural changes that could be made in the client's workplace to improve flexibility, well-being, and work–life balance?

Culturally Informed Radical Self-Care

The challenges of being a minority-identified practitioner are sometimes multiplied due to the lack of institutional practices that can provide safety, security, and culturally congruent understanding of well-being. Many BIPOC and female practitioners report discrimination in the workplace (e.g., Hennein et al., 2021), which can necessitate a need for self-care. Black feminist author Audre Lorde (2017) wrote many essays on how self-care in a capitalist, racist, sexist system is political and necessary. Lorde acknowledged the struggle of trying to maintain one's own identity and whole sense of self within a system known to be troubled with many forms of oppression. Therefore, a fully intersectional model for self-care acknowledges the reality of this suffering and the need to boldly preserve one's own sense of self.

An emerging term in practice, **radical self-care** (Chen et al., 2019) acknowledges the intersectional identity of a practitioner and that some forms of self-care are not as accessible to some people as they are to others. Due to lived experiences of racism and microaggressions, and the secondary trauma of witnessing police murders of innocent BIPOC individuals, the radical self-care model posits that minority practitioners engage in healing through "self-knowledge, critical consciousness, collectivism, strength, resistance, and hope" (Chen et al., 2019).

What is "radical" about this definition of self-care is that it should be considered normal and healthy to engage in self-care practices without needing to spend money, feel guilty, or feel like you are not contributing to your workplace when taking necessary time off to heal, rest, and rejuvenate. Experiencing the vicarious trauma of hearing about clients' experiences of discrimination and learning about victims being murdered by racist perpetrators can lead to intense feelings of survivor's guilt, sadness, and anger that are often difficult to manage and often inappropriate to bring to work with clients. Radical self-care might also include collective acts of self-care (e.g., healing circles, incorporating of food or prayer) and not solely individual acts of mindfulness and rest. For example, a manager could reimagine a work schedule for their working practitioners so that mental health days are common and encouraged to help manage work-life balance.

Many minority-identified practitioners experience a period of **impostor syndrome** (Hawley, 2019) in which they do not feel qualified or worthy of their role or position or that they need to work harder than others to prove their value to their organization. Individuals who experience impostor syndrome feel that they are not competent or intelligent enough, regardless of their actual past success and experience. The added stress of being one of few minority-identified practitioners in a work setting creates a potential burden in which the individual feels the need to constantly represent their culture and identity positively, given the lack of similar role models or staff in the agency.

Radical self-care acknowledges that factors such as race, gender, sexuality, religion, and/or socioeconomic background also impact the level of access to self-care in one's personal or professional space (Powers & Ensgtrom, 2019). For example, shopping might be a form of self-care for some people, yet low-income individuals might find shopping stressful because of the need to stretch limited resources to cover basic needs. Consider also if an individual has had past experiences of racism and being followed in a store in which she likes to shop. Would shopping at that store still be a form of self-care? Consider an Asian American professional experiencing vicarious trauma from reading about the hundreds of anti-Asian hate crimes that have taken place in the United States and throughout the world. This person might be having difficulty thinking, planning, and performing at their optimal level during the workday or be triggered by clients reporting experiences of hate and racism. This professional might need help from members of their personal or professional circle to find culturally relevant healing practices. Within an institution or agency, finding similar racially identified peers can also be beneficial to create spaces where vulnerable emotions can be shared and, collectively, healing and support become the workplace norm. Leadership, mentorship, and membership in local, regional, or national organizations can also help provide a safe professional space to find peers, implicit trust, and unity.

12.7 SETTING PROFESSIONAL BOUNDARIES

Regular self-care is important in reducing stress and preventing burnout. Maintaining a regular schedule and saying no to overly burdensome additional tasks or duties is a form of self-care. In professional practice, many social workers and psychologists manage their caseload by negotiating which days of the week or which hours of the day are spent on more stressful cases. For example, the emotional toll and secondary trauma of working with refugees for an entire day might lead a practitioner to revise their schedule and dedicate blocks of time on different days to working with such clients.

Importance of the Supervisory Relationship

Improvements in managing self-care can be sought by developing a strong rapport with one's supervisor. Clear communication about workplace expectations and caseload management can signal to one's supervisor a need to be flexible about the demands placed on any practitioner on-site and can provide comfort to a practitioner that their contributions are valid and enough for their share of the institution's workload. Supervisors can both model and verbalize what a healthy work–life balance looks like (Thompson et al., 2011), as well as create opportunities for trainees and colleagues to share in the responsibility of case management and not burden any one individual. Acknowledgment that human services careers can be challenging and draining, but also worthwhile and fulfilling, can help provide a more balanced workplace climate.

12.8 INSTITUTIONAL SUPPORT FOR SELF-CARE

Institutions can do more than provide individual-level services to promote self-care and wellness in their staff. Policies that offer more choice (e.g., working from home or telecommuting vs. in-office hours) and support employees' contributions to the workplace are ways that institutions can build self-care practices into their systems.

Institutions can be strategic in their hiring, retention, and workplace climate policies and practices to promote employee well-being. Facilities such as child care, accessible parking spaces, subsidized parking and transportation passes, gender-free restrooms, website and office materials translated in multiple languages, and visible ramps and elevators can help promote better well-being for more employees and clients as well. Policies that offer flexible work hours, the option of remote work on certain days, and building self-care days into the system can help promote wellness for all (Moen et al., 2011). The World Health Organization (2020) published several considerations for employees with disabilities for offices to prepare an amenable workplace climate during a pandemic. Many of these lessons (e.g., being able to work online and avoiding crowded locations) could be adapted for a post-pandemic society and may support employee wellness for all workers regardless of their ability or disability status.

Institutions can also be strategic in their hiring, retention, and workplace climate issues to promote well-being among all BIPOC staff. Imagine trying to diversify a mental health clinic and there is only one BIPOC therapist working in that space. This therapist might feel stress and isolation because of the lack of diverse peers and mentors, or find their time overtaxed due to extracurricular advising and mentorship. Overburdening such individuals with diversity and inclusion-related service constitutes an environmental microaggression and communicates an inconsistent track record on retention of diverse talent; as a result, some BIPOC staff might then lack trust in the institution and find that the workplace climate is harmful or discriminatory.

Imagine trying to schedule a work meeting on a weekend, when some employees are providing extra care to family members or children or would need additional funds or transportation to attend the meeting. What should a director do in this case to still engage in meaningful workplace discussions without causing excessive burdens on a team's long work hours (e.g., van der Hulst, 2003)? What would be a more balanced work policy? Perhaps the director creates options for all employees to Zoom in to a meeting and read and leave notes on a workplace message board. The most inclusive workspace will ensure that

TRY IT YOURSELF

In the scenario described above, what information would the director need to know to develop a flexible workspace for her program employees? What questions about ethics and confidentiality are needed to know that employees can work from home safely, access the internet, and have group discussions about caseloads without violating informed consent?

there are strategies in place to promote radical and holistic self-care for all its employees and to honor the identities and experiences of all staff, contractors, and volunteers.

As described previously, the employee–supervisor relationship can provide a great deal of support and valuable mentorship for staff, but what happens when an employee is receiving improper or microaggressive supervision? How can such a situation be managed? The responsibility for addressing inappropriate behavior or abuse of power should not be left to the employee alone. Insightful, proactive, antiracist, and anti-oppressive supervision demands thoughtful self-reflection on the part of supervisors and an examination of how programs hire practitioners and train students. Organizations should strive for diversity across all levels and implement processes and policies that protect employees from unfair supervisory practices.

SPOTLIGHT ON SERVICE-LEARNING

Think about these questions. They can also be the basis for small-group discussion.

1. How do human services professionals in your service-learning placement handle stress associated with their work?
2. What kinds of policies or practices are in place to support staff wellness?
3. What structural efforts is your organization using to prevent burnout, promote wellness among their staff, and reduce stress? What barriers prevent them from providing this support to staff?

SUMMARY

- Stress is defined as the body's reaction to a change, challenge, or demands.
- There are different types of stress. Stress can be short term or ongoing, and it is a normal part of development. Some stress is positive, whereas other stress is negative. Without social support or intervention, some stressors may be considered toxic, or associated with negative outcomes.
- The impacts of stress may be dependent on the timing of the stressors in development. The ACE study documented how multiple stressors and childhood trauma impacted adult outcomes.
- Stress can have a physiological impact on development. Stress can trigger the production of hormones such as adrenaline and cortisol, which are associated with negative health outcomes over time.
- The physiological stress response has been associated with four main responses known as fight, flight, freeze, or fawn.
- Resilience is the process of positive or successful adaptation despite adversity.
- Burnout is feeling physically and emotionally drained and exhausted due to workplace conditions and/or responsibilities. Human service professionals have demanding jobs and may experience burnout that can impact their workplace effectiveness and also their quality of life outside of the workplace.
- Compassion fatigue is when a human service professional shares in the emotional burden or trauma described by clients.

- Secondary trauma can occur as a result of compassion fatigue or when a practitioner's experience of the pain experienced by a client is internalized. Common symptoms include sleeplessness, difficulty concentrating, and hyperarousal.
- Challenges for BIPOC/minority practitioners can occur through interactions within the workplace with other staff, supervisors, or clients. Due to heightened stress within the workplace, some BIPOC professionals may experience a unique form of workplace burnout.
- Self-care is defined as activities used to preserve and improve one's own physical, mental, and emotional health.
- Radical self-care considers societal inequities may impact practitioners' ability to practice certain forms of self-care. It should not be radical for any practitioner to identify and address their needs for self-care but, rather, a normal part of professional practice.
- Institutions can promote policies and practices that support their employees' well-being. Institutions can be strategic in their hiring, retention, and workplace climate policies to ensure that all workers, including workers with disabilities and BIPOC workers, feel supported.

REVIEW QUESTIONS

Assessment Questions

1. What are two specific examples of how the timing, duration, and severity of stress affect a person's ability to adapt and cope?
2. What are different types of stress? How does stress differ based on its duration and nature?
3. How does chronic stress affect the body?
4. What is burnout? Why are BIPOC and other minority-identified practitioners especially susceptible to experiencing burnout?

Reflection Questions

1. What is an example of positive stress you have experienced? What coping skills did you gain from this experience? How have you applied these coping skills in facing other challenges?
2. What is the importance of radical self-care? Brainstorm some forms of self-care not listed in this chapter and categorize them based on whether they fit the radical self-care model.
3. Think about an institution you are connected to. What actions and policies does it implement to promote self-care and wellness? How could it do a better job of supporting self-care for employees, contractors, and volunteers?
4. How much self-care is part of your current routine? What activities could help you achieve the healthiest balance of work, rest, and personal life? How can you ensure that you hold yourself accountable for acting in support of your physical, mental, and emotional well-being?

REFERENCES

American Psychological Association. (n.d.). *Stress effects on the body.* https://www.apa.org/topics/stress/body

Bride, B. E., Radey, M., & Figley, C. R. (2007). Measuring compassion fatigue. *Clinical Social Work Journal, 35,* 155–163. doi:10.1007/s10615-007-0091-7

Brockie, T. N., Heinzlemann, M., & Gill, J. (2013). A framework to examine the role of epigenetics in health disparities among Native Americans. *Nursing Research and Practice, 2013,* 410395. doi:10.1155/2013/410395

Center on the Developing Child at Harvard University. (n.d.). *A guide to toxic stress.* Retrieved June 11, 2021, from https://developingchild.harvard.edu/guide/a-guide-to-toxic-stress

Centers for Disease Control and Prevention. (2020). *Violence prevention: About the CDC–Kaiser ACE study.* https://www.cdc.gov/violenceprevention/aces/about.html

Chen, G. A., Neville, H. A., Lewis, J. A., Adames, H. Y., Chavez-Dueñas, N. Y., Mosley, D. V., & French, B. H. (2019, November 15). Radical self-care in the face of mounting racial stress. *Psychology Today.* https://www.psychologytoday.com/us/blog/healing-through-social-justice/201911/radical-self-care-in-the-face-mounting-racial-stress

Chrousos, G. P. (2009). Stress and disorders of the stress system. *National Review of Endocrinology, 5,* 374–381. doi:10.1038/nrendo.2009.106

Cleveland Clinic. (2021). *Stress: Signs, symptoms, management & prevention.* https://my.clevelandclinic.org/health/articles/11874-stress

Corey, G. (2017). *Theory and practice of counseling and psychotherapy* (10th ed.). Cengage.

Duru, O. K., Harawa, N. T., Kermah, D., & Norris, K. C. (2012). Allostatic load burden and racial disparities in mortality. *Journal of the National Medical Association, 104*(1–2), 89–95. http://doi.org/10.1016/s0027-9684(15)30120-6

Felitti, V. J., Anda, R. F., Nordenberg, D., Williamson, D. F., Spitz, A. M., Edwards, V., Koss, M. P., & Marks, J. S. (1998). Relationship of childhood abuse and household dysfunction to many of the leading causes of death in adults: The Adverse Childhood Experiences (ACE) study. *American Journal of Preventive Medicine, 14,* 245–258.

Figley, C. R. (Ed.). (1995). *Compassion fatigue: Coping with secondary traumatic stress disorder.* Brunner/Mazel.

Frothingham, M. B. (2021, October 6). Fight, flight, freeze, or fawn: What this response means. *Simply Psychology.* https://simplypsychology.org/fight-flight-freeze-fawn.html

Gaba, S. (2020, August 20). Understanding fight, flight, freeze and the fawn response. *Psychology Today.* https://www.psychologytoday.com/us/blog/addiction-and-recovery/202008/understanding-fight-flight-freeze-and-the-fawn-response

Hambrick, E. P., Brawner, T. W., & Perry, B. D. (2019). Timing of early-life stress and the development of brain-related capacities. *Frontiers in Behavioral Neuroscience, 13.* https://doi.org/10.3389/fnbeh.2019.00183

Hawley, K. (2019). What is impostor syndrome? *Aristotelian Society Supplementary Volume, 93,* 203–226. https://doi.org/10.1093/arisup/akz003

Hennein, R., Bonumwezi, J., Nguemeni Tiako, M. J., Tineo, P., & Lowe, S. R. (2021). Racial and gender discrimination predict mental health outcomes among healthcare workers beyond pandemic-related stressors: Findings from a cross-sectional survey. *International Journal of Environmental Research and Public Health, 18,* 9235. https://doi.org/10.3390/ijerph18179235

Kazakou, P., Nicolaides, N. C., & Chrousos, G. P. (2023). Basic concepts and hormonal regulators of the stress system. *Hormone Research in Paediatrics, 96,* 8–16.

Larkin, H., Shields, J. J., & Anda, R. F. (2012). The health and social consequences of adverse childhood experiences (ACE) across the lifespan: An introduction to prevention and intervention in the community. *Journal of Prevention & Intervention in the Community, 40,* 263–270.

Lorde, A. (2017). *A burst of light: And other essays.* Ixia Press.

Mayo Clinic Staff. (2021). *Job burnout: How to spot it and take action.* https://www.mayoclinic

.org/healthy-lifestyle/adult-health/in-depth/burnout/art-20046642

McEwen, B. S. (2005). Stressed or stressed out: What is the difference? *Journal of Psychiatry and Neuroscience, 30,* 315–318.

McEwen, B. S. (2008). Central effects of stress hormones in health and disease: Understanding the protective and damaging effects of stress and stress mediators. *European Journal of Pharmacology, 583,* 174–185.

McGonigal, K. (2016). *The upside of stress: Why stress is good for you, and how to get good at it.* Penguin.

Moen, P., Kelly, E. L., & Hill, R. (2011). Does enhancing work-time control and flexibility reduce turnover? A naturally-occurring experiment. *Social Problems, 58,* 69–98. https://doi.org/10.1525/sp.2011.58.1.69

National Scientific Council on the Developing Child. (2008). *The timing and quality of early experiences combine to shape brain architecture.* Harvard University, Center on the Developing Child.

Pooley, J. A., & Cohen, L. (2010). Resilience: A definition in context. *The Australian Community Psychologist, 32,* 30–37.

Powers, M. C., & Engstrom, S. (2019). Radical self-care for social workers in the global climate crisis. *Social Work, 65,* 29–37. doi:10.1093/sw/swz043

Russell, G., & Lightman, S. (2019). The human stress response. *Nature Reviews Endocrinology, 15,* 525–534.

Shonkoff, J. P., Boyce, W. T., Cameron, J., Duncan, G. J., Fox, N. A., Gunnar, M. R., & Thompson, R. A. (2005). *Excessive stress disrupts the architecture of the developing brain* (Working paper no. 3, updated edition 2014). National Scientific Council on the Developing Child.

Smith, W. A. (2004). Black faculty coping with racial battle fatigue: The campus racial climate in a post-civil rights era. In D. Cleveland (Ed.) *A long way to go: Conversations about race by African American faculty and graduate students at predominantly white institutions.* (pp. 171–190). Peter Lang Publishers.

Thompson, E. H., Frick, M. H., & Trice-Black, S. (2011). Counselor-in-training perceptions of supervision practices related to self-care and burnout. *The Professional Counselor, 1,* 152–162. doi:10.15241/eht.1.3.152

van der Hulst, M. (2003). Long work hours and health. *Scandinavian Journal of Work, Environment & Health, 29,* 171–188. https://doi.org/10.5271/sjweh.720

World Health Organization. (2020, March 26). *Disability considerations during the COVID-19 outbreak.* https://www.who.int/publications/i/item/WHO-2019-nCoV-Disability-2020-1

GLOSSARY

ACCULTURATIVE STRESS Difficulty coping and adapting to a new host country's norms and environment.

ACTIVIST Person who participates in activities and/or campaigns to bring about social, political, or economic change.

ACUTE STRESS Short-term or time-limited stress created by a particular event or context.

ADVOCACY Work performed to change policies, practices, and conditions of clients served by human services practitioners.

AID TO FAMILIES WITH DEPENDENT CHILDREN (AFDC) was an entitlement grant program that provided cash welfare payments to eligible children based upon state determined criteria.

ALLOSTATIC LOAD Wear and tear on the body and brain that result from repeated or ongoing stress.

ASPIRATIONAL ETHICS Personal and professional behaviors required to engage in the best practice possible to provide services to clients and communities.

ASSET-BASED COMMUNITY DEVELOPMENT Strategies and methods of economic and social development that rely on community knowledge and skills to support community goals and objectives.

ASSET MAPPING An assessment of all of the existing resources and capacities in a community, including nonfinancial assets such as its culture, neighborhood groups, and mutual aid structures.

ATTRIBUTION THEORY Understanding the *why* behind a problem. Attribution theory considers the frames or forces used to explain and understand the causes of behavior or events.

BENEFICENCE Seeks to reduce potential harm associated with research and to maximize possible benefits.

BOARD OF DIRECTORS The board of directors is the governing body of a nonprofit organization, typically composed of volunteers.

BOUNDARY VIOLATION When rules, laws, and/or ethics (professional boundaries) have been violated in the helping relationship.

BURNOUT State of feeling drained and exhausted due to workplace conditions or responsibilities.

BYLAWS rules by which a nonprofit organization is governed. They address practical, legal, and ethical matters such as the size and responsibilities of the board of directors and conflict of interest policies.

CAMPAIGN An organized plan to achieve a goal.

CASE MANAGEMENT A collaborative process of assessment, planning, facilitation, care coordination, evaluation, and advocacy for options and services to comprehensively meet a client's needs.

CHILD WELFARE The health and well-being of children.

CHILD WELFARE SYSTEM Government agencies that work to protect the safety and well-being of children.

CHRONIC STRESS Stress that is ongoing and pervasive and can impair physical and mental functioning.

CLIENT CONFIDENTIALITY Keeping all information received from a client private, in accordance with state and federal laws, and professional ethics.

COGNITIVE-BEHAVIORAL THEORY This is the theory that says conscious thought, observable behaviors, and emotions all interact to create the landscape of an individual's mental health.

COMMUNITY DEVELOPMENT Organized efforts and programs designed to produce improvements, opportunities, structures, goods, and services that increase the quality of life, build individual and collective capacities, and enhance social solidarity within a given community.

COMMUNITY INVOLVEMENT Engagement in one's community by volunteering or participating in community activities.

COMMUNITY ORGANIZING When communities seek to disrupt the status quo and engage in efforts to pressure individuals and groups to create structural forms of change.

COMPASSION FATIGUE Effect of practitioners in helping professions sharing in the emotional burden or trauma described by clients; can lead to negative physical and mental health outcomes.

CONFIDENTIALITY The understanding between a client and professional that no personally identifying information about the client may be shared outside the professional relationship without the consent of the client, except in cases of potential harm to self or others.

CONFIRMATION BIAS The phenomenon of one's subjective experience and mindset accepting information consistent with our understanding of the world, and rejecting information that is inconsistent.

COUNSELING Providing assistance and guidance in resolving personal, social, or psychological problems.

CROSS-NATIONAL Refers to individuals who relocate from one country to another.

CULTURAL COMPETENCE The ability to effectively engage across cultural differences.

CULTURAL HUMILITY Acting in a way that acknowledges understanding difference is an ongoing process that must be engaged in with a growth mindset, ongoing and honest self-appraisal, flexibility, and willingness to be corrected by clients.

CULTURAL IDENTITY Refers to the level of affiliation, membership, and/or identification with being part of a particular cultural group.

CULTURE Refers to the set of customs, traditions, lore, behaviors, and beliefs that are typically passed down from one generation to another; also refers to a group of people who share similar traditions, or information about specific groups of people with a shared identity.

CULTURE-BOUND SYNDROME A disorder whose presentation, explanation, or characteristics are much more endemic to a particular cultural group or geographic area.

DECISION DILEMMA Situation in which a decision-maker is forced to make a choice and is held accountable for their action (or lack of it).

DIRECT PRACTICE Human services work in which a practitioner interacts directly with an individual, couple, family, or group.

DISPOSITIONAL ATTRIBUTION Emphasizing individual factors or characteristics to explain the result of a situation.

ECHO CHAMBER Self-selecting of information and relationships that affirm what we believe to be true about the world.

ECOLOGICAL MODEL A holistic perspective that begins to answer some of the broader questions about the individual and the situation by considering both individual and structural causes.

EMPATHIC CONFRONTATION Shedding light on a potential mismatch in motivation and behavior in a way that is constructive to the client.

EMPATHIC FEEDBACK A practice that includes providing honest summaries of what has been accomplished so far and reflecting back paraphrases and interpretations of a client's lived experience.

EMPATHIC SELF-DISCLOSURE When a practitioner uses personal insight to draw more of a connection between their experience and that of a client.

EMPATHY The ability to understand and share the feelings of another person.

EMPATHY GAP A form of bias that prevents a person from being able to understand the perspectives and experiences of others.

EMPIRICALLY SUPPORTED TREATMENT Treatment or intervention strategies for a specific population that have proven to be effective through study data.

ENTITLEMENT PROGRAM Program with benefits/services that are available to all individuals who meet eligibility requirements.

ETHICS The moral principles that guide a person's or organization's decision-making and actions.

ETHNOCENTRISM The belief that one's home country or ethnicity is superior to or more normative than that of another country.

EVIDENCE-BASED PRACTICE Using a combination of well-researched interventions with professional experience, ethics, client preferences, and culture as the basis for the delivery of service.

EXTERNAL STRESSORS Stressors caused by environmental demands.

FEMINIST THERAPY   An approach to therapy that significantly interrogates gender norms and socialization around expression of emotion; requires an intersectional perspective that is often empowering to clients.

FIGHT-OR-FLIGHT RESPONSE   Physical reaction to stress that prepares the body to either take action (fight) or retreat from the stressor (flight).

GLOBALIZATION   The interdependence and interconnectedness of international systems, including economies, governments, products, business, and media.

HARM PRINCIPLE   When a client is a danger to themself or others, certain boundaries, such as confidentiality, can be overstepped to ensure the client's safety. Decisions on acting in response to the harm principle should always be made in consultation with an advanced-level supervisor.

HARM REDUCTION   Any activity or policy that aims to reduce the potential harm of a particular activity.

HEAD START   Program that offers free high-quality early educational opportunities for preschool children.

HELPING RELATIONSHIP   The relationship between a human services practitioner and client, wherein the practitioner provides assistance of varying types.

HIGH-CONTEXT COMMUNICATION   Relying more on the tone and implicit meaning rather than just the words spoken.

HUMANISTIC   A person-centered approach to direct practice relationships, which emphasizes the importance of conveying empathy and unconditional positive regard.

HUMAN SERVICES   Broad range of occupations focused on helping meet basic human needs and solving social problems.

HUMAN TRAFFICKING   Recruitment, transportation, transfer, harboring, or receipt of people through force, fraud, or deception, with the aim of exploiting them for profit.

IMPOSTOR SYNDROME   Feeling of unworthiness experienced by some minority-identified professionals in which they do not feel qualified or deserving of their role, position, or success.

INDIVIDUALS WITH DISABILITIES IN EDUCATION ACT (IDEA)   requires states that received federal education funds to provide a free and appropriate public education to all children, including children with disabilities.

INFORMED CONSENT   When a client or subject acknowledges and agrees to what the research or treatment process will be like and understands they have the right to know more information about procedures and have the right to terminate their participation.

INTERNAL STRESSORS   Stressors caused by internal expectations, motivations, and demands.

INTERNATIONAL DEVELOPMENT   Organized efforts to bring resources, skills, and knowledge to economically disadvantaged countries.

INTERSECTIONALITY   A holistic conception that involves the interactions among multiple social inequalities and privileges. It considers the contributions of complex factors within and between individuals, families, communities, and the broader social and economic system.

JUST TRANSITION   Principle which holds that a healthy economy and a clean environment can and should coexist and that the process should not come at the cost of workers' or community residents' health, environment, jobs, or economic assets.

JUST WORLD BELIEF   The notion that you get what you deserve, and you deserve what you get, and that people are responsible for their circumstances.

LAND TRUST   Private agreement in which one party (trustee) holds the title to a property for the benefit of another party (beneficiary).

LIFE COURSE THEORY   The context that considers human development by exploring how specific experiences and social changes interact with growing and changing human beings over time, from birth to death.

LOGIC MODEL   A logic model is a tool used when developing programs to identify and test assumptions about the relationship between planned actions and expected outcomes.

LOW-CONTEXT COMMUNICATION   Relying more on the explicit words and meaning of the language being used.

MACRO PRACTICE   Practice that works to create large-scale systemic change.

MANDATORY ETHICS   Minimum legal professional practice required.

MEANS-TESTED   Type of program that requires recipients to meet specific income requirements to be eligible for benefits/services.

MEDICAID   Joint federal–state program that provides health insurance for low-income individuals and families and individuals with disabilities.

MEDICAL MODEL Based on assessment, diagnosis, and treatment of a problem.

MEDICARE Federal entitlement program that provides health insurance for older adults and other designated populations.

MESO PRACTICE Broader practice within groups, nonprofit organizations, institutions, and communities.

MICROAGGRESSION An unintentional slight or behavior that communicates invalidation, exclusion, or harm, typically toward members of minority communities.

MICRO PRACTICE Services at the micro level, via one-on-one practice involving direct interactions with individuals, families, and groups.

MICROSKILLS Basic practitioner skills in communication, listening, responding, reflecting, sharing, and providing feedback and summary to clients.

MINORITY Denotes a cultural group that is subordinate, less powerful, underresourced, and sometimes fewer in number.

MISSION DRIFT Mission drift occurs when a nonprofit organization accepts funding to do work unrelated to its mission.

MISSION STATEMENT A mission statement is a brief articulation of a nonprofit organization's purpose and primary goals.

MUTUAL AID ORGANIZATION Mutual aid is a decentralized organizational model sometimes used to provide critical services during disasters; it may also involve collective support for members.

NEEDS ASSESSMENT A needs assessment is a study conducted to identify specific social, economic, or other needs in a community that may be addressed by a nonprofit organization or other entity.

NEGATIVE STRESS Stress that can be acute or chronic, causes worry and anxiety, and can lead to mental and physical problems; also called *distress*.

NEW DEAL Series of programs established by the administration of President Franklin D. Roosevelt in the 1930s to provide jobs and economic relief and implement reforms in many industries.

NONMALEFICENCE Avoiding causing harm.

NONPROFIT ORGANIZATIONS Mission-driven organizations established for purposes other than generating profit, often educational or charitable organizations.

PATIENT PROTECTION AND AFFORDABLE CARE ACT (ACA) Legislation commonly called "Obamacare" that expanded access to health care for low-income individuals and workers who cannot obtain health insurance through an employer.

PERSON-CENTERED An approach to direct practice that stems from the work of Carl Rogers, wherein the practitioner focuses on conveying empathy and authenticity, unconditional positive regard, listening, and belief in the client's ability to change.

PHILANTHROPY Funding or a donation from a private individual or foundation.

POLICY A set of ideas, a plan, or a course of action officially established by a group such as an organization, business, or government body.

POSITIVE STRESS Stress that is associated with positive life events and tends to be short term and time-limited; also called *eustress*.

POSITIVISM A theory which holds that singular truths *are* attainable and that objective standards exist for making moral decisions.

POWER DYNAMICS When there is a perceived or real difference in relative status between the client and therapist.

PREVENTION SCIENCE Strategies that work to prevent or limit negative outcomes.

PREVENTIVE ETHICS The ethics of considering when and how ethical conflicts can be reduced or eliminated.

PRIMARY RESEARCH Data that are directly collected and analyzed by the person/organization or someone they hire.

PROFESSIONAL BOUNDARIES The rules, laws, and ethics that define the parameters of a human services practitioner and client interactions and relationship overall.

PROTECTIVE FACTORS Foster self-reliance and include environmental influences such as physical safety and opportunities for education and employment.

PSYCHOEDUCATION This is the term used for psychological education provided in a therapeutic setting.

PSYCHOLOGIZATION Using psychological terminology to indicate psychological distress (e.g., "felt depressed," "experienced anxiety").

PSYCHOTHERAPY Any psychological service provided by a trained, licensed professional that primarily uses forms of communication and interaction to address emotional, relational, and other problems in living.

RACIAL BATTLE FATIGUE Effect that many Black, Indigenous, and people of color (BIPOC)/minority individuals feel in a work setting when taking on extra tasks associated with promoting diversity and retention.

RADICAL SELF-CARE   Self-care that acknowledges the intersectional identity of an individual; a model that encourages minority individuals to engage in healing through self-knowledge, critical consciousness, collectivism, strength, resistance, and hope.

REDLINING   Discriminatory practice that limited who was eligible for a mortgage, thus ensuring that the sale of housing was mostly to White individuals and families.

RELATIVISM   A theory that highlights the context of human experience and history and suggests that perspectives of right and wrong may differ based on one's relative position or culture in society.

RESILIENCE   Process (and outcome) of adapting well ("bouncing back") when faced with adversity, trauma, or significant sources of stress.

RESTORATIVE JUSTICE   is an approach emphasizing accountability, making amends, and, when desired, facilitated meetings between victims, offenders, and other persons.

SAFETY NET   System of government programs designed to support individuals and families when they experience social or financial hardship.

SCHEMAS   Mental shortcuts that are created by our subjective experiences and beliefs being so powerful that it can be difficult to perceive people, events, or social phenomena objectively.

SECONDARY RESEARCH   Existing data that have been collected by someone else.

SECONDARY TRAUMA   Effect of practitioner's experience of empathically understanding the pain shared by a client.

SELF-CARE   Activities and strategies used to manage stress and support physical/mental health and well-being.

SETTLEMENT HOUSE   A way to provide social services for poor workers while creating a community of learning and fellowship.

SITUATIONAL ATTRIBUTION   Emphasizing environmental, structural, or policy-related factors or reasoning to explain the result of a situation.

SLIDING-SCALE FEE   A flexible fee-for-service system in which clients who are unable to afford the standard rate for treatment are able to pay a lower rate.

SOCIAL ACTION   Collective efforts and power to bring about positive change for communities.

SOCIAL DARWINISM   The idea that natural selection applies to humans the way it does to plants and animals.

SOCIAL LOCATION   refers to the unique way that factors such as race, class, gender, age, ability, religion, sexual orientation, and geography shape a person's experience.

SOCIAL POLICY   Broad term that refers to the ways that governments respond to basic health and welfare needs of a society; also called *social welfare policy*.

SOCIAL PROBLEM   Any condition or behavior that has negative consequences for large numbers of people, such as poverty, crime, hunger, homelessness, joblessness, and racism.

SOCIAL SECURITY   Federal program that provides pensions for retired workers and benefits for the disabled and dependents of deceased workers.

SOMATIZATION   Expressing psychological distress via somatic (physical) complaints such as a headache or racing heartbeat.

SPECIAL SUPPLEMENTAL NUTRITION PROGRAM FOR WOMEN, INFANTS, AND CHILDREN (WIC)   Nutrition support program for certain low-income women and children younger than age 5 years.

STAKEHOLDER ANALYSIS   Stakeholder analysis is a process to identify all of the individuals, groups, organizations, businesses, and other entities that are affected by or engaged with an issue.

STATELESS   Refers to individuals who are not recognized as citizens or nationals under the laws of any country.

STRESS   The body's reaction to a change, challenge, or demand, experienced as physical and/or emotional tension.

STRESSORS   Stimuli or events that cause a state of tension and strain.

SUPPLEMENTAL NUTRITION ASSISTANCE PROGRAM (SNAP)   Food assistance program for low-income families, including seniors and individuals with disabilities.

TEMPORARY ASSISTANCE FOR NEEDY FAMILIES (TANF)   Program that assists low-income families with basic needs using grants from the federal government.

THEORY OF CHANGE   An organization's research-based understanding of the kinds of interventions likely to be effective in addressing a particular need or problem.

TOLERABLE STRESS   Stress that is manageable if the person experiencing it has the resources and support to promote coping and adaptation.

TOXIC STRESS   Frequent or prolonged stress, often associated with trauma or the accumulation of risk factors.

TRANSNATIONAL Refers to individuals who maintain close personal, family, or business ties to multiple locations between their country of origin and country of residence.

UNCONDITIONAL POSITIVE REGARD An attitude adapted in direct practice work in which the practitioner avoids conveying negative judgments or feelings towards the client and identifies, focuses on, and communicates a belief in the client's inherent value and worth.

UNIVERSAL BASIC INCOME Model that provides individuals with a regular cash payment to be spent at the recipient's discretion.

VALIDATION When a listener affirms, supports, and understands a client's perspective and identity.

VALUES Fundamental beliefs that guide or motivate attitudes and actions.

VIRTUE ETHICS The ethics that do not separate the individual self from the professional self.

WAR ON POVERTY originated under President Lyndon Johnson and included anti-poverty policies such as Medicare and Medicaid, which were part of the Social Security Amendments of 1965.

WATCHDOG ORGANIZATION A nonprofit organization whose mission is to monitor and report on the performance of other nonprofit organizations.

WEIRD BIAS The existing body of research is mostly normed on a White, educated, industrialized, rich, democratic population.

WHITE SAVIORISM Biased beliefs and practices of White individuals who work with communities of color; residents of struggling BIPOC communities are seen as incapable of helping themselves.

INDEX

Page number suffixes indicate: *f*, figures; *b*, box; and *t*, tables.